I

JEWISH FRIENDS AND NEIGHBOURS

An Introduction for Christians

Marcus Braybrooke

**Braybrooke Press, 6 Portland House, Teignmouth
TQ14 8BQ marcusbraybrooke 4 @gmail.com**

In memory of my dear Mary
and to all my friends and colleagues
my thanks for your friendship and your encouragement.
as together we pray and work for
the coming of God's kingdom

Shalom

CONTENTS

INTRODUCTION

 This book gives me a chance to express my thanks to many Jews for their friendship and to acknowledge, with gratitude, how much we have in common as people of faith.

It may be helpful for readers if I share some of my own journey. I have been familiar with the stories of Joseph and Moses from childhood. In those days readings in church were always from both testaments and in my daily readings I include reading a psalm and readings from both testaments. It saddens me that in many churches, the Hebrew Bible is almost ignored or, if read, passages are selected to relate to the New Testament reading, rather than relating Jesus' ministry to the Biblical story of salvation.

I am also grateful that during my National Service in Libya, I was given a week's leave to visit Israel. This was in 1958 and I sensed the enthusiasm of those struggling to create a new nation whilst surrounded by hostile neighbours. The week was particularly important in two ways.

First, seeing the places where Jesus lived emphasised for me his full humanity and made me hesitant when studying theology at Cambridge to agree with the radical Bible criticism which questioned the historical accuracy of the Gospels. Secondly and equally important was the shock of a visit to the Chamber of the Holocaust on Mount Zion. The Shoah was then still shrouded in silence and I was overwhelmed by the evidence of such cruelty and evil.

In the nineteen sixties my wife Mary and I joined the World Congress of Faiths and the Council of Christians and Jews and we have been enriched by deep friendship with many Jews and people of other faiths, as well as Christians who have been deeply committed to interfaith understanding and friendship. It was at the suggestion of George Appleton, then Anglican Archbishop in Jerusalem, that Rabbi Hugo Gryn and I arranged a joint Christian-Jewish study tour to the Holy Land. Subsequently, I have been back many times, including a three month sabbatical at Tantur Ecumenical Centre, near Jerusalem.

It was a great surprise when I was invited to become Director of the Council of Christians and Jews, where I learned about the different branches of Judaism and the concerns of the community. At the time, Christians were beginning to repent of the centuries old anti-Jewish teaching of the Churches, which contributed to the soil in which anti-Semitism and Nazism could grow. Some theologians also affirmed the continuing validity of God's covenant with Jewish people and distanced themselves from the efforts to convert Jews to Christianity..My time at CCJ was cut short by illness, but already Rabbi Tony Bayfield and I had set up the Manor House Dialogue Group. Some six Jews and six Christians met regularly to discuss theological issues .Some papers were published in the book *Dialogue with a Difference*.

While there is a special agenda between Jews and Christians, it is clear that dialogue with Muslims is increasingly important.

It was a privilege to be asked by Sir Sigmund Sternberg to be a co-founder with him and Sheik Zaki Badawi of the Three Faiths Forum – now because its work has grown and includes people of many religions and world views – renamed the Faith and Belief Forum.

Because of the shared scriptures, my love of the land of the Bible, and continuing need to confront anti-Semitism, as well as many friendships, I hope this book will help Christians to a greater appreciation of the enormous contribution which Jews and Judaism have made to the world, to grow in their own Christian discipleship and to discover the personal enrichment of interfaith friendship and co-operation, which will bring nearer the day foretold by the Prophet Micah when people 'will beat their swords into ploughshares and their spears into pruning hooks. When nation will not take up sword against nation, nor will they train for war anymore and everyone will sit under their own vine and under their own fig-tree, and no one will make them afraid.'

FOREWORDS

Rabbi Professor Tony Bayfield
CBE, DD (Cantuar)

More years ago than I care to remember, I was an undergraduate at Magdalene College Cambridge. Three of my friends – one of whom had a car – were historians and would-be aesthetes: I tagged along for the ride when they went exploring the magnificent wool churches of the Essex-Suffolk border. Their interest was largely architectural. I was a Jew from a humdrum North East London suburb, my family members of a synagogue with a new multi-purpose building, designed and built down to what the community couldn't quite afford. Yet, ironically, it was me who sensed a religious dimension to those experiences of place.

In a book I co-compiled with Marcus – with Long Melford in mind – I wrote

'I look up to the roof soaring above me heavenwards. The prayers prayed in this place for centuries are almost tangible. Real prayers, honest prayers, true prayers, prayers which are heard. People reach out to God here, just as I strive to reach out to God in a synagogue. And if they reach out to God, God comes to meet them here. The smell, the flavour, the accoutrements may not be of my home, but God is at home here just as much as God is at my house.'

Some fifteen years after my undergraduate encounter and now an established rabbi, I was tempted away from my community in the southern suburbs to establish a new Jewish cultural centre – later to be named The Sternberg Centre for Judaism – in North West London. I was given *carte blanche*: but only after I arrived was told I had no budget! On a wing and a prayer, we built a range of programmes – cultural, educational and training for volunteers in community development and therapeutic support. And I also indulged my personal theological itch. For thirteen years I'd been rabbi of a small community in the wilds of Surrey, effectively PR representative to the wider Christian neighbourhood – giving talks to local organisations, visiting schools, speaking to church groups of many hues and enjoying endless cups of tea and biscuits. All of which was essential and rewarding but, characteristically, I wanted more!

The Council of Christians and Jews had recently appointed Marcus as its Director, who I discovered was also a graduate of Magdalene College Cambridge – and he too wanted more. Since its foundation in 1941/2, CCJ had taken on the Herculean task of engaging and building relationships of trust with a Jewish community indelibly scarred by the Shoah and deeply disturbed by the engrained nature of anti-Semitism in Western Society. Much invaluable work had been done and many urns of tea and trays of biscuits shared: Marcus was utterly devoted to the agenda – but he wanted to go further.

The Orthodox Jewish community had adopted the stance of the doyen of American Orthodoxy, Rabbi Joseph Soloveitchik, who was born in Imperial Russia 1903 and died in Boston 1993. He declined to enter the field of theological discussion with other faiths. Marcus and I both wanted that deeper engagement and dialogue at a theological level. He taught me that though place – those wool churches – can be important, it's the person who is transforming.

We set up a small ongoing dialogue group, meeting relatively infrequently but regularly, with no purpose beyond the impact of the group on its members. We met for a decade and built enduring friendships and deep trust. Marcus introduced me to John Bowden (SCM's remarkable managing editor), Richard Harries (later Bishop of Oxford), Alan Race (author of Christians and Religious Pluralism) and Sister Margaret Shepherd of the Sisters of Sion. I introduced Marcus to Rabbis Albert Friedlander (expert on reconciliation work), Jonathan Magonet (Bible scholar), Julia Neuberger (later to enter the House of Lords) and Norman Solomon (Orthodox scholar). Some of the papers are reproduced in Dialogue with a Difference. (1992).

Marcus brought both vision and wisdom to the process and to the group. He came with unique experience of other faiths, a profound commitment to Christianity and an equally profound openness to the other. His sensitivity, integrity and quiet humour were a key to the creation of a space imbued with personal warmth, trust and friendship in which people like me were able to engage in personal theology – in a way I hadn't been able to with my own colleagues! Marcus enabled me to realise that Christians and Jews are siblings, not identical twins, equal children of the Good Parent who has no favourites. I wasn't a sinful or deviant version of the other; I didn't need always to understand the other; I could question the doctrinal ethicality of the other. We could demand reflection and more clarity – but in so far as theological presuppositions and doctrines could not accommodate the indisputable reality of the faith of the other, then it was the theology and the doctrine that needed to change. Marcus the person – much more than my initial sense of place – taught me that.

And Marcus – despite wounds inflicted by institutional politics and the challenges of ill-health – has been teaching this life-changing insight through his numerous books and global travels ever since.

This brings me to this book. In the bad old days of comparative religious text books, religions were treated 'objectively', dispassionately and categorised – sacred buildings, festivals, life-cycle events, foods, attitudes to afterlife and so on. It was as if they were corpses laid side by side, duly dissected, fundamentally the same. But, of course, they're not – religions are alive not dead and each is *sui generis*, uniquely distinctive. Thankfully, we've moved on. There are now many fine books about a given faith, written by a knowledgeable member of that faith. These are indispensable and invaluable, but they do, inevitably, offer the particular view of an individual and represent how that person would like their faith to be perceived.

Occasionally – as with this book – we're treated to the portrait of one faith by an individual of another faith but one who has devoted much of his life to encounter and dialogue and does so with experience, empathy and understanding. Of course, it's a portrait by an outsider – one who cannot know what it fully feels like to be the other – but it does tell Christians how the Jews they meet, or are likely to meet, will appear. No-one knows better than Marcus how the clamorous range of British Jews present themselves – and that's the very considerable strength of this book. After all, how we see ourselves and how we appear to others are different facets of each living faith – and only God holds the complete picture.

Bishop Michael Ipgrave
Chair of the Council of Christians and Jews

I am thankful for the opportunity to write a foreword to *Jewish Friends and Neighbours*, which is an excellent resource designed to inform and to encourage Christians to share in dialogue. Marcus Braybrooke is somebody supremely well-qualified for this task, which has been at the heart of his life's work. Through his highly effective tenure as Director of the Council of Christians and Jews, and through the many other inter faith organisations in which he has played a pivotal role, Marcus has been deeply involved in networks and partnerships to deepen dialogue, advance understanding, and to promote co-operation between Christians, Jews and people of other faiths for over sixty years.

This book bears witness to the many friendships in the Jewish community which he has formed through this tireless activity, and to the ways in which those have enriched and extended his Christian faith. It also shows how he has always wedded to this practical experience a firm scholarly awareness of the issues involved. If at the end of this book you ask yourself, what is the one word you would take with you to describe the task of building Christian-Jewish relations, that word might well be 'complex' – a note which is sounded right at the beginning, with the first chapter headed 'Many ways of being Jewish'.

The other word you might take away would be 'urgent'. Against the long, troubled and shameful backdrop of two millennia of Christian-Jewish interactions, expertly and concisely presented in these pages, the growing signs of rapprochement between our two communities from the mid-twentieth century were a welcome resetting of the relationship, and as an important actor in that period Marcus, the author, is well-placed to sketch it. In the last decade, though, the resurgence of antisemitism has become sadly undeniable in our society and across Europe, as has its mutation into new variants. It is imperative that as Christians, repentant for our past behaviour and learning from our past mistakes, we should now stand in solidarity with Jewish friends and neighbours as together we work for God's kingdom of mercy, justice and peace. It is my hope and my prayer that this book will give its readers the confidence and the knowledge to do that.

Michael Sternberg,QC

KCFO of the Order of Merit
of the Federal Republic of Germany

I am delighted you have picked this book up and are thinking about reading it. It is a *tour de force* and a unique one at that. Not only will it tell you pretty much all you need to know about Jews in England, their history, their sects, their shared beliefs and differences (providing *en passant* a highly attractive and accessible understanding of the Jewish Religion) but it also deals so sensitively with such major topics in Judaism as the Holocaust, Holocaust Denial, the silence or indifference of the many, and the failure of the churches in dealing with the Shoah. The book covers too, in both an historical and analytic way, the creation of the State of Israel, who lives in Israel, why they do, why Israel is so important for so many Jews, and what hope there is for peace. As you would expect, there is a very valuable section on Jewish-Christian relations and a dialogue for a better world. This work is written in clear prose with an almost Orwellian directness: it is hard to put down once you have started to read it.

I believe that I am uniquely qualified to tell you all this. I was born in England, brought up in the Orthodox Jewish tradition, but I also attended a Jewish Public School which aimed to distil in its students the best of English and Jewish culture. After that, I went to Cambridge University; then I was called to the Bar. My father, the late Sir Sigmund Sternberg, was a tireless interfaith campaigner. He saw from his childhood in Hungary (when he was persecuted for being a Jew) how imperative it was for Jews and Christians to redefine their relations and to try to make better so much of what had gone wrong over the 2,000 years since the birth of Jesus.

Importantly for anyone who simply wants a "Vade Mecum" as to how the Jewish communities in this country are organised in terms of Ashkenazim, Sephardim, the various strands of synagogues, beliefs, and structures, this provides a masterly analysis.

The work describes the many ways of being Jewish; it provides a highly sensitive and accurate description of how Jewish communities are so varied, together with their history in the British Isles. It is beautifully written and compelling. At the end, in a section entitled "Conclusion," Marcus Braybrooke describes a Jewish tradition, of which I was ignorant, of parents writing an ethical Will or *Tzava* for their children. This is a custom which goes back to the time of Isaac. In one such *Tzava*, a father asks his children "Why be a Jew?" Here Marcus touches upon the importance for the world of the Jewish people. He does this in a way which is both brief and highly convincing, referring as he does, to Judaism being the longest continuous culture within

Western Civilization. His answer to why Judaism needs to exist is that it is a precious system of belief and action to guide an individual through the world. This is deeply heartening.

There are so many aspects of this work which are pleasing. In particular the quotations from a profusion of literary sources are highly effective. One is a letter written in 1940 by a Jewish mother to her child in the Warsaw Ghetto, shortly before they were murdered. Its citation is both heart breaking and highly appropriate.

The book contains surprises. Even though I have been part of a Jewish tradition in this country for nearly 70 years, I learned so many new things. Not least of these was about a novel called *Reuben Sachs* by Amy Levy (1861-1889). This is a story by the first Jewish student at Newnham College, Cambridge, in the 19th Century. Overall, the grasp of historical detail which *Jewish Friends and Neighbours* displays is riveting. For example, I never knew that Beatrice Potter wrote about a pathetic scene at the landing stage when Jewish newcomers arrived in East London at beginning of the last century; although I was aware of the tensions between Jews and non-Jews when so many arrived, in the early part of the 20th century, as a result of the cruel actions and inactions of the Russian Government.

 After I finished reading the book, I found myself making a list of all the people I wanted to give it to. This of course includes Christians, Muslims, Jews, and so many of differing faiths and beliefs. I wanted all of them to read it, because this book is in its way one of the very best current descriptions of almost all aspects of the Jewish Community in this country; indeed it is a book which tackles so many important and difficult issues with great understanding and compassion. I could go on telling you more and more about this book. I won't. I think what you need to do now is to start reading the first chapter. You will not be disappointed.

1. SETTING THE SCENE

Toppling statues of those who made money from owning slaves may rightly express our abhorrence of slavery, but it does little to eradicate the legacy of racism which still haunts our society. In the same way condemnation of anti-Semitism by Governments and Churches has not removed this hateful virus from society. When I was Director of the Council of Christians and Jews, I sometimes compared anti-Semitism to weeds in a garden. You pull them up: but then, if you go away for a couple of weeks, the weeds are as big as ever. The same is true of anti-Semitism, which a Runnymede Report called *A Very Light Sleeper*.

Archbishop William Temple once said that you cannot be 'anti an anti'. My hope in writing this book is that others will come to share the enormous enrichment that I have found by reading the scriptures that are revered by Jews and Christians and by learning more about the long history of the Jewish people and a little of the wealth of Jewish learning. I hope also they will feel a little of my love for the Land in which Jesus, a faithful Jew, witnessed to the love of God for all God's children.

Sadly faith has to be lived in a world which is often torn apart by conflict and tragedy and true friendship grows as we learn to share each other's pain. The causes of anti-Semitism are complex. Tragically the traditional anti-Jewish teaching of the churches and, too often, the persecution of the Jewish people, has reinforced it. Christians, by meeting their Jewish neighbours and by learning more about Judaism and Jewish history are better equipped to help to eradicate anti-Semitism it. Moreover, their life and faith will be enriched.

The Council of Christians and Jews, with its many local branches, the Faith and Belief Forum, the World Congress of Faiths and local interfaith groups all provide opportunities to meet Jewish neighbours and to learn more about their way of life. I this book will encourage more church-goers to share this journey.

Before we start, there is luggage to leave behind. Judaism today – in its many varieties – is post-Rabbinic. It grows out of efforts of rabbinic scholars and teachers in the first centuries of the Common Era to rebuild the Jewish community after the Romans in the year 70 CE destroyed the Temple in Jerusalem, rendered the priests powerless and put an end to the sacrificial system.   This means that a knowledge of the Hebrew Bible - which sadly too many Christians today lack - does not provide us with an understanding of contemporary Judaism. The Hebrew Bible was, of course, also formative for the Early Church. Indeed many scholars now see the parting of the ways between the two communities as a gradual process and picture Rabbinic Judaism and the Early Church as two branches growing from common roots.

Perhaps here I should pause to say that I use the phrase 'Hebrew Bible' rather than Old Testament because the latter may suggest that it is out of date and has been replaced by the 'New Testament' – although at my age I would hope the word 'old' means 'venerable and to be respected' rather than 'antiquated and passed it.' In the same way, for dates I use CE – Common Era - and BCE – Before the Common Era – rather than AD -Anno Domini (Latin : "In the year of (our) Lord") and BC –'Before Christ.' Certainly for Christians the coming of Jesus Christ is the decisive event, but sensitivity to other people's feelings helps friendship to grow.

It is also important to emphasise that Jews are not a race or an ethnic group, but a people united by ties of family, history and culture. Membership is by birth or by choosing to join the community.

As we shall see the history of the Jewish people is complex, because so often they have suffered persecution or expulsion. In the second century CE, most of the Jews in Judah and Galilee were expelled by the Romans. Already there were Jewish communities in Babylon and in Mediterranean cities – living in what is called the Diaspora. For some centuries, Spain was an important centre, until in the fourteenth century, Jews were forced to convert or leave the country. From about that time, the largest Jewish communities, mostly living in Ghettos, were in Eastern Europe. Gradually, in the nineteenth century, restrictions on Jews living in Western Europe were lifted. At the end of the century many Jews fled the pogroms in Russia and made their homes in Western Europe or the USA. Some settled in Palestine and during the British Mandate from 1918-1947, the number increased.

Any growing sense of belonging was shattered by the Shoah – as Jews often call the Holocaust. Out of the eleven million people murdered by the Nazis, mostly in concentration camps, more than half were Jews. The six million were about one third of the total Jewish population at the time. Survivors lost family members and the grandchildren of those murdered cannot forget. The horror is a challenge to all who believe in a Loving God.

For many Jews, Israel is their protection – whether or not they live in the Land. Criticism of the actions of those in power is legitimate, but too often such criticism is a mask for anti-Semitism.

Many Christians visit the Holy Land each year.' Sadly, with an abundance of holy sites to visit, they often meet few of those who live in the Land and should beware of superficial judgements.

Of course, as a Christian, I have not grown up in a Jewish home and shared from childhood in the festivals. Yet as a follower of Jesus, who was Jewish, and because of our shared scriptures, my love of the land of the Bible, and the continuing need to confront anti-Semitism, as well as many friendships, I hope this book will help Christians to a greater appreciation of the enormous contribution which Jews and Judaism have made to the world, to grow in their own Christian discipleship and to discover the personal enrichment of interfaith friendship and co-operation, which will bring nearer the day foretold by the Prophet Micah when 'nation will not take up sword against nation ... and no one will make them afraid.'

2. MANY WAYS OF BEING JEWISH

Who Is A Jew?

A Church Fellowship invited the local Rabbi to come and speak. Eight o'clock came and went. The vicar apologised for the delay and hoped the Rabbi would soon arrive. An attractive young lady at the back called out, 'I've been waiting here for the last twenty minutes.' The vicar assumed that the rabbi would have a beard and a large black hat.

The Jewish people are very varied. There is a traditional joke that if two Jews discuss a matter, there are at least three opinions. In the first century of the Common Era (CE), when the rabbis were clarifying Jewish teaching, they recorded the different opinions of two great rabbis, Hillel and Shammai, saying that both 'were the words of the living God.'

A major question today for Jews, as perhaps for all people of faith, is how to be true to one's religion in the modern world. As we meet some Jewish communities, we shall see that there are many very different responses to this challenge. In the words of Rabbi Jonathan Magonet 'There are extreme positions: for example, denying the tradition entirely and attempting to live a totally secular, uncommitted Jewish life; or denying the secular and creating a religious world as if the secular challenge did not exist. There are a number of shades of accommodation between the two.'[1] The response, of course, affects numerous aspects of daily life.

Rabbi Jonathan Magonet illustrates this in the decision he and his wife made about their children's education. Should they go to a Jewish school and perhaps feel somewhat isolated from the wider society or go to a state school and be uncomfortable with their Judaism? The Rabbi decided on a compromise: their primary education was at a Jewish school, their secondary education at a state school. Freud, it seems, would have agreed with him. Although a strong critic of the Jewish religion, Freud believed in the persistence and distinctiveness of the Jewish people. He recognised that anyone born a Jew could not escape this identity and needed to be aware of it – even if he explained 'the distinctiveness of the Jewish people in terms of wholly secular values.'[2]

Often it may be sometime before one recognises that a neighbour or colleague at work is Jewish. Indeed, there may be some dispute about whether or not a person is Jewish, partly because of disagreements, which we discuss below, between Orthodox and Progressive Jews. Traditionally, anyone with a Jewish mother is a Jew. Although almost all Jewish males are circumcised, birth, not circumcision, makes a person Jewish. Even if a person with a Jewish mother who never goes to the synagogue and even marries a person of another faith, he or she remains a Jew.

The situation in the Jewish world before the Emancipation, which began in the late eighteenth century, was very different. Whereas in the Middle Ages and early Modern Period it was possible, indeed relatively common to invoke the language of "heresy", and the ban (*herem*) was pronounced on individuals and groups that refused to conform to the dominant mode of Jewish life or practice, nowadays such language is rarely heard, and pluralism is not only something that is remarked on by sociologists but is accepted by most Jews as a fact of life.

The label "Jewish" is available to any person or group wishing to lay claim to it: there is no universally acknowledged way of "being Jewish." Ultimately, what counts is membership of the "Jewish people", rather than fidelity to any particular creed or praxis. This extends to the recognition that a Jew does not need to believe anything in particular: the rejection of supernatural beliefs, a logical outcome of the Enlightenment, is seen by many not as abandoning of Judaism, but as a legitimate form of Jewish self-expression'. The pluralism of the contemporary Jewish world is true, but relations within the community are not always irenic. There are tensions, as we shall see, between Orthodox and Progressive Jews. In Israel there are sharp disagreements between religious and secular Jews.

Ben Gurion, the first Prime Minister of Israel, asked countless Jewish figures across the world for their definition of 'Who is a Jew?' The answers were so different that Ben Gurion decided there was no satisfactory answer to the question.[3] In part the difficulty of definition turns on whether being Jewish is determined by birth or faith. When the state of Israel was established the Law of Return made clear that anyone by virtue of his (sic) being a Jew and being willing to take part in settling the land had an inherent right to live in Israel – unless his or her presence was judged to be a danger to public health or welfare. When, however, a Polish-born Jew, Samuel Rufeisen, who had survived the Holocaust in White Russia and had become a Carmelite monk, arrived at Haifa, he was refused citizenship, although allowed to live in Israel. The Supreme Court subsequently made clear that the Law of Return did not apply to a Jew who had converted to Christianity.4 This is why, as we shall see later, most Jews reject the claims of 'Messianic Jews', who recognise Jesus as the Jewish Messiah, still to be Jewish.'

How Many Jews Are There?

It is estimated that there are about 14.7 million Jews in the world, with 6.6 million in Israel. Of the Jews who live outside Israel in the Diaspora, nearly 5.5 million live in the Americas. Only about one and a half million Jews now live in Europe, although before the outbreak of the Second World War and the mass murder of Jews by the Nazis, of a world population of nearly seventeen million, ten million Jews lived in Europe.[5]

The largest Jewish communities in Europe are in France, the United Kingdom and Russia. The number of Jews in Britain is just under 284,000, according to the Institute for Jewish Policy Research. Three out of five live in the Greater London Area – particularly in the Boroughs of Barnet, Brent and Harrow. There are also sizeable communities in Manchester, Salford, Leeds and Glasgow.

It is difficult to be sure of the figures for the various strands of Judaism, because in some traditions membership is based on households rather than of individuals. There are rather over 80,000 Jewish households. About half the Jews in Britain are members of a synagogue. Of these rather over half belong to the central orthodox United Synagogue; 10% to Strictly Orthodox Synagogues and about a third to Reform or Liberal synagogues.[6] We shall look at the differences later in the book.

The Diaspora

To understand some of the varied ways of being Jewish we need to look back over many centuries. Already, before the destruction of Jerusalem by the Romans in 70 CE, many Jews were living in dispersion in different parts of the Roman Empire. Indeed St Paul, who grew up in Tarsus in Asia Minor, usually began his preaching at the local synagogue in the places to which he travelled. There was also an important Jewish community in Babylon, which dates back to the sixth century BCE, when Jews were driven into Exile following the first destruction of Jerusalem in 593 BCE. The Babylonian community, under its Exarch, was highly influential in the Middle Ages and although now scattered, it survives to this day. In Europe, following the conversion to Christianity of the Emperor Constantine, Jewish privileges were withdrawn and many Jews suffered from discrimination and persecution. In those countries, which later came under the rule of Islam, Jews were regarded as second-class citizens (*dhimmi*), although granted security of life and property.

During the early Middle Ages, some Jews prospered, especially in Spain, where their international connections and ability to lend money and pay taxes was useful to princes and barons. Usually they had to live apart in ghettoes. Their situation, which was always precarious and dependent on the good will of the powerful, deteriorated in the later Middle Ages. The Crusades provided an excuse to attack 'the enemy within.' Jews also became the victims of slanderous allegations and prejudice. They were expelled from England in 1290 and subsequently from other countries – most significantly from Spain in 1492 and Portugal in 1497. These Jews from Spain, known as Sephardim, settled in different Mediterranean countries, most of which were under Muslim rule. Some Jews, known as Marranos, were baptized, but often suffered at the hands of the Inquisition because they were suspected of secretly practising Jewish rites.

The distinction between Sephardi Jews and Ashkenazi Jews from Europe continues to this day. The differences are not theological. They are on matters of food and ritual practice. For example the prayer shawls worn by Sephardi Jews are usually made of silk, whereas the Ashkenazi wear shawls made of wool. Such variations result from different cultural conditions, local customs and obedience to different legal authorities.

The majority of Ashkenazi Jews have their roots in Eastern Europe. By the middle of the seventeenth century the Jewish population of Poland was more than 150,000. Even after the deadly attacks during 'The Deluge' (1648-1667), many Jews remained in Poland. It was there in the eighteenth century that two remarkable men, with very different approaches, Rabbi Elijah ben Solomon (1720-97), better known as the Gaon of the Lithuanian city of Vilna, and Rabbi Israel ben Eliezer (c.1700-60), who is better known as Baal Shem Tov or the Besht, led revival movements that are still influential. We shall meet them again later in the book.

Emancipation And Assimilation

The late eighteenth century saw profound changes, which have had a lasting effect on Jewish life. The small number of Jews who settled in America in the eighteenth century enjoyed full freedom from the beginning. It was taken for granted that the American Declaration of Independence, which stated that 'We hold these truths to be self-evident that all men are created equal, that they are endowed by the creator with certain unalienable rights, that among these are life, truth and the pursuit of happiness,' applied to Jews.

In France, it was not so obvious that the French Revolution's claim that 'all men are born, and remain, free and equal in rights' included Jews. It was a matter of heated debate. The answer was yes, but to Jews as individuals not to Jewish communities, which usually had a measure of self-government. The Parisian deputy Clermont-Tonnerre famously said, 'Everything for the Jews as citizens, nothing as a nation.'[7] The armies of the French Republic, as they spread across Europe, brought emancipation to Jewish communities. Napoleon, who would not refer to Jews but only to 'French citizens of the Mosaic faith' subjected Jews in France to some discrimination, but these restrictions were swept away when the monarchy was restored. In other Western European countries Jewish emancipation took longer.

In Poland, even at the start of the twentieth century, most of the large Jewish population were restricted to the 'Pale of Settlement' and lived the traditional life of the ghetto. Jews in Russia continued to suffer from prejudice, persecution and periodic pogroms, which, in the late nineteenth century, drove many Jews to settle in Western Europe or America.

Emancipation provided great opportunities, which many Jews gladly seized and became active members of the community. But there was a price. Was it possible to enter fully into European society and retain one's Jewish faith and way of life? The boss might insist on a Jew working on a Saturday (the Sabbath). Did Jewish dietary laws allow an observant Jew to eat in the home of a Gentile? Jews have adapted in different ways to their changed situation. Some strictly observant Jews, often labelled Ultra-Orthodox, may choose to live, as far as possible, apart from the wider society. Modern Orthodox Jews hold that a person can continue to live according to the God-given Torah and, at the same time, share fully in the modern world. Progressive Jews are also committed to living as faithful Jews, but are ready to make changes to inherited practices, recognising that the Torah is both human and divine.

Secular Jews see Judaism as a cultural tradition and set of ethical values, not as a religion. A few people that are Jewish by descent totally reject their Jewish inheritance and some others convert to another religion.[8]

These, of course, are very broad categories and few of us are totally consistent in how we live. As we go on, we shall learn more about the many ways of being Jewish, but it helps to be aware of the historical differences between Sephardi and Ashkenazi Jews and the different theological approaches of Ultra-Orthodox, Modern Orthodox, Progressive and Secular Jews. These distinctions are compounded by the very varied situations in which Jews in different countries find themselves.

Zionism

In Western Europe, the challenge of the nineteenth century was how to be both a faithful Jew and a modern citizen. Towards the end of the nineteenth century, some Jews were forced to ask again whether they were fully accepted by and integrated into Western society. Renewed pogroms in Russia forced many Jews to flee from Eastern Europe and to seek a new life in America or Western Europe. The pogroms also raised the question in the minds of some Jews of whether they would ever be secure until, like other nations, they had a country of their own. Theodor Herzl (1860-1904) became convinced that this was the case by the shocking anti-Semitism in France at the time of the trial of Alfred Dreyfus (1859-1935), who was falsely accused of betraying military secrets to the Germans. Herzel, whose *Der Judenstaat* (The

Jewish State) was published in 1896 became the prophet of Zionism.

The Shoah

Although in the first part of the twentieth century a number of Jews settled in Palestine, all too soon millions were to be murdered by the Nazis. Rising anti-Semitism in much of Europe in the early twentieth century, culminated in the genocide of some six million Jews. The Holocaust or Shoah was a horrific and defining event in world history, which we shall reflect on in a later chapter. It left an indelible mark on the survivors and it shattered Jewish communities across Europe.

Rabbi Dow Marmur, in his *The Star of the Return*, argued that the old paradigm ended with the Shoah and a new one began with the foundation of the state of Israel. His own life reflected this. Having fled from Poland to escape the Nazis, he was for several years a rabbi in England and then Canada before settling in Israel.[9]

Other people have chosen different paths. To generalise, there are those Jews who have wanted to rebuild the traditional pre-war way of life in Eastern Europe; others, who have committed themselves to building and defending the state of Israel; and others who in Western Europe and the USA seek to live both as faithful Jews and as participants in the modern world.

Rebuilding Jewish Life

For much of the last seventy years, Jewish energy has been focused on rebuilding Jewish communal life. The energy with which this has been achieved is amazing, but at the same time many Jewish communities in the West are declining partly because of 'marrying out' and partly because of the corrosive influence of the modern world. This means that whereas in the last fifty years the priority has been to rebuild Jewish communities, today it is to reinvigorate Jewish faith and practice – which is similar to the challenge which faces all faith communities in the West today.

The Birth Of Israel

The last seventy years have also seen the birth and growth of the State of Israel. Some Jews who had made a good home for themselves and their families in Western Europe and America were, at first, unsympathetic to the idea of a Jewish state. Increasingly the majority of Jews became convinced that a nation state was essential for their long term security. Israel provided a home for many of the survivors of the Holocaust and other refugees, as well as Jews who fled from Arab countries and later for Jews when they were allowed to leave Russia.

A considerable number of Jews from Western Europe and America chose to make *aliyah* and to settle in Israel, but, even now, more Jews still live in the Diaspora than in the Jewish state. They are, usually, deeply committed to Israel's survival and prosperity, but not necessarily supportive of all the policies of the government. The relationship of Jews in the Diaspora to Jews in Israel is an important issue.

What Of The Future?

Survival and Revival are perhaps the key words to describe Jewish life in the twentieth century. Survival is still a question in the twenty-first century, although the threat is different. Elliot Abrams warned in 1997 that 'As an ethnic, cultural or political entity, they (American Jews) are doomed...Jewish ethnicity is no proof against American culture.'[10] Norman Cantor was equally gloomy. He ended his lengthy book *The Sacred Chain,* with these words, 'The Jewish people as a whole, as an ethnic entity, is threatened with erosion and communal extinction. What the Holocaust began physically will, in the twenty first century, be accomplished culturally. The Jews are going home into the mist of history.'[11] If this is true, it would be a tragedy not just for Jews, but for all people of faith.

In the twenty-first century, the Jewish world is, increasingly, concentrating on the future and how to survive in a pluralist society. It is a question facing every faith community. One answer is to retreat into a fundamentalism or isolation from the modern world, another answer is to be absorbed into the dominant secular culture. For others, the focus is on the contribution Jews can make to the healing of the world (*tikun olam*).

This means that the agenda for Christian-Jewish dialogue, which has mostly been determined by the past, also needs to change. Christians and Jews, together with Muslims and other people of faith, need to ensure that faith is life-giving not life-taking. Only together will people of faith be able to rescue religion from extremists and ensure that religion is a resource for the healing of the world.

Jonathan Sacks, a former Chief Rabbi, has expressed this hope in several of his writings. Thirty years ago he wrote in *The Persistence of Faith*: 'I am convinced that religions can be both faithful to their traditions and answerable to the imperative of tolerance. They can come to terms with other cultures without sacrificing their identity. They can be responsive to social change without at the same time assenting to every ephemeral shift in moral mood. Not only do I believe this to be possible, I believe it to be necessary...In the beginning, God created the world. Thereafte, He entrusted us to create a human world, which will be, in the structures of our common life, a home for the Divine presence. That command still addresses us with its momentous challenge, the persisting call of faith.'[12]

3. BRITISH JEWS

When did Jews come to Britain? Did Shakespeare, whose vivid portrayal of Shylock in The Merchant of Venice is world famous, ever meet a Jew? He was cerainly aware of the abuse heaped on Jews and, in Shylock's words, asked, 'Hath not a Jew eyes... senses, and passions as a Christian.' Jews had been banned from Britain for nearly three hundred years. They were expelled by King Edward I in 1290 and not re-admitted until 1656, when Oliver Cromwell was Lord Protector.

Although some Jews may have lived in Britain in Roman times, the earliest evidence of an organised settlement dates to the reign of King William I, following the Norman Conquest in 1066. A site known as 'Old Jewry' is to be found in the City of London, close to Bank Underground station. There was a Jewish community in Oxford as early as 1075. A few years later there are references to their school and to a synagogue. Clifford's Tower in York still witnesses to the massacre of Jews, which took place there in 1190. There were about 3,000 Jews in England, when Edward I ordered their expulsion. At least the King gave orders to the wardens of the Cinque Ports that the refugees were not to be harmed when they left and to ensure 'that their passage is safe and speedy.' The exiled Jews, unless they were impoverished, had to pay for their crossing![13]

After their expulsion from Spain, some Jews, known as Marranos (who feigned conversion to Christianity), settled in London. Maybe Shakespeare knew some members of this community. Probably Christopher Marlowe, who wrote *The Jew of Malta* in 1590, had met some Jews on the Continent and may have based the character of Barabas on Lopez Dr Roderigo, a Portuguese Marrano, who was a medical attendant to Queen Elizabeth.[14]

Re-Admission of the Jews

In 1650 Menasseh ben Israel of Amsterdam began to campaign for the return of Jews to England. In 1655 he led a delegation to London and at a conference in Whitehall a petition was presented to Oliver Cromwell. In this the Jews asked for 'security to meet privately in our particular houses for our Devotions' and 'being we are all mortal,' they asked also for a place of burial.[15]

There is no record of a decision or of a formal reply, but a Spanish and Portuguese (Sephardi) congregation was established in 1656. Their first synagogue was in Creechurch Lane in the city of London, but a beautiful new synagogue, Bevis Marks, modelled on the Portuguese synagogue in Amsterdam, was opened in 1701. Sephardi Jews continued to come to Britain throughout the eighteenth century, but even by 1800 there were only 2,000 in London. By that time, the Ashkenazi Jews, who began to settle towards the end of the seventeenth century, were nearly ten times as numerous. Ashkenazi Jews came mostly from Holland and Germany, where they were suffering persecution.[16]

Some Jews were very poor. 'Jewish pedlars became a familiar sight in the English countryside from early in the eighteenth century. Soon their activities also extended to the towns: selling, besides beguiling trifles, old clothes, fruit, dried herbs and so on.' Other Jews were very rich. The Mendes and da Costas were the wealthiest Sephardi families and the Harts and Franks the richest Ashkenazi. In the nineteenth century, the de Rothschilds and the Monetfiores were very wealthy. In between, others were, in Jane Austen's phrase, "in trade." Some were shopkeepers, others specialised in providing clothing and equipment to naval ratings and officers. There were a few who were pharmacists or dentists.[17]

Emancipation

Jews in Britain suffered the same disabilities as Non-Conformists and Papists. They could not take public office and were excluded from some professions, but there was no specifically anti-Jewish legislation. There were occasional outbreaks of anti-Semitism in the eighteenth century. Indeed when a bill to facilitate the naturalisation of foreign-born Jews was passed, the protests were so strong that the bill was quickly repealed. The nineteenth century saw the gradual removal of most of these disabilities, although the campaign for political equality was of little interest to many Jews. Henry Mayhew, who made a study of the London poor in the eighteen fifties, said, 'I was told by a Hebrew gentleman (a professional man) that so little did Jews themselves care for "Jewish emancipation", that he questioned if one man in ten, activated solely by his own feelings, would trouble himself to walk the length of the street in which he lived to secure Baron Rothschild's admission to the House of Commons.'[18]

Although the Reform Act of 1832 increased the number of people given the vote, only a small number of wealthy Jews benefited from these changes, as the franchise was still restricted to those with property. Four years earlier, Wellington's Tory Government had repealed the Test and Corporation Acts, which required holders of public office to be members of the Church of England. An amendment in the Lords, introduced by the Bishop of Landaff, however, inserted into the declaration required of those taking office the words 'on the true faith of a Christian.' Jews, Unitarians and atheists were still excluded from public office.' 19 This restriction does not seem to have been much applied to local government. A number of Jews had held office prior to 1828 and they continued to do so. Parliament was a different matter. Lionel de Rothschild was five times elected to Parliament between the years 1847- 1857, but, because he was not prepared to take the required oath, he was not allowed to take his seat. Sir David Salomon, however, who was elected for Greenwich in 1851, did take his seat, but was then expelled.

Eventually, the government overcame the bishops' opposition to changing the oath. Baron de Rothschild at last took his seat in July 1858. He continued as a member until 1874 - although there is no record that he ever spoke on the floor of the House! Other Jews were soon elected and if the Jewish population is compared to the total population of the country, Jews were, as Geoffrey Alderman says, 'soon "over-represented" in the Commons – a state of affairs that has persisted ever since.'20 Jewish members of Parliament were expected by their fellow believers to keep a watching brief over Jewish interests, although there were some complaints that the community did not receive the co-operation and assistance from some of the Jewish members of Parliament, which it had a right to expect. Some MPs, however, insisted that their responsibility was to *all* their constituents – an interesting example of the continuing question of how

Jews saw themselves in relation to the country's Christian majority.

Disraeli

Although Benjamin Disraeli was baptised into the Church of England at the age of twelve, he was widely regarded as Jewish.[21] It has been said that 'Conversion meant that Jews who had absented themselves from the synagogue became Christians who did not attend Church, except where bourgeois respectability demanded it.' Conversion was a way to escape the disabilities of being a Jew. Disraeli remained a Christian with unorthodox views. Even so, Disraeli was accepted in Jewish society.

There was a saying that 'in three places water is useless – in the ocean, in wine and in the baptism of Jews.' The German poet and essayist, Heinrich Heine, expressed well the attitude of many nineteenth century emancipated Jews. He wrote: 'From the nature of my thinking you can deduce that baptism is a matter of indifference to me and that I do not regard it as important even symbolically... The baptismal certificate is the ticket of admission to European culture.'[22]

Louise de Rothschild expressed 'a sort of pride in the thought that he (Disraeli) belongs to us - that he is one of Israel's sons.'[23] At the time Jewishness was interpreted more in racial terms than it would be today. Popular Jewish notions of who was a Jew were quite broad. It is often asserted that in the age of emancipation Jews preferred a national or ethnic definition of Jewishness, rather than one based on religion, because only this definition of Jewishness allowed them to participate fully in the life of the modern nation state. *The Jewish Encyclopaedia*, published in New York at the beginning of the twentieth century, included Disraeli in its list of Jews who showed intellectual leadership. The editors of the *Encyclopaedia* did not exclude 'those Jews who were of that race, whatever their religious affiliations may have been.' Twentieth century authors tend to avoid reference to Disraeli's Jewishness, but more recently Jewish authors have revisited his Jewishness.

The public tended to regard Disraeli as Jewish – cartoonists certainly did. In 1880, a cartoon in the magazine *Fun*, with the caption 'Shylock and his Pound of Flesh,' exaggerated 'Disraeli's "semitic" features. The whole attitude of his body is one of volatile menace.'[25] Usually Disraeli was portrayed as effeminate and as a fop, although in his novel *Coningsby* he himself emphasised the manliness of Jews Disraeli himself never ignored his Jewish background and expressed it in his novels. He did not, however, allow this to affect his political judgement. In the crisis following the massacre of thousands of Serbs in Bulgaria, who had risen up against their Turkish rulers, Disraeli refused to act despite pressure from the Jewish community and from Gladstone and his vocal supporters.

Anti-Semitism in Britain

The extent of anti-Semitism in the mid nineteenth an early twentieth centuries is disputed. Certainly Jews were barred from many clubs. It has been said that at the time 'Jews were accepted not for who or what they were, but according to terms set by the English majority and cast in the liberal rhetoric of toleration and universalism.'[26] As a result the aim of many Jews was to gain acceptance in society. In the mid-nineteenth century, Anglo-Jewry, in the words of Judge Finestein, was 'dominated by considerations of public image.'[27]

Jews felt they needed to prove that they were worthy of the

rights and freedoms that they were now allowed. The *Jewish Chronicle*, which was founded in the early 1840s - just as the West London Reform Synagogue was being established - helped literate and thoughtful members of Anglo-Jewry to orientate themselves as Jews in relation to the dominant culture of mid-Victorian Britain. The J.C, as the *Jewish Chronicle* is known, provided them with 'a Jewish gloss on the major intellectual developments of the day and formulated a response which they could adopt.' This explains why several articles were devoted to explaining Christian belief.[28]

Scholarly research stressed the duration of Jewish settlement in Britain and the contribution that Jews made to the "host" society. 'Jewish writers,' Geoffrey Alderman says, 'were expected to describe the community to the non-Jewish world in glowing, even angelic terms.'[29] Aguilar Grace Aguilar's (1816-47) *History of the Jews in England* was published in 1847 – the year of her death. In it, she wrote, 'Jews are still considered aliens and foreigners ... little known and less understood. Yet they are, in fact, Jews only in their religion – Englishmen in everything else.' Writers such as Benjamin Farejon Benjamin (1833-1903) and Samuel Gordon Samuel (1871-1927) gave idealized pictures of the 'English Jewish gentleman.'

From the Preface to the Fifth edition of Benjamin Disraeli's Coningsby or the New Generation, May 1849

In considering the Tory scheme, the author recognised in the Church the most powerful agent in the previous development of England, and the most efficient means of that renovation of national spirit at which he aimed...

In asserting the paramount character of the ecclesiastical polity and the majesty of theocratic principle, it became necessary to ascend to the origin of the Christian church and to meet in a spirit worthy of a critical and comparatively enlightened age, the position of the descendants of that race who were the founders of Christianity. The modern Jews had long laboured under the odium and stigma of mediaeval malevolence. In the dark ages, when history was unknown, the passions of societies, undisturbed by experience, were strong, and their convictions, unmitigated by criticism, were necessarily fanatical. The Jews were looked upon in the middle ages as an accursed race, the enemies of God and man, the especial foes of Christianity. No-one, in those days, paused to reflect that Christianity was founded by the Jews, that its Divine Author, in his human capacity, was a descendant of King David.

Church doctrines avowedly were the completion, not the change of Judaism; that the Apostles and Evangelists whose names they daily invoked, and whose volumes they embraced with reverence, were all Jews, that the infallible throne of Rome itself was established by a Jew; and that a Jew was the founder of the Christian Churches of Asia.

The European nations, relatively speaking, were then only recently converted to a belief in Moses and in Christ; and, as it were, still ashamed of the wild deities whom they had deserted, they thought they atoned for their past idolatry by wreaking their vengeance on a race to whom, and to whom alone, they were indebted for the Gospel they adored. In vindicating the sovereign right of the Church of Christ to be the perpetual regenerator of man, the writer thought the time had arrived when some attempt should be made to do justice to the race which had founded Christianity.

The writer has developed in his book *Tancred* the views respecting the great house of Israel which he first intimated in "Coningsby." No one has refuted them, nor is refutation possible; since all he has done is to examine certain facts in the truth of which all agree, and to draw from them irresistible conclusions, but which reason cannot refuse to admit.

Reuben Sachs

Reuben Sachs by Amy Levy (1861-89) – the first Jewish student at Newnham College, Cambridge – is a more realistic novel. It is the story of romantic love sacrificed on the altar of wealth. 'The world it describes, of a coterie of Jewish families in Maida Vale and Bayswater, is a world in which men are preoccupied with making money, and their womenfolk with displaying whatever it can buy. The book shows how Jewish values had been corrupted in the process.'[31] The *Jewish Chronicle* condemned the book and noted that wealthy members of the Jewish community exerted themselves to provide for poor Jews, so that they did not become a burden on the state.[32]

> *Charles Dicken's Good Jew*
>
> *'For instance' Fledgby resumed, 'who but you and I have ever heard of a poor Jew?' The old man, raising his eyes from the ground with his former smile, replied, 'The Jews often hear of poor Jews and are very good to them,*
>
> 'From *Our Mutual Friend*, 1863

The Jewish Chronicle

After emancipaion in 1860s the *Jewish Chronicle* continued to assist Anglo-Jewry in working out the identity of British Jews as citizens. 'It helped to delineate the relationship between the Jews and the state, and explored ways to combine the obligations of citizenship with the preservation of Judaism and the Jewish tradition. At the same time it sought to integrate Jews into English culture without jeopardising their Jewishness.' This difficult task became even more urgent during 1880s and 1890s under the impact of mass immigration and anti-Semitism. The Jewish Chronicle was also influential in encouraging the establishment of communal institutions and by creating a Jewish public opinion, which demanded them. The *Jewish Chronicle* subsequently kept a critical watch on these institution. By the late nineteenth century Jewish gentlefolk had gained an entrée into English society. Edward, Prince of Wales, (later King Edward VII) enjoyed the company of wealthy and cultured Jews, especially if they shared his great interest in horse racing. This *modus vivendi*, however, was threatened by the arrival of a large number of impoverished Jewish immigrants from Russia and Eastern Europe, following the pogroms of Tsar Alexander III Tsar (1881-1894).

The editor of the *Jewish Chronicle* warned of the danger: 'The constant flux of foreign co-religionists so different in speech and habits as they are from the general population, must tend to keep alive the lingering feeling that Jews are not and cannot be Englishmen, which still holds possession of so many minds.'[34]

Immigrants From Eastern Europe

The number of Jews in Britain in the eighteen-eighties was between fifty and sixty thousand, of whom more than two thirds lived in London. By 1914, the number had risen to about a quarter of a million. 'The cruel action of the Russian Government,' the *Jewish Chronicle* complained in 1903, 'has unsettled and introduced a grave feature into the whole course of Anglo-Jewish development.'[35] As early as 1888, Chief Rabbi Nathan Adler had urged his colleagues in Eastern Europe to discourage Jews from seeking entry to Britain.[36] Indeed some Jewish leaders supported calls to check the influx and to limit the number of immigrants allowed to enter the country, lest their arrival caused an anti-Semitic backlash.

The great majority of the new comers settled in East London. Many were destitute and some in the Jewish community provided and cared for them. Even so, the new comers were often exploited.

Beatrice Potter

Beatrice Potter described the scene at the landing stage. 'There are a few relations and friends awaiting the arrival of the small boats filled with immigrants: but the crowd gathered in and about gin-shop, overlooking the narrow entrance of the landing stage are "dock loungers" of the lowest type and professional "runners." ... They seize hold of the bundles or baskets of the new comers, offer bogus tickets to those who wish to travel forward to America or promise guidance and free lodging... In a few days, the majority of these, robbed of the little they possess, are turned out of the "free lodgings" destitute and friendless.'

Beatrice Potter mentions the valiant, but not very successful efforts of an official of the Hebrew Ladies' Protective Society to look after unprotected females.[37]

A number of the immigrants found work in tailoring or shoe making 'sweat shops.' As one victim wrote, 'the room we worked in was used for cooking also, and there I had to sleep on the floor... A young woman worked the machine from eight in the morning till nine at night, for three shillings a day... I had to get up in the morning about half past five and we finished at night between ten and eleven.'[38] There were complaints from some of the local community that the newcomers were undercutting them and that because of them rents were rising. A clergyman noted: 'When visiting the poor when times were bad, I often heard the weary complaint, "It's them Jews. Time after time I heard that lament. Many men and women, struggling to keep a home over their heads, but driven out of work by the foreigner, who "could live on less", and would take less and work longer, have said to me, "What's the use? The Jews are coming by thousands and there will be nothing left.""[39]

An extract from the report of the Royal
Commissionon Alien Immigration

'They have no sort of neighbourly feeling... A foreign Jew will take a house, and he moves in on a Sunday morning, which rather, of course, upsets all the British people there, who like to laze in bed. Then his habits are different. You will see houses with sand put down in the passages instead of oilcloth or carpet.'[40]

There were also the usual complaints about the aliens' way of life and warnings about the dangers to - what would now be called - 'social cohesion' of having a large number of people who 'remained apart and not merely held a religion differing from the vast majority of their fellow countrymen, but only intermarried among themselves.'

It was a time when the Yiddish press flourished. Many of the accusations made against the immigrant Jewish community were unjustified. They did not constitute a health hazard and they observed housing regulations.Jewish leaders were, however, aware that "peculiarities" of dress, language and manner did give rise to prejudice and tried to coax newcomers away from them. 'The great drive within the Anglo-Jewish community was to Anglicise the immigrants by all means possible.'Education was recognised as the long-term answer. It would provide newcomers with the skills necessary to improve their standard of living and would help them to be at home in British society. The use of Yiddish was discouraged and the importance of learning English emphasised. It was hoped English would have a 'distinctly civilising influence upon them.

This could create difficulties at home and also with names. In one family, the father who was a learned Hassidic Jew from Eastern Europe insisted that the children only spoke Yiddish at home. 'If he saw me reading an English book... he would throw it in the fire.' Names could also be a problem. When one pupil started at Manchester Jews' School, the headmistress asked 'What is your name?' 'Tauba,' the girl replied. 'Tauba's not a name. Ask your mother what she would like,' replied the headmistress. The girl's mother wanted to keep 'Tauba,' but the headmistress chose 'Matilda' instead. Finally they compromised on Tilly. The girl had been named Tauba after her grandfather Nonetheless despite the problems the policy achieved its objective. Whereas Yiddish is still spoken in some Jewish communities in New York, it almost died out in Britain. If children attended Board schools they learned traditional English playground games and read popular comics. Equally, as a Board of Trade Report noted, 'Pupils enter the (Jews' Free) school Russians and Poles and emerge from it almost indistinguishable from English children.' Free English classes were provided for adults and newcomers were introduced to British sports. A Jewish Lads' Brigade and a Jewish Girls' Club were set up. The price for this was that young Jews knew little about their culture and few could speak Hebrew. In the 1920s the leaders of the Anglo-Jewish community tried to encourage interest in Hebrew and in Jewish history and religion. The Jewish Lads Brigade was attacked for failing to provide religious teaching. Jewish clubs continued to play football and cricket matches against Jewish boys may have dated non-Jewish girls, few married 'out.' 'My parents would be so upset.'[50]

Just as the newcomers and, more so, their children were being turned into British Jews, the question of Jewish identity was raised in a new form by the growth of Zionism. This had as its goal the national self-determination of the Jewish people by the creation of a Jewish state. The story of Zionism will be told later. The point here is that 'Political Zionism, embracing as it must the notion of Jewish statehood and thus of Jewish nationality, struck at the very heart of the process of social, cultural and political assimilation of which Anglo-Jewish leadership was so proud.'Chief Rabbi Herman Adler said, 'since the destruction of the Temple and our dispersion, we no longer constitute a nation; we are a religious communion. We are bound together with our brethren throughout the world primarily by ties of a common faith. But in regard to all other matters we consider ourselves Englishmen and we hold that in virtue of being Jews it is our duty and privilege to work as zealously as possible for the welfare of England.'[52] Samuel Montagu (the first Lord Swaythling), said he felt himself 'to be more of an Israelite than an Englishman.'[53]Even if the leadership was mostly lukewarm about Zionism, there was quite a lot of popular support for it in the Jewish community. In 1915 nearly 50,000 British Jews signed a petition calling for the establishment of a 'publicly recognised, legally secured home for the Jewish people in Palestine.'[54]The question of identity was also highlighted during the First World War. Whereas Jewish leaders in Britain emphasised that the British war effort had the support of the whole Jewish community, popular anti-German hysteria did not always distinguish between Germans and Jews – some of whom were victims of the widespread xenophobia.

There is an amusing story of a Jew who had been badly injured in the War who attended a rally at which Fred Brocklehurst was telling the crowd that 'Britain is for the British: Send all foreigners back.' The man asked the speaker, 'What is the position of a man who came over here from Russia long before the war and brought up a family here? He's got half a dozen sons all fighting in the British army, several of them wounded – would he have to go back to Russia?' Fred Brocklehurst replied, 'It's a hard case, but we couldn't make any exceptions.' So the soldier said, 'I went on my crutches toward the platform and I threw a crutch at him. ... In those days a wounded soldier could commit murder and get away with it.'[55]

The Balfour Declaration and Zionism

Jews who were sympathetic to Zionism watched with delight the progress of British troops in the Middle East. They also welcomed The Balfour Declaration of the British government's support for a Jewish homeland. The importance of the Balfour Declaration is discussed more fully in the chapter on Israel. Here it is interesting to note that The Balfour Declaration, was not popular with a number of Jews – some of whom formed a League of British Jews 'to uphold the status of British subjects professing the Jewish religion' and resisting 'the allegation that Jews constitute a separate political entity.'[56]

A letter to the *Times*, published on May 24th, 1917, from the Conjoint Committee of British Jews, expressed forcefully the views of the opponents of Zionism.'Emancipated Jews in this country regard themselves primarily as a religious community, and they have always based their claims to political equality with their fellow-citizens of other creeds on this assumption and on its corollary – that they have no separate national assumptions in a political sense. They hold Judaism to be a religious system.'[57] Less than five hundred British Jews settled in Palestine during the first decade of the Mandate. By the mid-thirties, however, the Jewish community was becoming united in its support for Zionism. This was partly out of common feeling for Jews in Palestine who were faced by Arab hostility, partly in opposition to government moves to limit Jewish settlement in the Land – following the unpopular Passfield White Paper, published in 1930 - and most of all because of the growing fear of the anti-Semitic menace of the Nazis in Germany.

The Holocaust

The Shoah or Holocaust is discussed more fully in a later chapter. Of course, no one in the nineteen thirties would have believed that such a horror was possible: but there was growing alarm about news of Hitler's persecution of Jews. The Jewish community became increasingly resentful of the Government's moves to restrict the number of Jewish refugees from Hitler's Germany. More generous policies would have saved many more lives. The government, however, wished to avoid creating a 'Jewish problem' by allowing 'a flood of the wrong type of immigrants.'[58]

After the outbreak of war, a clear Declaration that Jewish refugees would be granted asylum in any part of the British Empire would have saved lives. Even after the war, survivors were cruelly refused entry to Palestine. But if the government can be criticised, the Jewish community cannot escape some blame.

Chief Rabbi Hertz told a Jewish audience in Finchley, 'While we are sitting in this hall ... hundreds of our brethren are being murdered. One feature of this unparalleled tragedy is the general indifference. Anglo-Jewry does not know what is going on, and the few who do, do not seem to care much.'[59] On the other hand, help that was given by both Jews and non-Jews to refugees and especially to refugee children who came unaccompanied on the Children's Transport (*Kindertransport*) needs to be remembered, even if the experience was profoundly traumatic for most of the children.

With the liberation of the death camps, the public gradually became aware of the unbelievable horror of the Holocaust. (My mother said she hid the papers when they first reported the atrocities as she did not want my sisters and I, as children, to read what had happened).

For almost twenty years there was an eerie silence about the Holocaust. Yet the Shoah, as Jews usually now call it, has overshadowed Jewish life for more than fifty years, just as much as the State of Israel has been a cause to be championed.

The legacy of the Holocaust affected British Jewry in many ways. One affect was on the size of the community, as a considerable number of Jewish refugees from Hitler made their way to Britain. Some 80,000 Jewish refugees from Central Europe were admitted in the period from 1933-1939. Another 70,000 came during the war years.
In the aftermath of the war about another 70,000 displaced persons or refugees came to Britain. Not all of these were Jewish and some were only temporary residents. Even so with less than half a million Jews in Britain the refugees were a sizeable proportion of the total. Their presence added to the enormous task of rebuilding Jewish institutions and community life, which had been, like most features of British life, shattered by the war. Yet among the refugees were many distinguished scholars and rabbis who made a big contribution to this task.

British Jewry also could not be unaffected by the dramatic changes in the wider Jewish world. As already mentioned, in 1939 of a total of about 17,000,000 Jews in the world, about 10,000,000 lived in Europe.

Rebuilding Jewish Life

After the War, America and then Israel became the major

homelands.60 Wartime evacuation and conscription led to the establishment of new Jewish communities in several cities, including Amersham, Beaconsfield, Guildford, Peterborough, St Albans, Windsor and Worcester. Moreover, some rural areas had Jewish residents for the first time. As a result the number of buildings registered for Jewish worship increased from 310 in 1934 to 428 by 1952. After a decline in the latter part of the last century, there are now again just over 400 synagogues. Even so, only about half of the Jews in the UK belong to a synagogue. In part this is because Jews who 'marry out' – that is to say who marry a non-Jew – are less likely to be observant: but there has been a more general decline in the numbers of both Christians and Jews who regularly attend a place of worship.

To redress the decline and to ensure that this generation has 'Jewish grandchildren' education and programmes for young people and adults designed to encourage Jewish continuity are now a priority.

Certain issues have continued to unite the Jewish community. One is support for Israel. For some years, until the collapse of Communism, campaigning for Jews in the Soviet Union was a unifying factor. Sadly, too, the ever-present threat of anti-Semitism.' 61

Two recent initiatives have been taken to strengthen the sense of Jewish identity. In 2010 the Jewish Museum, which was founded in 1932, moved to Camden. It houses a major international-level collection of Jewish ceremonial art. The museum's *Holocaust Gallery* includes items and filmed survivor testimony from Leon Greenman, who was one of the few British subjects to be interned in the death camps section at Auschwitz. The museum also has exhibitions recounting the history of Jewish life in England, supported by a diverse collection of objects. There are also collections of paintings, prints and drawings, and an archive of photographs, consisting mainly of photographs from the 1900s to the 1940s.In 2013, JW3, the first Jewish Community Centre and arts venue was opened in North West London. The aim is to transform the Jewish landscape in London by helping to create a vibrant, diverse and proud community, inspired by and engaged in Jewish arts, culture and community. By the end of its first year over 225,000 people had visited it.

What of the Future?

Jews continue to play an important role in British life – in government, public affairs, law, business, medicine, the arts and many other fields. Yet, Rabbi Tony Bayfield, who was for many years Head of Britain's Movement for Reform Judaism, views the future with anxiety. 'My overriding perception is of a community riddled by fear and anxiety: at the internal threats of diminishing numbers and a crisis of meaning beyond identity; and the external threats of never-ending anti-Semitism, the rise of populism and the consences for democracy all over the Western world.'[62]

Similar anxiety has been voiced by some of the Ultra-Orthodox Jews. In 2020, one headline in the *Jewish Chronicle* was 'No future for Orthodox Jews in Britain, says Rabbi Aaron Klein.' The report continues that 'One of the leading educational figures in Stamford Hill has warned there is "no future" for Orthodox Jews in Britain unless government proposals on regulating independent schools are changed.'[63] In June 2019, the *Jerusalem Post* had the headline, 'Could 300,000 Jews flee the UK.[64] After the 2019 General Election, The Chief Rabbi, still expressed concern about the future.[65]

4. RELIGIOUS DIVERSITY

If people do decide to join a synagogue, there is plenty of choice. Most often, people will continue in the tradition of their parents. The reasons that people join a synagogue are varied. It is not always because of belief, but because of what a congregation has to offer - 'for example: a nursery, a school or a *cheder* (a religious Jewish supplementary school).' Another motive for joining a synagogue may be the wish to secure a service when needed, such as burial, which is unavailable or less desirable elsewhere, thus utilising their membership as a means to an end. Others join perhaps to meet fellow Jews or to give their children some sense of what it means to be Jewish. 'There are also those who join because they feel responsible for the continuity of Jewish life generally, the continuity of their own congregation, or their family's traditions.' Affiliation to a synagogue, according to a report published by the Board of Deputies, is not synonymous with religiosity. 66

Christians, therefore, need to recognise that membership of a synagogue may not necessarily suggest strong belief and remember that Judaism is practised as much in the home as in the synagogue.

Moreover, at a communal level, British Jewry now offers multiple ways for individuals and groups to become attached and involved, such as political, welfare, cultural, or leisure activities. Jewish schools also have become increasingly important. It has even been said that "schools have now become the new *shuls*"(a Yiddish term for synagogues).

The trends mentioned above are to be seen in all sections of British Jewry, except the Strictly Orthodox. It is time now to try to distinguish the various traditions of belief and practice in British Jewry. The terms which groups use of themselves may be different from those that outsiders use of them, so any general descriptive phrase is not entirely accurate but merely intended as an aid to those who are not Jewish.

Orthodox Judaism
Sephardi Jews

As we have seen, the first Jews to return to Britain in the seventeenth century were Sephardim or descendants of the Jews, sometimes called Marranos, who had been expelled from Spain and Portugal and who had settled in various Mediterranean countries. They often spoke Ladino. It may be that a hidden Marranos community had already settled in the sixteenth century. Although, Sephardi ritual and mode of Hebrew pronunciation are different from that of Ashkenazi Jews, the distinction between Sephardi and Ashkenazi Jews is now largely one of family origin, as both Sephardi and Ashkenazi Jews may belong to Orthodox or Progressive synagogues. The Sephardi tradition is particularly maintained in the Spanish and Portuguese synagogues at Bevis Marks and in Maida Vale and Wembley.

Ladino

Ladino, otherwise known as Judeo-Spanish is the spoken and written Hispanic language of Jews of Spanish origin dating back nearly a thousand years. The language originally developed from Old Castilian Spanish and included many elements of Hebrew and Aramaic. Ladino did not become a specifically Jewish language until after the expulsion from Spain in 1492. When the Jews were expelled from Spain and Portugal, they were cut off from the further development of the language, but continued to speak it in the communities and countries they emigrated to. In Amsterdam, England and Italy, those Jews who continued to speak 'Ladino' were in constant contact with Spain, allowing them to continue to speak the Castilian Spanish of the time. However, in the Sephardic communities of the Ottoman Empire, the language borrowed words from Hebrew, Arabic, Greek, Turkish, and even French, and became increasingly different. This led to major splits in dialects of the language, forming into two primary regional dialects: "Oriental" and "Western."

Ashkenazi Jews

The Sephardim were soon followed by Ashkenazi Jews from Central and Eastern Europe. Because the Ashkenazi came from various places - some of which were rural - they were a diverse community. Gradually, as the Jewish immigrants to Britain became more settled, centres of worship were established. Important early Ashkenazi synagogues were the Great Synagogue - built in 1722 and rebuilt in 1790 - The Hambro synagogue, built in 1725 and the New Synagogue, founded in 1761. Most Ashkenazis spoke Yiddish. When they used Hebrew they differed from the Sephardim in pronunciation, in their liturgical melodies and in the details of their prayer rituals. There were approximately 13 million Yiddish speakers on the eve of World War II. That number was much reduced by the Shoah.

Yiddish

Yiddish is the third principal literary language in Jewish history after classical Hebrew and (Jewish) Aramaic. The language is characterized by a synthesis of Germanic, derived from medieval German, recombined with Hebrew and Aramaic. The word for the sun *(zun)* comes from Germanic; the word for the moon *(levóne)* from Hebrew; and the word for "probably" is from Aramaic *(mistáme)*. During the second half of the history of the language, a Slavic element (largely from neighbouring Polish, Belarusian, and Ukrainian dialects in Eastern Europe) was acquired, providing a new layer.

Famously Yiddish words for God include the universal deity, *got;* the more personal deity interested in human fate, *der éybershter* (from Germanic); one called out to in second person (or in third, as an exclamation), *rebóyne-shel-óylem* (from Hebrew); the more philosophical *rebóyne deálme* (Aramaic); and the emotional, homespun God invoked by Slavic-derived endings in *tátenyu zísinker* and *gótenyu*.

Here is one well known Yiddish saying:

A mensch tracht un Got lacht - Man plans and God laughs

The United Synagogue

In 1879 the Hambro and the United synagogues with some others came together in 1870 to create the United Synagogue, which now has about 40 member synagogues and 20 affiliated synagogues. The present membership is about 100,000 or 39,000 families. From early in the eighteenth century the rabbi of the Great Synagogue was recognised as the spiritual leader of British Jews and came to be known as the Chief Rabbi.[69] The United Synagogue can be said to represent 'modern Orthodoxy,' but its dominant position has increasingly been challenged by the growing number of both 'Ultra-Orthodox' and 'Progressive Jews' – to use convenient but not very precise terms.

Although the first Reform synagogue – the West London Synagogue – was opened in 1842, it may be more helpful first to mention other Orthodox communities.

Strictly Orthodox (Charedi) Judaism

If the membership of Orthodox synagogues is declining that of Strictly or Ultra-Orthodox synagogues is growing. Indeed some predict that Ultra- Orthodox Jews will make up the majority of British Jews before the end of this century, as high birth and low death rates drive population growth. According to a study in 2015 by the Institute for Jewish Policy Research, the growth among the strictly orthodox population is fuelled by a birth rate of seven children per mother, compared with 1.98 per mainstream Jewish woman. (The overall birth rate in the UK is 1.93; for Christians it is 1.53 and for Muslims 3.25.)[70]

The Federation Of Synagogues

The Federation of Synagogues was established in 1887 to link the growing number of small synagogues in the Eastend of London set up by Jews who had recently arrived from Russia and Eastern Europe. These immigrants on the whole shunned established synagogues and Jewish schools. Instead they established their own religious infrastructure, often centred on a *chevra* or fraternity. In Leeds, to give one example, immigrants did not attend the *Englische Shool* or the Great Synagogue in Belgrave Street, but founded the Great House of Study (in the early 1870s), the Central Synagogue in Templar Street (1885), the *Mariempoler Chevra* in Hope Street (1885) and the Polish Synagogue in Byron Street (1893). In East London also a large number of *chevrot* sprung up – some, with names such as the Warsaw Synagogue, indicating where the community had come from. Many of these fraternities could not afford a full time rabbi, but some could, and soon 'a veritable academy of rabbis from Eastern Europe became concentrated in the capital.'[71] These distinguished rabbinical scholars from Russia, Lithuania and Poland, in the eyes of orthodox Jews, were fully competent to authorise marriages and divorce, and to license *schochetim*, who performed approved ritual slaughter or *Schechita*.

The most influential of the rabbis was Werner Avraham Aba Werner (1837-1912), who had been a *Dayan* in Lithuania and rabbi in Helsinki, who became rabbi to the *Chevra Machzike Hadath* (Society of the Upholders of the Religion), which was an alliance of two strictly orthodox communities, one of German immigrants and the other of Russian and Polish settlers.

In 1898, the community moved into the Spitalfields Great Synagogue, at the corner of Brick Lane and Fournier Street. It now became a distinct and independent community, authorising its own marriages and divorces and setting up its own religious school. The community also arranged for its own kosher supplies, regarding existing arrangements as lax and expensive. This threatened the financial viability of the existing Shechita Board, but also was seen by Chief Rabbi Adler as a challenge to his authority. Eventually a settlement was reached in 1905, which allowed the *Machzike Hadath* to keep some of its institutions, in return for recognition of the overall authority of the Chief Rabbi 'provided that he acts in accordance with the Code of Jewish Law.'[72]

The passing of the Aliens Act in the same year (1905) helped to curb the already diminishing number of Jewish immigrants. Nonetheless, twenty-five years of large scale immigration had changed the nature of British Jewry. A new synagogal body now existed which reflected the different social, cultural and political outlook of communities, which did not share the ethos of 'English Jewish gentlemen.' The Federation was quick to support Zionism. Indeed, the differences continue to this day. The Federation has played no part in the election of the Chief Rabbis. It still has its own Beth Din (or Court),

Kashrus Board and Burial Society. The Federation today has 18 constituent synagogues and 8 affiliated congregations – (*kehillos*) mostly in the Greater London area.

Union Of Orthodox Hebrew Congregations

Another strictly Orthodox grouping is the Union of Orthodox Hebrew Congregations. Not all the adherents of the *Machzike Hadath* accepted the 1905 agreement with the Chief Rabbi and as a result they constituted the North London *Beth Hamedrash.* Dr V Schonfeld (1880-1930), a Hungarian, who was the presiding Rabbi of the *Adath Israel* synagogue in North London, soon became their leader. Several like-minded groups linked themselves to the *Adath Israel,* initially for burial purposes. In 1926 they established the Union of Orthodox Jewish Congregations - the name was later changed to the Union of Orthodox Hebrew Congregations (UOHC) – with the purpose of protecting traditional Judaism. Eventually after considerable reluctance by the Chief Rabbi, the *Adass* gained permission to authorise marriages and divorces, on condition that full information was subsequently sent to the Chief Rabbi's office.

The movement further developed under the leadership of his son Dr Solomon Schonfeld Solomon (1912-84). Solomon Schonfeld was a determined opponent of Zionism. He championed the establishment of independent orthodox primary and secondary education. Through his efforts, some 3,700 Jewish children and adults were rescued from the Nazis. UOHC's relations with the rest of the Jewish community have never been easy. In 1971 it withdrew from the Board of Deputies after concessions had been made to Progressive Jews. It has not returned, although the Board of Deputies, which speaks for all Jewish communities, continues to represent its interests.

Many of the post-war refugees, who settled mainly in

Stoke Newington, Stamford Hill, Hendon, Golders Green and Manchester, attached themselves to synagogues of the Union of Hebrew Congregations, thus reinforcing the growth of Strict Orthodoxy or 'Ultra Orthodoxy' as this tradition is sometimes called. Some however belonged to new groups, which have become increasingly influential.

Hasidic

Among the newcomers, two groups stand out: Lubavitch and Satmar.

Lubavitch

Lubavitch's roots lie in the Hasidic revivalist movement in eighteenth century Poland, founded by Baal Shem Tov – often known as the Besht – whom we shall meet again later. Within Hasidism, some people led by Shneur Zalman of Liady (1745-1813) emphasised the importance of the intellect. This tendency became known as Habad (sometimes Chabad), which is an acronym of the initial letters of three Hebrew words, which mean Wisdom, Understanding and Knowledge. Shneur Zalman's successor in leadership of Habad was his son Dov Baer, who settled in the Russian town of Lubavitch (1773-1827) – hence the name 'Lubavitch.' His successor was his son-in-law Menahem Mendel of Lubavitch (1787-1866). The sixth leader of the group, Rabbi Joseph Isaac Scheerson (1880-1950) settled in Brooklyn, New York. His son, the seventh Lubavitcher Rebbe was Rabbi Menahem Mendel Schneerson (1902-1994), who established a worldwide network of educational institutions and also a major publishing house.

Lubavitch has a special appeal for young people. In 1968, at the opening of Lubavitch House in London, the Lubavitcher Rebbe said: "This precisely is the basic function of the Lubavitch Centre: to gather Jewish children - children in the plain sense of the word, as well as "children" in terms of knowledge of

G-d, His Torah and Mitzvot - to reveal their inner soul and true essence, so that they recognise that "You are the children of G-d, your G-d," and should forge the golden chain of their ancestral tradition to the point of veritable self-sacrifice for the preservation of the Jewish way of life, the way of the Torah and Mitzvot."

Lubavitch is pro-Zionist and makes determined efforts to win back secularised Jews to a strict orthodoxy. Its relation to the modern world is complex. The aim is to reshape reality through traditional Jewish symbols and values and so bring about the coming of the Messiah. To do this, devotees are willing to use all modern media to spread the message. Young devotees also leave their homes and *yeshivas* (places of study) to encounter non-practising Jews on the streets. One of their best-known campaigns is the *tefillin* ritual, in which a person is invited to put on phylacteries in the midst of secular surroundings, thereby publicly reaffirming his or her Jewish identity.[74] Some Lubavitch rabbis now serve United Synagogues. As a result Lubavitch influence within Orthodox Judaism in Britain has grown and strengthened the move towards stricter observance. There are now over a dozen centres in Greater London and rather more in the rest of the UK.

Satmar

Satmar is less influential because its members are separatist. As far as possible, they avoid contact with modern society and seek to preserve their traditional values and way of life. They are anti-Zionist and unlikely to say prayers for the State of Israel.

Gateshead has become a centre of Talmudic study. The town is home to a small community of ultra-Orthodox Jews and is known worldwide for its educational institutions and *yeshivas* – most of which are to be found in a small area of rather less than one square mile. The Gateshead Talmudical College, also known as Gateshead Yeshiva, has a particularly high reputation. In London, members mainly live in Stamford Hill. There are about 30,000 members of the movement in the UK.

Although members of the 'Ultra-Orthodox' movements are unlikely to engage in dialogue with Christians or to participate in events arranged by the Council of Christians and Jews, Christians need to be aware of their growing influence and of the pressure they put upon the Chief Rabbi, especially if he makes any move toward Progressive Jews.

Progressive Judaism

Progressive Judaism is an umbrella term used for non-Orthodox movements, which include Reform, Progressive and Liberal Judaism. There are over 1,200 congregations around the world – both large and small, some established and others just starting. The World Union for Progressive Judaism, at the urging of Lily Montagu, was established in 1926. Members are committed to embracing pluralism, modernity, equality and social justice as core values and believe that such values are consistent with a committed Jewish life.

Progressive Judaism in Britain is represented by two organizationally distinct denominations – Liberal Judaism and Reform Judaism. Rabbis for both movements are trained at the Leo Baeck College in London. In the USA the largest denomination is Conservative Judaism, which occupies the middle ground between Orthodox and Reform Judaism. American Reform Judaism is probably closer to British Liberal Judaism.

The Movement For Reform Judaism

Just as the Ultra-Orthodox numbers are growing so are those of Progressive movements. As in the early nineteenth century some emancipated Jews entered more fully into European society, they became uncomfortable with aspects of Jewish worship and practice. Israel Jacobson, a German Jewish financier and communal leader initiated reforms. At a school he established in Westphalia, he allowed Christians to teach general subjects. He also introduced hymns and some prayers in German. In 1810, he built the first Reform Temple, close to his school. Soon afterwards he moved to Berlin and founded a temple there. Then, in 1819, a Reform Temple was opened in Hamburg by Eduard Kley, who had previously been a preacher with the Berlin Reform Group. In 1819, the Hamburg Temple issued a prayer book, which omitted repetitions and medieval poems.

In London, the issue was more the inconvenience to Jews who lived in the West End of having to attend worship at Bevis Marks synagogue, which was in the city. There were also some complaints about the lack of decorum during services. One of the governing rules of Bevis Marks was that no other Sephardi synagogue was to be built within six miles of it. It was suggested that a branch synagogue should be opened in the West End, but this was rejected by the governing body of Bevis Marks, who also insisted that any changes in ritual had to be agreed by the authorities of the whole community. Twenty-four gentlemen decided to ignore this ruling and to establish a new congregation to include both Sephardi and Ashkenazi Jews – eighteen of the gentlemen were Sephardim and six Ashkenazi Jews.

Despite the anger of the Orthodox authorities, the West London Synagogue of British Jews was opened in January 1842 in Burton Street, close to Euston. The synagogue moved to its present building in Upper Berkley Street in 1870. A Reform Synagogue was opened in Manchester in 1857 and another in Bradford in 1873. Yet by the outbreak of the Second World War in 1939 there were only six Reform congregations. Initial reforms were modest and it was only after the First World War that men and women were no longer required to sit apart.

It was not until the 1930s that Reform Judaism began to develop significantly, partly thanks to refugees from Germany. Amongst them were some outstanding rabbis, including Rabbi Ignaz Maybaum and Rabbi Werner Van der Zyl, whom I had the honour of meeting when the World Congress of Faiths, for the first time, held its annual All Faiths Service at the West London Synagogue in 1967. In the 1930s, the Senior Minister at the West London Synagogue was Rabbi Harold Reinhart, who was a graduate of the Hebrew Union College at Cincinnati. Under his guidance, a new Reform prayer book was completed in 1931 and new headquarters were opened in 1934.

Synagogues were also founded in the expanding suburbs of Golders Green and Edgware as well as in Glasgow. In 1942 these synagogues formed the Associated British Synagogues and in 1948 set up their own Beth Din or law court, thereby affirming the total independence of the movement, which in 1958 became the Reform Synagogues of Great Britain (RSGB). In 2005, the movement changed its name to 'The Movement for Reform Judaism' – an umbrella movement often just called Reform Judaism. In 1956, a theological seminary was established and is now situated at the Sternberg Centre for Judaism. It is named after the great non-orthodox German Jewish leader Leo Baeck (1873-1956), who came to Britain as a Holocaust survivor.

There are now just over 50 autonomous Reform synagogues in Britain, with a membership of more than 35,000 men, women and children, which is nearly twenty per cent of UK synagogue affiliations. Reform Judaism seeks 'to engage with Jews "where they are"... It offers authentic, pluralist Judaism, rooted in tradition yet in dialogue with modernity.'[75]

Liberal Judaism

The Liberal Jewish movement in Britain dates back to the beginning of the last century. The prime mover was Lily Montagu, who was the sixth child of Samuel Montagu, a leading member of the Federation of Synagogues. Lily became increasingly unhappy with the oppressive orthodoxy imposed on the family by her father. Her unease was partly because of her own deep spirituality and because Orthodoxy provided no formal role for women in its organisation. She recognised that many Jews were alienated from the faith by strict orthodoxy. At the age of fifteen she had a mental crisis, from which she emerged with the conviction that she was called to minister to the Jewish community. As a woman, it was impossible for her to become a rabbi. Instead she immersed herself in social work in the Jewish East End. She was also attracted by the views and personality of Claude Montefiore (1858-1938), who was propounding a 'de-nationalized and de-ritualized' theology of Judaism.[76] Accepting a modern critical view of scripture, Claude Montefiore rejected the Orthodox belief that Torah was the very word of God. To be a good Jew, he said, was to bear witness to 'righteousness in action and truthfulness of the heart.'[77] Claude Montefiore also wrote a sympathetic commentary on the Synoptic Gospels.

By the 1890s, Lily Montague was conducting a very flexible service in English for children and had composed a book of *Prayers for Jewish Working Girls.* In January 1899, she published an essay in the *Jewish Quarterly Review,* of which Claude Montefiore was a co-editor. She condemned the 'materialism and spiritual lethargy' of Anglo-Jewry and called for a new form of Judaism in which 'all that was valuable and lovely in the ancient faith' would be preserved in 'forms acceptable to emancipated minds.'[78]

Following from this The Jewish Religious Union was formed in 1902. Lily Montagu seems to have hoped that the body could achieve reform in the whole Jewish community – indeed at the time relations between Orthodox and Reform Jews were quite cordial. By 1909, when the name was changed to The Jewish Religious Union for the Advancement of Liberal Judaism, it was clear that an independent body was coming into being. The first Liberal Jewish Synagogue was opened in Marylebone in 1911, with Israel Mattuck (1883-1954) as its rabbi. In 1925, the synagogue moved to larger premises in St John's Wood Road –near to Lords cricket ground.

Liberal Judaism was strengthened by the influx of refugees from Continental Europe. In 1944, the movement became the Union of Liberal and Progressive Synagogues (ULPS). There have been on-going but inconclusive moves to bring Reform and Liberal Judaism together - like the discussions between the Church of England and the Methodist Church. In 1964 the ULPS agreed to become a partner in Leo Baeck College.

Liberal Judaism describes itself as 'the dynamic cutting edge of |modern Judaism' There are now some 40 Liberal synagogues or regional groupings.[79]

In 2014 Reform and Liberal Judaism formed an alliance to increase collaboration between the two movements in areas such as student chaplaincy, social justice and social action and to strengthen existing joint work at Leo Baeck College as well as representation on cross-communal institutions. Liberal and Reform leaders stressed that that the two movements would retain their autonomy and distinct identities.

Other Movements

Masorti

'The Jacobs Affair'

Somewhere between Orthodox and Progressive Judaism is the Masorti movement, which describes itself as 'traditional Judaism for modern Jews.' It grew out of the so-called 'Jacobs affair.' Rabbi Dr Louis Jacobs Louis (1921-2006), who was born in Manchester, was both a graduate of London University and of the Gateshead Yeshiva. He soon gained a reputation as a distinguished Talmudic scholar, but he did not accept the usual Orthodox view that every word of the five Books of Moses – the Pentateuch – had been dictated to Moses by God. He explained this in his book *We Have Reason to Believe*, which was published in 1957, without any censure by the Chief Rabbi. Indeed, Chief Rabbi Dr Brodie approved Dr Jacobs' appointment to the staff of Jews College - with the understanding that he would succeed Rabbi Dr Epstein as Principal of the College. Yet when in 1961, Epstein was, against his will, forced to resign, Dr Jacobs was not offered the post. As Louis Jacobs was neither promoted nor dismissed, he chose to resign.

He was then asked to return to the New West End Synagogue where he had previously been the rabbi. This appointment required the approval of the Chief Rabbi, which Dr Brodie was prepared to give, provided Dr Jacobs would retract his views about the nature of Divine revelation. Dr Jacobs refused to do this. The members of the synagogue nonetheless resolved to appoint him, despite the Chief Rabbi's objections. The United Synagogue Council responded by dismissing the Synagogue's honorary officers. As a result, over 300 members of the synagogue resolved to form an independent congregation, led by Louis Jacobs 'to work for the return of the United Synagogue to its own traditions of tolerance and the "Progressive Conservatism" referred to in the preamble to its Bye-laws.'[80] Eventually the congregation established the 'New London Synagogue.' Subsequently, with the establishment in the nineteen-eighties of a few other synagogues with a similar approach, the Assembly of Masorti Synagogues was set up. (Masorti is the Hebrew for tradition). This has a membership of over one thousand.

At issue, as Dr Jacobs himself recognised was the question of what was meant by Orthodoxy. 'I repeatedly said,' he wrote, 'that if Orthodoxy denotes fundamentalism, I was not Orthodox and did not want to be Orthodox. But if Orthodoxy meant, as it had in Anglo-Jewry, an adherence to traditional practice, then I could claim to be Orthodox.'[81] He pointed out that no one could think that the saying in the Pentateuch that 'And the Lord spoke unto Moses saying' was intended to convey the thought that these words, too, were spoken by God to Moses.'[82] But Jacobs went further than that. He made clear that, in his view, the creation narrative in Genesis could not be squared with the findings of modern science. He saw the creation of *Torah* as a dynamic process and accepted the principle of historical development.[83] Jacobs also rejected the view that the matter was one only for scholars and that members of a congregation should not be troubled by this. He held that the disagreement between fundamentalism and non-fundamentalism was one that any lay person could understand.[84] The second part of the Jacobs affair took place at the same time as Christians were arguing about *Honest to God* - a provocative book written by the then Bishop of Woolwich, John Robinson. The 'Honest to God debate' was about the image of God whereas the 'Jacobs affair' was about the authority of scripture

The Masorti Community

Masorti is affiliated to the World Council of (Conservative) Synagogues, whose membership has includes strictly observant Jews like Louis Ginzberg, Abraham Heschel or Louis Finkelsten who see 'no incompatibility between the acceptance of the findings of critical scholarship and complete loyalty to the Halakhic process.[85]

There are now some fourteen Masorti Jewish communities with a total membership of about 4,000.

Oxford

Mention also needs to be made of the unique Oxford Jewish Community. It welcomes Jews of every persuasion and whatever their level of observance. Services for Orthodox, Masorti and Progressive Jews are held there, sometimes simultaneously. The Centre provides for all the Jews in Oxford, be they permanent residents, students or just visitors passing through. The community recognises that there is no single kind of Judaism that fits everybody, no one size that fits all.

Reconstructionism

Reconstructionism is a modern movement founded in America by Mordecai Kaplan (1881-1983), who was born in Lithuania but was taken to the USA when he was nine. Kaplan, who adopted a naturalistic philosophy, rejected the view that God was a Person or Being outside and beyond the universe. God, he said, was best understood as a power present in the universe and in the human psyche that makes for righteousness. The commandments derive from the God within the Jewish soul. They remain important but their meaning is reinterpreted. He compared the Sabbath to an artist standing back from his or her work. In the same way we need a Sabbath to stand back from daily life so that we can see its meaning. Judaism, for Kapla, was a preparation for a moral life and contributed to the health of society.

The movement dates from 1922, when the Society for the Advancement of Judaism was founded in New York. The magazine *Reconstructionist* was started in 1935. There are a few Reconstructionist congregations in America, but not in this country. Nonetheless Kaplan's re-interpretation of Judaism, which could be compared to the Christian 'Sea of Faith' Movement, has been quite influential.

Leadership In The Community
The Chief Rabbi

Traditionally the Chief Rabbi has been seen as the spokesman for all British Jews. The growth of Reform and Liberal Judaism, however, has meant that leaders of other traditions now have a more public role. For example, the Jewish representative who lays a wreath at the Cenotaph on Remembrance Sunday changes from year to year. During the nineteen eighties (when I was Director of the Council of Christians and Jews), CCJ had only one Jewish President – namely the Chief Rabbi. Already Progressive Jews were asking for their own CCJ President. Now, most major traditions are represented.[86]

The Chief Rabbinate of England is an institution that first arose in the 18th century, initially evolving from the Rabbinate of the Great Synagogue in London, and gradually extending its influence to encompass both Britain's provincial Jewish communities and those across the British Empire. That it evolved independently of a secular power, rather than being instituted by civil authorities, marks it out as unique within the European Rabbinates.

It was not until the final decades of Aaron Hart's incumbency, in the middle of the eighteenth century, that the office of 'Rabbi of the Great Synagogue' became synonymous with that of 'Chief Rabbi of Britain', with provincial Ashkenazi communities, members of which often had links to London congregations, voluntarily subscribing to his spiritual authority. As Chief Rabbi he provided answers to Halachic (Jewish legal) enquiries, accreditation for Shochetim (those whose work is to slaughter animals according to kosher requirements) and issued marriage licenses to his spread-out disciples. The new title also evolved from a communal desire for official representation, akin to the Archbishop of Canterbury's role in Church life. Unanimous recognition of the position's dual nature did not occur until 1758 however, when the Hambro synagogue – an early 18th century breakaway faction of the Great Synagogue – acknowledged the authority of incoming Great Synagogue Rabbi Hart Lyon. This concord was short-lived, as disagreements between the two London communities over the selection of the next Great Rabbi led to the Hambro installing their own Rabbi in 1765, Meshullam Solomon, who (unsuccessfully) bestowed upon himself the mantle of Chief Rabbi of the British Ashkenazi population. The schism even divided the prominent provincial community of Portsmouth for a time, but following Solomon's departure from England in 1780, the Chief Rabbinate once again became an institution recognised by all provincial communities as the unequivocal heart of English, and later Imperial Jewry.

Since then, the British Jewish community has evolved beyond the auspices of the United Synagogue (instituted in 1870 to unite Orthodox congregations) with younger movements not officially recognising the Chief Rabbi as their representative. Nevertheless, the present Chief Rabbi Mirvis maintains healthy relations with their respective leaders in his bid to unite British Jewry.[87]

The Board Of Deputies

It is, however, the Board of Deputies of British Jews that speaks for the community. The Board dates from 1760 when seven Deputies were appointed by the elders of the Sephardi congregation of Spanish and Portuguese Jews to form a standing committee and pay homage to George III on his accession to the throne. Shortly thereafter the Ashkenazi Jewish congregation from Central and Eastern Europe similarly appointed their own "Secret Committee for Public Affairs" to deal with any urgent political matters that might arise, and safeguard the interests of British Jews as a religious community, both in the British Isles, and in the colonies. They soon began to meet together as occasions arose, and then on a more frequent basis; by the 1810s they appear to have united as one body, named the London Committee of Deputies of British Jews. In the mid-18th century, the body was dominated by Moses Montefiore, the Sephardi lay leader of British Jewry, and Nathan Adler, the Ashkenazi Chief Rabbi. It adopted its current name in 1913. During its history, some of the major divisions in opinion have been between Sephardi and Ashkenazi and between religious and lay leaders.

Today, to quote from its website, 'The Board of Deputies delivers tangible results. Our elected leadership is supported by a professional team without parallel in our community. The work of the Board of Deputies reaches those in positions of influence in towns and cities across the UK, including those who have little exposure to the Jewish community. It is through tools such as the innovative 'Jewish Manifesto' series that we have been able to extend our reach further than ever across the whole of the UK.

The Board of Deputies works in a range of areas on a host of issues. We work to combat antisemitism from wherever it emanates, to express our community's bond with the State of Israel, to defend Jewish education and to educate wider society about Judaism and build bridges through interfaith relations. We are also the foremost point of contact for London's diplomatic community, and the UK affiliate of the European Jewish Congress and World Jewish Congress.'[88]

Recently, the Board has been very active in alerting the wider public to the growth of virulent anti-Semitism.

What Of The Future?

Geoffrey Alderman ended the revised 1998 edition of his *Modern British Jewry* on a depressing note. 'British Jewry stands on the verge of the next millennium more disorganised, and more divided, than ever before. Its demographic decline continues in a seemingly irreversible fashion... Religious polarization now affects almost every communal initiative... [This is] symptomatic of a much deeper malaise, stemming perhaps, from a complete breakdown of communal identity.

Judaism once united the Jews of Britain; now it divides them. Zionism once united the Jews of Britain, and indeed provided them with an alternative ethnic identity; now it divides them too. A substantial proportion of British Jews do, however, claim to feel secure in British society, and no longer think of themselves as living in exile. It may be, therefore, that in the next century much of what we now regard as modern British Jewry will disappear, submerging itself within a species of secular ethnicity while retaining picturesque memories of its Jewish origins. However, there may still be recognizably British Jews, a strange and largely suburban-dwelling remnant, small in numbers but rich in the distinctively Jewish contribution that it is still capable of making to British society.'[89]

Much the same could be said of the traditional churches. Alderman's remarks highlight the problems facing many established faith communities. Elliott Abrams says of America that 'as religion has been driven to the margins of American life, Jews have become less Jewish.'[90] Whether American Jews can commit themselves anew to the goal of survival, to reversing the demographic patterns that threaten their collective future, depends on whether they *still believe they are above all else members of a religious community*. As an ethnic, cultural, or political identity they are doomed.'[91]

The situation, however, is not as bad as Alderman suggests. Synagogue membership is stable and perhaps increasing – especially of Ultra-Orthodox Jews. There have been important developments in higher education. The Oxford Centre for Hebrew and Jewish Studies, which was the brainchild of David Patterson (1922-2005), who was an expert in the study of Hebrew literature – attracts scholars from around the world. The Woolf Institute in Cambridge, under the energetic leadership of Ed Kessler, has expanded rapidly and offers a wide range of courses to promote understanding of and between Islam, Judaism and Christianity.[92] The Sternberg

Centre has also grown rapidly and is home for a number of important initiatives. The Spiro Ark, which continues the work of the Spiro Institute, uses innovative teaching methods to help develop a learning community. Limmud is a cross-communal, adult education initiative. Its residential winter conference and its summer and regional events all attract a good attendance.

There is concern too for the next generation. According to the Partnership for Jewish Schools, in 2018, there were 120 Jewish schools, attended by 37,000 children. These schools range from the ultra-orthodox same-sex to more secular mixed schools. There are both primary and secondary schools and state and fee-paying schools. Although predominantly in London, there are Jewish schools in Glasgow, Birmingham, Liverpool, Leeds and Manchester, although in some of the pupils are not Jewish. There are none in Wales or Northern Ireland.[93]

Organization such as the Faith and Belief Forum and the Council of Christians and Jews provide opportunities for pupils who are at faith schools to meet with children of other religions. The Faith and Belief Forum's 'Parliamentors Programme, which has received a United Nations award, brings small teams of university students of different faiths and non-religious beliefs together to network and learn the skills they need to effect real change in their communities. They are mentored by Members of Parliament.

Another sign of growth is the increasingly important role that women are playing in the life of the community. In 1975, Rabbi Jackie Tabick, was the first woman in British reform to be ordained. Orthodox Judaism has not followed this example, but in 1991, the then Chief Rabbi sanctioned the first women-only Sabbath service, although women were not permitted to read from the Torah scroll.

5. DIFFERENCES OF BELIEF AND PRACTICE

Belief

The key issue that divides Orthodox and Progressive Jews is the authority of both the written and oral Torah. There is a rabbinic saying that 'Moses received Torah from Sinai and passed it on to Joshua, and Joshua to the Elders, and the Elders to the Prophets; and the Prophets passed it on to men of the Great Assembly.' For Orthodox Jews, the authority attached to scripture - the written Torah - also applies to its rabbinical interpretation, the Oral Torah. Both are said to be *Halakhah leMoshe m'Sinai* - dictated by God to Moses essentially as they exist today. Traditionalists accept there may be some scribal errors but are cautious about the use of Biblical criticism, which tries to identify the date and context in which the books of the Bible were written. In the words of one modern Orthodox writer, 'The Torah must be seen as a record not of man's spiritual genius, but of God's will communicated to mortal and finite man... No interpretation of Judaism is Jewishly valid if it does not posit God as the source of Torah.'[94] Yet, as David Ariel says, in his book *What do Jews believe?*, 'the traditional notion of the divine authorship of Torah is not as fundamentalist or literalist as it appears and represents a far more complex phenomenon. Concerning the divine origin of Torah, Jewish tradition itself is far more diverse and accepting of other approaches.'[95]

Some Orthodox scholars make use of modern critical scholarship. For example, Rabbi Dr Norman Solomon, a very open-minded and scholarly Orthodox Jew, has written, 'Our attitude towards sacred text, in particular the Bible and the Talmud, has changed under the impact of modern scholarship. We have learned to see them as the record of the Israelite and Jewish response to God over a period of some thousands of years, and in varying cultural environments. We therefore try to relate statements to their social-historical contexts, and we recognise the views, which then emerge, as attempts, not always perfectly executed and by no means always mutually consistent, to grapple with major issues. Bible and Talmud are not "proof texts" but guides to life, aids to our rediscovery and reformulation of the teachings and insights they enshrine.'[96]

According to Orthodox Judaism, Jewish law today is based on the commandments in the Torah, as viewed through the discussions and debates contained in classical rabbinic literature, especially the Mishnah and the Talmud. Orthodox Judaism thus holds that the *Halakhah* represents the "will of God", either directly, or as closely to directly as possible. To the Orthodox Jew, *Halakhah* is a guide, God's Law, governing the structure of daily life from the moment he or she wakes up to the moment a person goes to sleep. It includes codes of behaviour applicable to a broad range of circumstances (and many hypothetical ones). There are a number of meta-principles or over-arching values that guide the halakhic process, especially when a new issue arises. Examples of Halakhik meta-principles are: *Deracheha Darchei Noam* - the ways of Torah are pleasant - *Kavod Habriyot* - basic respect for human beings - and *Pikuach Nefesh* - the sanctity of human life.

Modern Orthodox authorities are willing to accept that under scrupulous examination, identical principles may lead to different applications in the context of modern life. They recognize that some elements of the law were decreed or added as 'fences' around the law so as to warn people that they were in danger of breaking a law. Those Jewish theologians, who choose to emphasize the more evolutionary nature of the *Halacha* point to a famous story in the Talmud where Moses is magically transported to the House of Study of Rabbi Akiva and is clearly unable to follow the ensuing discussion.

'When Moses ascended into heaven, he saw God occupied in making little crowns for the letters of the Torah. Upon asking what these might be for, he received the answer, "There will come a man, named Akiva ben Joseph, who will deduce *Halakot* from every little curve and crown of the letters of the Law." Moses' request to be allowed to see this man was granted; but he became much dismayed as he listened to Akiva's teaching; for he could not understand it.'[97]

There is significant disagreement within Orthodox Judaism, particularly between Ultra-Orthodox and Modern Orthodox Jews, about the extent and circumstances under which the proper application of *Halakha* should be re-examined as a result of changing realities. As a general rule, Ultra-Orthodox Jews believe that whenever possible the law should be maintained as it has been practiced through the generations. For some it is a principle of belief that *Halakhah* never changes and regard higher criticism of the Talmud and indeed of the Bible as inappropriate, and almost certainly heretical.

Progressive Judaism rejects the traditional view that the Torah is '"the word of God" given (by direct inspiration or in some other way) by God to Moses.'[98] W. Gunther Plaut, the editor of *The Torah: A Modern Commentary*, explains that

'The commentary proceeds from the assumption that the Torah is a book which had its origin in the hearts and minds of the Jewish people.' The question, then, is what if anything does God have to do with the Bible? Why is it any more significant than other ancient literature, other than its role in shaping Western civilization? Plaut's answer is 'we believe it is possible to say: the Torah is Israel's distinctive record of its search for God. It attempts to record the meeting of the human and the Divine, the great moments of encounter. Therefore, the text is often touched by the ineffable Presence. The Torah tradition testifies to a people of extraordinary spiritual sensitivity. God is not the author of the text, the people are: but God's voice may be heard through theirs if we listen with open minds.'[99]

Likewise, Rabbi Tony Bayfield summarizes his discussion in this way: 'I'm not dismissing or downgrading the Torah text nor the infinite number of meanings generations have found and continue to find in it. But I am insisting that even the primary text is an interpretation of our ancestors' experience of God, not the experience itself. *The text of Torah is itself interpretation.*'[100]

It follows that if God is not the author of the Written Torah, even less is the Oral Law directly given by God. Jonathan Romain says, 'Reform Judaism, is in this sense 'non-*Halakhik* for it does not accept the theory, methodology or practice of Orthodox interpretations of Judaism: the Torah is not regarded as the literal word of God: subsequent rabbinic rulings are not accepted as binding; and many centuries old practices have been abolished. Even if many observances are the same, the reasons behind them are often different from the *Halakhik* ones... Reform always takes account of the *Halakhah* and regards it as the starting point for all decisions, but it does not feel bound by *Halakhah*.'[101]

Practice

For many Jews, differences in practice are more important than the theological ones. It is also true that each individual member of a religion needs to work how her or his faith guides her or his daily life. Even so it may be helpful to give some examples of how the differences of approach affect practice.

Sabbath Observance

According to the *Halakhah*, Jews are not permitted to discuss their business affairs on the Sabbath: they should not handle money; they should not carry anything from a public to a private place. They should not ride in an automobile, even if driven by a non-Jew, nor switch on electric lights or use any electrical appliances – although time-switches are permitted.'[102] In the Reform tradition 'a redefinition of work permitted on the Sabbath has been undertaken. The object is to preserve the original spirit of the Sabbath command – a day of pleasurable rest and spiritual refreshment which is marked by refraining from normal work... turning on a light [is allowed] as it enhances rather than detracts from the Sabbath... Driving on the Sabbath is allowed if it is used to attend a synagogue or visit relatives, but not if it is to go shopping.'[103] Progressive Judaism puts more weight on the individual's decision on what behaviour is appropriate and to following his or her conscience. It must be remembered, however, that in every community people make adjustments to the demands of modern life.

'Mixed Faith Marriage'

Although 'marrying out' (marrying a non-Jew) is discouraged, about a quarter of Jews choose a non-Jewish partner.

Dr David Graham, a senior research fellow at Jewish Policy Research, found that 'Intermarried Jewish men are four times less likely to raise Jewish children than intermarried Jewish women.' Even if the child is brought up Jewish, he said, his/her parents' differing ethnicities "at least doubles" the chance of the child intermarrying. He added that in a mixed marriage, the Jewish partner is far less likely to maintain Jewish customs and tradition. 'Intermarried Jews exhibit far weaker levels of Jewish practice and performance than in-married Jews. For example, 91 percent of in-married Jews light candles on Friday night at least occasionally, compared with 36 percent of intermarried Jews."[104]

For some years there was an opportunity for those planning a 'mixed faith marriage' to come to a day gathering entitled, 'I'm Jewish, my partner isn't'. I was invited, as a Christian priest, to be present to see fair play. One issue that always came up was having a Christmas tree, which highlighted the question of in which faith should children be brought up. Sometimes, it was a matter of which parent was 'most religious', others wanted their children to learn about both faiths, and perhaps most often the question was evaded.

Anya Topolsiki highlights the pain that can be caused by a refusal to cross boundaries.

Anya who is Jewish and her husband, who is a practicing Catholic and a former seminarian, had an interfaith wedding. Their ketubah (Jewish marriage contract) included their promise 'to strengthen each other in our respective faiths and to raise our children as both Jews and

Christians.' When, tragically, their young daughter died, they wanted an interfaith funeral: but within twelve hours of the child's death, Anya's local rabbi told her, 'On principle, I am opposed to officiating at an interfaith ceremony.' A visiting rabbi was more sympathetic and the funeral was 'a moment of beauty and peace.' Anya, however, discovered real difference between the prescribed Jewish ritual for mourning (*Shiva*) and the Christian lack of one: but also that Catholicism has much to say about the afterlife, whereas Jews focus on life in this world rather than 'the world to come.' She was pained that her non-Jewish husband was not counted as part of the *minyam* - the minimum of ten people needed - to say *kaddish*, (the mourner's prayer).[105]

From *Ritual Participation and Interreligious Dialogue*

Homosexuality

There is a similar division of opinion about homosexuality and whether blessing of a civil partnership – often called a 'gay-marriage' – should be allowed. Orthodox Jews, bound by biblical and rabbinic law only condones sexual relationships between a man and a woman who are married. Most Orthodox Jewish authorities continue to regard homosexuality as sinful, although some accept that homosexuality is a condition and think it is a matter that should be left to the individual's relationship with God.

Rabbi Dr Julian Shindler, of the Office of the Chief Rabbi, has made clear that 'there is no prospect of the mainstream Orthodox community permitting same-sex commitment or marriage services.[107]

Reform Judaism is fully opposed to discrimination on any grounds. As the Cardiff Reform Synagogue says on its website, 'Living Judaism is unconditionally committed to the principle of equality, both before God and in Jewish communal life. We recognise the frequently disorientating effect of change in the social sphere particularly, but we are absolutely committed to the full implementation of principles of equality – not least between women and men and between heterosexuals and homosexuals.'[108]

Reform Judaism allows individual rabbis to make their own decision whether or not to participate in some form of 'commitment ceremony' although the term 'gay-marriage' should be avoided. 109

Same Sex Marriages

Orthodox Jews hold that same-sex relationships are not allowed by Torah. In 2009, however, Liberal Jews became the first mainstream religious organisation in Britain to sanction a 'gay marriage service.' The ceremony may take place in a synagogue or a private venue. A liturgy called 'Covenant of Love' was produced to coincide with the Civil Partnership Law. Rabbi Danny Rich, Liberal Judaism's chief executive said, at the time, 'When civil partnership comes into force, Liberal Judaism will be in a unique position to meet the needs of lesbian and gay people.'[110] Rabbi Elizabeth Tikvah Sarah of Brighton and Hove progressive Synagogue also has said that 'the Civil Partnership Act is a historic milestone, granting legal status and recognition to lesbian and gay partnerships. Liberal Judaism champions justice, equality, compassion and inclusion; the new liturgy ensures that these values are put into practice as far as lesbian and gay Jews are concerned, by enabling lesbian and gay couples to celebrate their partnership in a Jewish framework.' [111] Since 2014 all Progressive Jews recognise same-sex marriages and allow services to be held in synagogues. As one Reform rabbi said, "We regard same-sex marriages as fully equal and the requirements are the same."[112]

Although there have been differences between Reform and Liberal Jews – as for example, at one time, Liberal Jewish prayer books opened from left to right. In recent years, the two traditions have come closer together, as the Liberals have reintroduced many traditions that were previously abandoned. For example, Liberal Jews now often wear head coverings in the synagogue and make more use of Hebrew in the service.

Shared Beliefs

The theological differences, however, between Orthodox Judaism and Progressive Judaism appear at present irreconcilable. Yet in every religion, there are over-arching concepts shared by most members of that faith, which create a prevailing paradigm - even if interpretations of these concepts differ. The 'Thirteen Principles of Faith', identified by the great philosopher Maimonides (1135-1204), are often taken as a summary of what Jews believe. In the Orthodox Prayer Book they are printed after the Ten Commandments and spoken of as the 'Jewish Creed.'[113]

The Ten Commandments

Maimonides' Thirteen Principles Of Belief

I believe with perfect faith that the Creator, blessed be his name, is the Author and Guide of everything that has been created and that he alone has made, does make and will make all things.

I believe with perfect faith that the Creator, blessed be his name, is a

Unity, and that there is no unity in any manner like unto his, and that he alone is our God, who was, is, and will be.

I believe with perfect faith that the Creator, blessed be his name, is not a body, and that he is free from all the accidents of matter, and that he has not any form whatsoever.

I believe with perfect faith that the Creator, blessed be his name, is the first and the last.

I believe with perfect faith that the Creator, blessed be his name and to him alone, it is right to pray, and that it is not right to pray to any being besides him.

I believe with perfect faith that all the words of the prophets are true.

I believe with perfect faith that the prophecy of Moses our teacher, peace be upon him, was true and that he was the chief of the prophets, both of those that preceded him and of those that followed him.

I believe with perfect faith that the whole Law, now in our possession, is the same that was given to Moses our teacher, peace be upon him.

I believe with perfect faith that this Law will not be changed, and that there will never be any other law from the Creator, blessed be his name.

I believe with perfect faith that the Creator, blessed be his name, knows every deed of the children of men, and all their thoughts, as it is said, It is he that fashions the hearts of them all, that giveth heed to their deeds.

I believe with perfect faith that the Creator, blessed be his name, rewards those that keep his commandments and punishes those that transgress them. I believe with perfect faith in the coming of the Messiah, and, though he tarry, I will wait daily for his coming.

I believe with perfect faith that there will be a resurrection of the dead at the time that it shall please the Creator, blessed be his name, and exalted be the remembrance of him for ever and ever.

Sacred Myths

David Ariel, 'an engaged historian of Jewish thought', whom we have already met, speaks of the 'sacred myths' or 'central themes and fundamental beliefs of Judaism', which are interpreted in many varying ways.

These are the ones he identifies:

'Hear, O Israel, the Eternal is Our God, the Eternal is One.'

'It is difficult to imagine Jewish identity,' writes Ariel, 'without a belief in God.' He recognises that for some Jews today, especially after the

Holocaust, belief in God is a stumbling block. There is, he says, no one authoritative Jewish conception of God.

Maimonides said that God can be known by his acts, not in Godself. As God said to Moses 'You cannot see my face, for no-one may see me and live.'[114] Maimonides' reflections were much influenced by Greek philosophers, such as Aristotle. His is an impersonal God compared to the 'God of Abraham, God of Isaac, and God of Jacob' of the Bible, which has no hesitation in using anthropomorphic language. Some Jewish thinkers emphasise the otherness or transcendence of God, some speak more of his immanence or presence with the faithful in their prayer or study of Torah.

God is Creator and Sustainer of the universe, but not to be identified with Nature. Hence the Biblical attack on Baal worship. God is a God of mercy and justice, who upholds the moral order. God is also Lord of history.

'In the image and likeness of God'

Human beings are created in 'the image and likeness' of God.[115] The meaning of this has been much discussed, but this belief emphasises the uniqueness, dignity and worth of each human being. The God of the Bible is a God who is on the side of the poor and marginalized. To human beings, as God's stewards, are entrusted the Animal world and the realm of Nature. Equally care of the body was seen by Hillel the Elder as an act of piety.[116]

The Bible affirms the physical and spiritual unity of the human being in contrast to the soul-body dualism of much Greek and Indian thought Jews do not believe in original sin. Rabbis taught that a human being has two impulses - one was for good (*yetzer ha-tov*), the other for evil (*yetzer har-ra*). The virtuous, however, did not escape suffering, although perhaps they would be rewarded in the world to come. Jews have seldom tried to explain the mystery of suffering and do not see it as redemptive. Instead emphasis should be on alleviating and curing it.

Relationship to God

Through the centuries Jews have been conscious of a special relationship with God – thinking of themselves as 'the chosen people.'This belief, together with Sabbath observance and obedience to Torah, has enabled the Jews, despite so much suffering, to be the only people of the Western ancient world to survive into the modern world. Central to Jewish history is the concept of covenant – that God rescued the Israelites from slavery in Egypt and gave them the Torah as the basis for living together as a moral community. Many of our ideas today of welfare provision and human rights derive from the people who were called to be 'a light to the Gentiles.'

'To love mercy'

Judaism emphasises behaviour rather than belief. 'What does the Lord require of you?' asked the prophet Micah. His answer was, 'To act justly and to love mercy and to walk humbly with your God.'[117]

The Messianic Hope

Maimonides claimed to have perfect faith in the coming of the Messiah, 'even though he tarry.' Traditionally Jews have looked for the coming of a personal Messiah and a number of people have claimed that role. Today some Jews prefer to speak of a Messianic kingdom. However it is expressed, this Messianic hope continues to inspire many Jews to work for a more just and peaceful world.

Judaism, writes Jonathan Sacks, 'is the guardian of an ancient but still compelling dream. To heal where others harm, mend where others destroy, to redeem evil by turning its negative energies to good: these are the mark of the ethics of responsibility, born in the radical faith that God calls on us to exercise our freedom by becoming his partners in the work of creation.' 'That,' he adds, 'seems to me a life-affirming vision: the courage to take the risk of responsibility, becoming co-authors with God of the world that ought to be.'[118]

It is a vision to unite Jews of different traditions and believers of all religions.

6. AT HOME

You have been invited to the home of an observant Jewish family. If you have been asked to the Sabbath evening meal, you should be there in good time, well before sunset and the lighting of the candles.

Mezuzah

As you go in you might notice a little box on the right-hand side of the doorpost, which contains a mezuzah. It is placed there in obedience to the instruction in the book of Deuteronomy to 'Write them [the words of God] on the doorpost of your home and at your gate.'[119]

The words are from Deuteronomy, verses 6, 4-9 and 11, 13-21. They begin with the command, 'Hear, O Israel: The Lord our God, the Lord is one. Love the Lord your God with all your heart and with all your soul and with all your might.' A mezuzah is a reminder of God's presence in the home and the obligation to obey the Torah.

There may even be a mezuzah on the doorpost of each room. When the mezuzah is fixed to the door of a new home, there is a simple ceremony, which includes the beautiful words:

In this gate,
May there come no sorrow.
In this dwelling,
May there come no trouble.
Through this door,
May there come no panic,
In this area,
May there come no conflicts.
In this place,
May there be blessing and peace.[120]

The Sabbath

It has been said that 'more than the Jews have kept the Sabbath; the Sabbath has kept the Jews.' The Sabbath recalls God's creation of the world. The task was finished in six days. So, on the seventh day God rested and blessed the seventh day and made it holy.[121] Subsequently, as a reminder of this, God, in the Ten Commandments, forbade all work - even by servants or resident aliens or animals[122] The Sabbath was also a remembrance of God's rescue of the Israelites from slavery in Egypt.[123]

The Sabbath has traditionally been a time when the family and community come together. Abstention from work has allowed time for spiritual and physical renewal and strengthening of family ties. Modern life may make this more difficult. Families are scattered and if teenagers have non-Jewish friends, then Friday is a night to go out with them. Yet most practising Jews keep up the tradition. As one mother told me, 'I try to bring in the Sabbath by attending synagogue on the Friday evening, followed by a family dinner with all the regular traditional prayers and rituals. Sometimes I will attend synagogue on a Saturday morning and occasionally run youth activities. In the afternoon, I tend to relax at home, sometimes with a family lunch, otherwise reading or going for a walk.' Others say the same: 'I will have Friday night dinner with my family or another family' or 'At home with the family on Friday night.'

The prohibition of work on the Sabbath is one of the Ten Commandments. The Bible does not define what is work. Jews will vary in how strictly they obey this command. Is using the telephone to speak to a relation work? Some years ago after a spate of robberies on Friday evenings from Jewish homes in Golders Green, permission was given to Orthodox Jews, if this happened, to telephone the police. Many years before, after a band of Jews, who refused to defend themselves on the Sabbath had been massacred, it was agreed 'If anyone attack us on the Sabbath day, whoever he may be, we shall resist him; we must not all be killed, as our brothers were in the hiding places.'[124] Saving life takes priority over the command not to work.

There are less life-threatening decisions? Is gardening work or relaxation? In a very Orthodox Home, as I noticed in Jerusalem, the lights may be left on throughout the Sabbath – turning them on or off may count as work. I also recall the wonderful sense of quiet and peace in Jerusalem on a Sabbath afternoon when I was there. In some hotels in Israel, on the Sabbath, the lifts stop automatically at every floor so no one has to work by pressing a button for the lift.'

If work is forbidden on the Sabbath, a lot of work is put into getting ready for it: there is food to prepare – cooking should be avoided during the Sabbath itself – the house to be cleaned and the table to be laid and made attractive.

Sabbath runs from sunset on Friday to sunset on Saturday – so Sabbath starts quite early in winter and not till late in the evening in the summer. So then there is the question, should the youngest members of the family stay up for the Sabbath meal?

There are detailed rules about objects usually associated with work, which, for example, should not be moved on the Sabbath. Other rules prohibit carrying certain objects outside the private domain of one's home into the public domain of the street. So you could wheel a baby carriage within the home and garden, but not along the road. You should not go out with gum or food in the mouth. In some areas, the Jewish community create an eiruv or eruv, which encloses several blocks. The *eiruv* then counts as a private domain where carrying is permitted.

There are thirty-nine general categories of labour that are forbidden on the Sabbath, which are known as the 39 *Melachot*. They derive from the instructions for making the Tabernacle (Mishkan) in chapter 35 of the book of Exodus,. These thirty-nine rules are usually divided into six groups: *Field work; Making Material curtains; Making Leather curtains; Making the beams of the Tabernacle; Putting up and taking down of the Tabernacle and the Tabernacle's final touches, which include kindling or extinguishing a fire.*[125]

For example, a person should not move an object, such as a hammer, or telephone book or pen that is normally associated with work. 'However one is allowed to move these object if (a) they are needed for an activity permitted on Shabbat and nothing else can perform that task, e.g. a hammer to open a coconut, or a telephone book as a booster seat; or (b) the place the object occupies is needed, e.g. if a pen is on a chair where you want to sit. [127]

Some of the rules may seem strange to an outsider. Even for someone who is Jewish it may take time to become 'shabbat observant.' Yet in observing them, a person is constantly reminded of God's presence and calling in every aspect of life.

For many Jews, in the words of a Chief Rabbi of Belgium, 'The Sabbath is the high point of the week – as the Talmud says – half devoted to God (the study of Torah, prayers and songs), and half to human renewal (plenty to eat, rest and the satisfaction of marital needs).'[128]

The start of the Sabbath is marked by the lighting of two candles by the mother, who then covers her eyes and recites a blessing: 'Blessed are you, Lord, our God, sovereign of the universe, who has sanctified us with His commandments and commanded us to light the lights of Shabbat (Amen).' 'Lighting the candles,' as one child put it, 'transforms my room into a river of light.' As the Psalmist said, 'Your word is a lamp [or candle] to my feet and a light for my path.'[129]

The lighting of the candles is followed by the Shalom aleichem - 'Peace and Welcome to you, Servants of God...' This is usually followed by the reading from the book of Proverbs 'in praise of a wife of noble character who is worth far more than rubies,' and then a blessing of the children.[130]

Perhaps looking round you have noticed the kiddush cups. They are used in the blessing of wine and bread in the Kiddush or Sanctification of the Sabbath, which precedes the meal. You may also have noticed a spice box to be used at the ceremony marking the end of the Sabbath - the Havdalah. The 'scent' of the Shabbat is to be carried into the working week.

An alternative wording of the blessing to welcome the Sabbath

---

God of might, Light of the world
bless us with a perfect blessing in Your presence. Enlighten our eyes
with Your light and Your truth, just as we light the Sabbath candles
before You, and so make a spirit of trust and love dwell in our homes.
Guide us with the light of your presence, for in Your light we see
light. Send Your blessing to every home of Israel and to the whole
world, and set peace and eternal blessing upon them. Amen'

Kosher

The kitchen is a place for the visiting Christian to beware – if the couple keep Kosher. One of the basic rules is not to mix meat and dairy products. And if you are looking to make yourself a meat sandwich, don't expect to find any ham or bacon. Families will vary how strictly they keep kosher, but few Jews would eat pork products and most usually avoid shellfish. The meat will probably have been bought from an approved butcher who only sells meat from animals, which have been ritually slaughtered according to the rules of Shechita, which requires the animal to be killed by a single stroke across the neck by a very sharp knife.

One of my correspondents said, 'I will not have forbidden foods in the house but I do not buy kosher meats. I am careful about other products that they do not contain forbidden foods.' Some families will have separate crockery – perhaps blue for milk and red for meat. As another correspondent wrote, 'My house is fully kosher; I have separate cutlery and crockery for meat and milk. Out of the house I will only eat kosher meat. I will eat in a non-kosher restaurant but make sure only to eat vegetarian food.'

The Hebrew word kashrus, or kosher, means 'pure' or 'fit to eat.' The kosher laws were given to the children of Israel by God in the Sinai desert, as recorded in chapter eleven of the Book of Leviticus, and chapter fourteen of the Book of Deuteronomy,. The detailed working out of these laws by the rabbis was recorded in the Mishnah and Talmud (writings discussed more fully in the next chapter). To these were added various 'safeguards' to prevent unintentional breaking of the laws. The rules of kosher cover the animals and allow cattle and game that have 'cloven hooves' and 'chew the cud' to be eaten.

Dairy products must derive from kosher animals. They must not be eaten at the same time as meat. This is because of the Biblical verse 'You may not cook a young   animal in the milk of its mother.'[133] As you may not know where the milk comes from, not only are milk and meat not to be mixed, but they may not be eaten at the same time. Jewish hotels will usually have two dining rooms: one where meat is served and one where only dairy products and vegetables are available. After eating meat, a person will abstain from milk for perhaps three or more hours. After dairy consumption, no interval is required before meat may be eaten.

For its 4,000-year history, the observance of kosher has been a hallmark of Jewish identity. Perhaps more than any other commandment, the kosher laws emphasise that Judaism is much more than a "religion" in the conventional sense of the word. To the Jew, holiness is not confined to holy places and times outside the everyday; rather life in its totality is a sacred endeavour. Even the seemingly mundane act of eating is a Godly act and a uniquely Jewish experience.

Eggs of kosher birds may be eaten, but they need to be inspected to ensure they do not contain blood. Only fish with fins and scales, such as salmon or herring, may be eaten. Shrimps, crabs and lobsters are forbidden. Care has to be taken that there are no insects on fruit or vegetables. There are also rules about kosher wines.

Modern methods of food production, where more than 80% of food in Supermarkets contains pre-processed ingredients, makes full compliance with all the rules of kosher difficult. Hospitals and airlines now usually have kosher meals available. 134

Marriage

The couple you are visiting have just been to the wedding of two Jewish friends. They show you some of the photographs and tell you about the wedding. Rabbis encourage couples to get married in a synagogue, but weddings may sometimes take place in a garden or a hall. Whatever the venue, the actual marriage takes place under a chuppah or canopy, which is held on four poles and may be decorated with flowers. Although families may have their own traditions and there are some differences between Orthodox and Reform ceremonies, Jewish weddings have a common pattern.

The ceremony begins with a blessing of the cup of wine, from which both partners drink, and which is a symbol of joy. Then follows a blessing of the wedding which ends with the words, 'Blessed art thou, O Lord, who sanctifiest thy people Israel by the rite of the canopy and the sacred covenant of wedlock.'164

The groom gives the bride a ring. The marriage contract or ketubah, which is in Aramaic, is then read out, followed perhaps by a summary of it English. It is signed by two witnesses (edim). A glass is then broken as the bridegroom steps on it. This is a reminder of the Destruction of the Temple and also expresses the couple's awareness that although they are happy, others are sad. The guests wish the couple good luck with the traditional word 'mazeltov.' The beautiful Seven Benedictions are pronounced at the completion of the service:

> *Blessed art thou, O Lord Our God, King of the universe, who hast created joy and gladness, bridegroom and bride, mirth and exultation, pleasure and delight, love, brotherhood, peace and fellowship. Soon O Lord our God, may there be heard in the cities of Judah, and in the streets of Jerusalem, the voice of joy and gladness, the voice of the bridegroom and the voice of the bride, the jubilant voice of bridegrooms under their canopies, and of youths from their feasts of song. Blessed art thou, O Lord, who makest the bridegroom to rejoice with the bride.'135*

Judaism does not have the same ambiguity about human sexuality that is to be found in some Christian traditions. A man is expected to marry and be fruitful: there is no honouring of celibacy 'Sexual shame is foreign to Jews' writes Rabbi Julia Neuberger. 'Sexual delight is part of what the Sabbath is all about.'136 In the eighteenth century Rabbi Jacob Emden Jacob wrote, 'The wise men of other nations claim there is disgrace in the sense of touch. This is not the view of the Torah and our sages... To us, the sexual act is worthy, good and beneficial even to the soul.'137 Women's entitlement to sexual pleasure is also recognised. The book of Exodus says that a husband's obligations include 'food, clothing and "onah", which some rabbis interpret as sexual satisfaction.138 Some forms of contraception have usually been accepted.

It is not necessary to go into all the legal issues. Some Orthodox Jews do not recognise marriages conducted by a Reform or Liberal rabbi as valid. In Israel, Orthodox rabbis have a monopoly – only they can conduct a wedding. Some non-observant Israelis, therefore, fly to Cyprus to get married there.

Divorce

Jewish Beth Din or Rabbinic Courts now deal mainly with questions about divorce and conversion. Jews always regret the break-up of a marriage, but Jewish law allows for divorce. A couple must obtain a civil divorce and satisfy the requirements of the state. They may also wish to obtain a *get* or Jewish document of divorce, which cancels the kettubah and allows either partner to marry again in a synagogue, although problems arise if one partner refuses to agree.

Death

Homes, which are the setting for times of joy, also are the backdrop for occasions of sadness. It is at home that a person would wish to die and it is there that the mourners are comforted. Modern society means that elderly people who can no longer look after themselves may be cared for in a Jewish Care Home, but if they are still in their own home and are very ill, relatives will gather and sit with them. As death approaches, a person should make confession of his or her sins and pray, 'Make known to me the path of life: in thy presence is fullness of joy; at thy right hand bliss for evermore.'139

Jewish funerals are arranged quickly - within twenty-four hours if possible. A prayer, including the words, 'Open the gates of mercy' is said at home before the funeral. At the funeral psalms are read and a blessing said which speaks of God reviving the dead and keeping faith with those that sleep in the dust. Orthodox teaching discourages cremation. There are special Jewish cemeteries.

In early times, according to the Talmud, families would compete to dress the corpse in splendid and costly garments. This could be a burden to the poor. Rabbi Gamaliel, therefore, left instructions that he should be buried in a simple linen shroud. Still today, Jews are usually buried in a shroud.

The funeral itself is simple. As the pall-bearers bring the body to the grave, they stop seven times to remember the seven 'vanities,' which are mentioned in the book of Ecclesiastes. The coffin is lowered into the grave and the relatives shovel earth into the grave. The mourners then return to the cemetery hall to recite Kaddish. As people leave the cemetery – known as 'the house of eternity' or 'house of the living' - they wash their hands. It is usual to wish the bereaved a long life.

In the immediate period of mourning, the bereaved are given much support. For the first seven days (shivah), a memorial candle is lit in the home. The bereaved are encouraged to stay at home and family and friends visit and often provide food. For the following thirty days the mourner returns to normal activities, but refrains from entertainments.

For a year after the death, the mourner should recite the Kaddish each day (and thereafter on the anniversary of the death).

The Kaddish

Glorified and sanctified be God's great name throughout the world which He has created according to His will. May He establish His kingdom in your lifetime and during your days, and within the life of the entire House of Israel, speedily and soon; and say, Amen. May His great name be blessed forever and to all eternity.

Blessed and praised, glorified and exalted, extolled and honoured, adored and lauded be the name of the Holy One, blessed be He, beyond all the blessings and hymns, praises and consolations that are ever spoken in the world; and say, Amen. May there be abundant peace from heaven, and life, for us and for all Israel; and say, Amen.

He who creates peace in His celestial heights, may He create peace for us and for all Israel; and say, Amen.

It is perhaps surprising to those who are unfamiliar with this prayer that there is no reference to death. The theme of Kaddish is, rather, the Greatness of God, who created all things. It is said that 'people should give praise for the evil that befalls them even as they give praise for the good.'[170] The Kaddish also is a prayer for peace. It is sometimes said that the only true comfort in the case of the loss of a loved one is to be able to view the passing of the beloved individual from the perspective that that person's soul was gathered in, so to speak, by the One who had provided it in the first place.

The example is often given of Beruriah, the wife of Rabbi Meir. She consoled her husband, upon the death of their two sons, with these words,
'A soul is comparable to an object which was given to us - to each individual, to his or her parents and loved ones, to guard and watch over for a limited time. When the time comes for the object to be returned to its rightful owner, should we not be willing to return it? With regard to our sons, let us therefore consider the matter as "The Lord gave, and the Lord took back, may the Name of the Lord be Blessed!"

Yahrzeit

On the anniversary of the death – the yahrzeit - mourners light a memorial candle at home. It is also the time for erecting a gravestone and pryers. It is customary when visiting a grave, as well as at the funeral, to place a small stone on it - in a hot country flowers would soon wither. A *minyan* of ten people should be present for the Kaddish to be recited.

Special Clothes

If there are some Jewish men in the house when you visit, they may be wearing a small head-covering, known as a kippah. This is worn as a sign of respect to God. Orthodox Jewish men are likely to cover their heads at all times whereas Progressive Jews may only wear a kippah when they go to the synagogue or at times of prayer. In Orthodox communities married women usually cover their heads in public – wearing a wig (sheitel) or headscarf.

Orthodox Jewish men will also wear *teffilin* when they pray in the morning – except on Sabbaths and festivals. *Teffilin* are cubical leather boxes containing handwritten texts of scripture. They are worn in obedience to the instruction to tie the commandments 'as symbols on your hands' and to bind them 'on your foreheads.'[142]

The wearing of fringes (*tizit*) on the four-corners of one's garment is also commanded.[143] Some Jews wear a small four-cornered vest every day. They will almost certainly wear a larger and more impressive four-cornered garment with fringes (*tallit*) when they go to the synagogue and when they pray. The Sephardi custom is to make blue and white tallits of silk, whereas the Ashkenazi tradition is to make them black and white and of wool. In Reform synagogues some women now wear tallits. Rabbi Barbara Borts has said, 'Wrapping myself up in a tallit concentrates my mind, it is a constant reminder of my purpose. The tallit is like a cocoon, allowing for the possibility of a deeper change within, whilst separating me off from the outside world.'[144] These traditions help people to remember God's commands and that they are always in his presence.

We have been invited to accompany our friends to the synagogue. Men will be expected to cover their heads and will be given a kippah.

A Jewish boy wearing a *kappah* and a *tallit*

7. AT THE SYNAGOGUE

If the home is central to the life of Jewish families, the synagogue is the focal point for the community. Synagogues provide the spiritual, social and material foundations for communal life, and as such, they are vital to the Jewish community and its continuity.[145] A synagogue's traditional functions are reflected in three Hebrew synonyms for synagogue. It is the house of prayer - *bet tefillh*; the house of assembly – *bet knesset*; and the house of study – *bet midrash*. Sometimes Jews will refer to the synagogue as *shul* – a Yiddish word from the German word '*Schule*' for school. Especially in America, some Reform and Conservative congregations use the word 'temple.' In Britain most congregations use the word 'synagogue', although sometimes *Bet HaMidrash* is used.

History

Despite the importance of the synagogue in Jewish life

for over two thousand years, little is known about its origins. There are no explicit references to a synagogue in the Hebrew Bible. It is often suggested that the synagogue dates back to the exile of the Jews in Babylon, following the first destruction of the Temple in 586 BCE. If so, it would have been a small meeting place for prayer. The prophet Ezekiel, who lived among the exiles in Babylon, said 'This is what the Sovereign Lord says: Although I sent them far away among the nations and scattered them among the countries, yet for a little while I have been a sanctuary for them in the countries where they have gone.'(Ezekiel 11, 16 in the New International Version translation). The Authorised King James Bible has 'I will be to them as a little sanctuary in the countries where they shall come.' The meaning of the verse is, therefore, in doubt but the Talmud identifies the 'little sanctuary' with the synagogue.[146] Psalm 74, which bewails the destruction of the Temple, also says in the Authorised King James Bible 'they have burned up all the synagogues of God in the land.' The Jerusalem Bible has 'every sacred shrine' and the New International Version has 'every place where God was worshipped in the land.'[147]

Be that as it may, by the first century CE, the synagogue was a well-established institution. Philo speaks of a synagogue in Rome; the Mishnah, which, as shall see, is a compilation of decisions of the Oral Torah, speaks of a synagogue at the Temple itself and the Gospels say that Jesus preached in the synagogue at Nazareth.[148] On his missionary journeys, Paul's first address was usually at a synagogue.[149]

The importance of the synagogue increased significantly after the second destruction of the Temple in 70 CE by the Romans. The prayers of the synagogue replaced the sacrifices, which had been offered in the Temple. Moreover, because synagogue worship emphasized language rather than ritual, a more elaborate liturgy developed. The ending of sacrifices also meant that the priesthood was no longer needed and the leadership of the community passed to rabbis who were to develop the Oral Torah. Moreover the people now took part in the liturgy and were no longer just spectators.[150]

The Building

The architecture of the synagogue often reflects the style of public buildings of the country where they are situated. I once went on a tour of Oriental synagogues in Jerusalem, and in some, as in a Mosque or an Indian temple, people took off their shoes and sat on the floor. The famous Altneu synagogue in Prague is built in the Gothic style. In the nineteenth century, synagogues in the West often had an oriental style as a reminder of the oriental origins of Judaism. Some were similar to churches, (although, not built as a cruciform and without spires!).

Twentieth century synagogues reflect contemporary styles of building - the Beth Abraham Synagogue at No 46, The Ridgeway, in Golders Green, is just an ordinary semi-detached family house. The Hechal Yehuda Synagogue, built in 1979 by architect Itzhak Toledan, is all in white concrete. The scallop-like shape has given it the nickname 'the seashell synagogue.'

In the USA, the synagogues designed by Percival Goodman were assertive, modernist structures, reflecting his belief that the vocabulary of modern architecture could be transformed into something rich enough to express powerful religious feeling. His goal was to design synagogues that interpreted Jewish tradition in modern ways and he saw the architect as critical to the process of expressing religious identity in the 20th century.

London has some historic synagogues. The first place of worship after the Re-admission of Jews to Britain, as already mentioned, was in the upper floor of a house in Creechurch Lane in the City of London. A plaque marks the spot. It opened in 1656, but was soon too small. The diarist Samuel Pepys visited it in 1663 and was shocked. 'Men and boys in their vayles [prayer shawls] and women behind a lattice out of sight. But, Lord! To see the disorder, laughing, sporting and no attention but confusion in all their service.' Pepys was obviously unaware that it was the festival of Simchat Torah, when it is acceptable to sing loudly and dance joyfully.[151]

A beautiful new purpose-built synagogue, erected in the near-by Bevis Marks Street, was opened in September 1701. The construction was undertaken by a Quaker, Joseph Avis, who returned to the wardens 'such profits as he had made' as he felt he should not accept any financial gain for the 'building of a House of God.' The outside is quite simple and like the chapels built at that time by 'Dissenters' – Puritans and others who were not members of the Church of England.

The interior is impressive and modelled on the Amsterdam synagogue. There are seven ornate hanging chandeliers - one for each day of the week – which are still used on High Holy Days. The splendid wooden Ark is built in the classical baroque style. Its central feature is the Ten Commandments in Hebrew. Bevis Marks is still used for worship by the Sephardic Community, although the most active of the Spanish and Portuguese synagogues is in Lauderdale Road in Maida Vale.

Bevis Marks Synagogue

The Great Synagogue for Ashkenazi Jews in London was built in 1722. It was a beautiful and historic synagogue, but sadly it was totally destroyed during a bombing raid in May 1941.

The building in Brick Lane, which once housed The Spitalfields Great Synagogue, has had an interesting history. The building was erected in 1743 by French speaking Hugenot refugees, who had come to London to escape persecution. It was called 'Neuve Eglise.' In 1819, the Hugenots sold the building, which became a Wesleyan chapel. In 1898 it became the home of the Machzikei Hadath community and became known as the Spitalfields Great Synagogue. The Synagogue at its height was very influential and regarded as a 'Torah fortress in Anglo-Jewry.'

After the Second World War, the congregation declined

sharply and the community moved to Golders Green to a modern building, designed by Sir Charles Nicholson. The building in Brick Lane is now a mosque.

The plan of the Nozil Synagogue in Warsaw

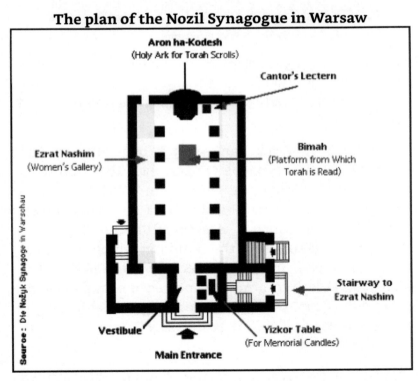

The Nożyk Synagogue in Warsaw, the city's only pre-war synagogue to survive the destruction of the Jewish Ghetto by the Nazis. On May 16, 1943 when the ghetto was firmly under Nazi control, as a symbolic act, the Germans blew up Warsaw's Great Synagogue.

The Scrolls

The scrolls have a special sanctity of their own. God's word is written on them. Great care, therefore, is taken in the preparation and preservation of the scrolls. The material used is parchment from an animal that is kosher. To ensure there is no mistake the scribe or *sofer* constantly re-reads his work. It is also checked by other scribes. The writing of the text is in columns, beginning at the right upper edge of the column. Each column consists of perhaps forty lines of equal length. Words should not be broken up, so the sofer carefully spaces the words. There are still sofers at work today, although they may use computers to help with spacing.

Square writing has been used for two thousand years. Classical Hebrew writing consists only of consonants, so the reader needs to know the grammar or memorise the vocalisation. In many ancient civilizations scriptures were memorised before they were written down. The ink used is a deep permanent black and the sofer uses a quill from a ritually clean bird – often a goose. A scroll may be repaired, but when it is past repair, it is put in a jar and buried – as may have been was the case with the Dead Sea Scrolls – or stored in a special room called a *genizah*. The Cairo Genizah, attached to the Ezra synagogue, was rediscovered at the end of the nineteenth century and found to contain an original version of Ecclesiasticus – the Book of Ben Sira – and a vast number of other documents which reflect the life of the community - some of which are now at the Cambridge University Library.

The Scrolls have ornate castings or dressings, topped by a silver crown

The Torah Procession

A central feature of a morning Sabbath service is the Torah Procession, for which everyone stands. A scroll is taken from the ark to the reading desk. Passages from the Five Books of Moses and the Prophets are read.

Traditionally in most Orthodox synagogues the reading desk or bimah is placed in the centre of the synagogue. In Reform synagogues, however, the bimah may be a platform in front of the ark, with a prominent pulpit to emphasise the importance of the Rabbi as a preacher. The Rabbi and the Cantor have seats on the platform

Old Jerusalem Hurva Synagogue

The House Of Prayer: Bet Ha-Tefilla.

The synagogue is a place of prayer where morning and evening services are held every day, with special emphasis on the Sabbath worship. The Hebrew word *Tefillah*, which rather misleadingly is usually translated as 'prayer' 'implies an act of self-judgement or intercession on one's own behalf before God, or the expression of hopeful sentiments.'[154] *Tefillah* includes liturgical worship and personal prayer. Louis Jacobs noted that the prayers in the Bible are of private persons with their individual needs, whereas from the earliest Rabbinic times onwards, the emphasis is on public prayer, although it is acknowledged that private prayers are also essential. The word *davening*, from Yiddish, is also used for prayer, especially when accompanied by swaying or gentle rocking.

One girl recalled, 'Ever since I was a young girl I loved davening. In elementary school one girl a week got to bring home a special decorated *siddur* (prayer book), and I always felt so privileged when it was my turn, I cherished that siddur. There was a joy to learning how to daven and davening out loud. [156]

The first siddur, which literally means 'order', was compiled in the ninth century by Rav Amram Gaon, who based it on the traditions of Jews living in Babylon.[157] The Hebrew word for liturgy is *avodah*, which also means service or work. 'So prayer is not primarily an expression of personal desire for communion with God, but the fulfilment of a task laid down by God.'[158] (Christian monks and nuns call daily worship 'the office').

Sabbath Morning Service

Although an *Erev Shabbat* service may have been held on Friday evening, it will be sufficient to try to describe the Sabbath morning service. This outline is based on the beautiful *Forms of Prayer* of the Movement for Reform Judaism. The basic pattern of worship is similar in synagogues of other traditions.

The service, after a number of Opening Prayers, begins with the 'Morning Blessings,' which are of a personal nature. They are followed by the 'Verses of Song' that prepare the community for the formal 'statutory' part of the service. Introduced by the 'call to prayer,' this section focuses on the Shema – 'Hear, O Israel, the Lord our God, the Lord is One' - with its blessings. It is followed by the Amidah, which is the central 'standing' prayer. At the heart of the service, and special to the Shabbat, is the reading from the Torah with its accompanying prophetic text, known as the Haftarah. Following the various prayers for the Jewish people and the community, some congregations include an additional Amidah. This is a way of copying the practice of the Temple, where an additional sacrifice was offered on the Sabbath and Festivals. The concluding prayers and songs prepare people to return to the outer world. The Sabbath service will normally include a sermon. This is an outline, but each section deserves some detailed comment and quotation.

Forms of Prayer suggests some thoughts for the congregation as they prepare to worship. The service, it says, 'offers us a different world, one which may give a perspective on our life.'[159]

A time of silence, before the service is commended and donning the tallit or prayer shawl helps to shut off 'outer noise and the busy-ness of life.' Usually the service begins with Opening Prayers.

Some congregations begin with the Morning Blessings. These were originally recited at home as a person woke up and prepared for the day. They start with thanksgiving or blessing for the gifts of our bodies – both for our physical being and for our soul. Thirteen short blessings are a vivid reminder of the goodness of God, who provides for every need. Some congregations study a portion of Torah at this point. The Morning Blessings end with two passages – one of which, from the Sephardi tradition, recognises the tension between affirming God's presence in our lives today and the messianic hope that one day God's rule will be accepted throughout the world. 'God rules, God has ruled, God shall rule for ever.'[160]

The opening prayers include ones for a just society, for the community, for the family of Israel and for the 'Gift of Women'.

Two prayers with a universal appeal are 'For the Future' and for 'One Humanity'.

God, we thank You, for Your gift of hope, our strength in times of trouble. Beyond the injustice of our time, its cruelty and its wars, we look forward to a world at peace when people deal kindly with each other, and no one is afraid. Every bad deed delays its coming, every good one brings it nearer. May our lives be Your witness, so that future generations bless us. May the day come, as the prophet taught, when "the sun of righteousness will rise with healing in its wings." Help us to pray for it, to work for it and be worthy of it. Blessed are You God, the Hope of Israel. God of the spirits of all flesh,

You created one human being,
so all humanity are one.
You created us in Your image,
so all are equal in your sight.
In a world so vast,
may all find for themselves a home.
In a world so small,
let us make space for one another.
In times of conflict
may we help to bring understanding.
In times of bitterness and hate,
may we offer healing and love.
When faith erects barriers,

may our understanding of You build bridges.
When faith is betrayed or misused,
give us courage to seek Your truth.[162]

With the Verses of Song, attention moves from the
personal to the communal relationship with God. It
begins with praise to God: 'Blessed be the One at whose
word the world exists;' and concludes with 'Praised be
Your name forever.' In between a number of Psalms and
other songs of praise are read or sung.

The next section of the service begins with the Sh'ma
- preceded by, at least, two blessings and followed by
one blessing. The Sh'ma is the central affirmation 'Hear
O Israel, the Eternal is our God, the Eternal is One,'
followed by the command to 'Love the Eternal your God
with all your heart, and all your soul, and all your
might...' The command is amplified in various ways, for
example, with reference to putting tassels on the corner
of clothes. The Temple ritual used to include a recitation
of the Ten Commandments, but this was omitted from
synagogue worship in case such prominence to the Ten
Commandments would devalue the rest of the Torah.

This section ends with the Amidah, which, as we have
seen, was instituted by the rabbis as a substitute for the
daily sacrifices in the Temple. The 'standing prayer' or
'eighteen benedictions', as it is known, is as if one were
addressing a sovereign. It begins with three verses that
acknowledge God's power over us and God's holiness. It
ends, as one leaves the 'royal' presence, with expressions
of gratitude and the hope for a favourable response.

Now it is time for the Torah Service. This symbolically
re-enacts the events at Mount Sinai when Moses went up
the mountain and brought the Torah down to earth, to
read it to the assembled people. The Ark is opened and a
Torah scroll is removed and carried in procession to the

bimah, where a portion of the Torah is read. During the procession, members of the congregation often touch the scroll with a corner of their prayer shawl. The scroll may be elevated and after suitable blessings, the Torah passage is read. The reading is followed by further blessings. The Ashkenazi elevate the scroll at this point in the service, saying, 'This is the Torah that Moses set before the children of Israel, given by God through Moses.'

The reading from the Books of Moses is followed by a reading from the *Haftarah*, the second part of the Bible. This is taken from the *nevi'im* or 'the prophets,' including the historical books starting with Joshua as well and also includes the twelve 'minor prophets.' In the Reform tradition the reading may be from the third section of the Hebrew Bible, known as *K'tuvim*, or the 'Writings,' of which the Book of Proverbs is one. The *Haftarah* is preceded and followed by a blessing.

The *Haftarah* is followed by prayers, including one for the Sovereign, as representative of the country at large. This continues the practice advocated by the prophet Jeremiah who told the exiles in Babylon: 'Seek the peace and prosperity of the city to which I have carried you into exile. Pray to the Lord for it, because if it prospers, you too will prosper.[194] There is a prayer for the State of Israel, and there are ones for consolation, for healing, for the community. On appropriate occasions there are prayers for International or Interfaith Understanding or for Justice and the Environment.

After the prayers, the Torah scroll is returned to the Ark. Psalms are sung and the Amidah may be repeated. The concluding prayers include the Aleinu, which focuses on building the kingdom of God and the relationship of the children of Israel to the wider society and then the

Mourners' Kaddish. After a concluding hymn or song, there is a blessing.

Forms of Prayer includes two alternative Torah services. The traditional service centres on the revelation at Sinai. Torah Service II relates more directly to the revelation of Torah and the covenant between God and Israel. Torah Service III uses a minimum of ritual so that time can be devoted to studying the Torah text.

The house of study – bet ha-Midrash
Torah

The synagogue is a place of worship and also a place to study Torah. The *Mishnah* says, 'These are the things whose fruit a man enjoys in this world while the capital is laid up for him in the World to Come: honouring father and mother, deeds of loving-kindness, making peace between a man and his fellow: and the study of the Torah is equal to them all.'[163]

The Ethics of the Fathers lists forty-eight 'excellences' by which the Torah is acquired. The list includes 'By the hearing of the ear, by the ordering of the lips, by understanding of the heart... by being one that is beloved, that loves God, that loves mankind, that loves well-doing, ...that shuns honour and boasts not of his learning.' The Ethics also says, 'This is the way of the Torah: a morsel of bread with salt to eat, water by measure to drink; thou shalt sleep on the ground and live a life of hardship, while thou toilest in the Torah. If thou doest thus, happy shalt thou be.'[164]

Many Jews, both well-known scholars and humble but faithful people whose names are forgotten, did indeed devote a great part of their lives to the study of Torah. It was regarded as a sin to waste a moment that could be devoted to study. God's word 'was a lamp for their feet and a light for their path.' [165]

Rabbis emphasised that Torah study took them into the presence of the Transcendent God. 'If two sit together and occupy themselves with the words of Torah, the divine Presence abides in their midst.'[166] This sense of Kedusha or Sanctification of God's name was 'the experience of becoming momentarily aware of the impact of the divine transcendence on the world on the world.' transcendence[167]

The great Jewish thinker Moses Maimondies said,
'Every man in Israel is obliged to study Torah, whether he is firm of body or a sufferer of ill-health, whether a young man or of advanced age with his strength abated. Even a poor man who is supported by charity and who is obliged to beg at doors and even one with a wife and children is obliged to set aside a period for Torah study by day and by night, as it is said, "You shall meditate therein day and night."'[168]

But what is meant by Torah? This is a difficult question. The Torah reveals the pattern of life required of anyone who wishes to love and obey the God of mercy and most Jews have regarded the Torah as a delight. As the Psalmist said
Oh, how I love your law
I meditate on it all day long...
How sweet are your words to my mouth
*Sweeter than honey to my tongue.*169

David Hartman, a leading Israeli rabbi, said that he gave a lecture to some Christians on 'Joy in the Law.' 'One of the basic problems for my audience,' he commented, 'was that they could not imagine how the Law could be a source of delight because in their experience joy and law were opposite experiences.'

There is, as we shall see, a festival known as *Simhat Torah*, which means 'Rejoicing in the Law.' It comes at the end of *Sukkot* or Tabernacles. The scrolls are taken from the Ark and carried in procession around the synagogue, accompanied by singing and dancing. All the children are called up together to a portion of Torah and then blessed and given apples and sweets.

The Pentateuch

The word 'Torah' is used in different ways. It may refer to the five books of Moses, the Oral Torah of the rabbis or the entire body of Jewish interpretation, study and learning. Jews often call the Hebrew Bible *Tenakh* or *Tanach* – the word is an abbreviation of the first letter of the three Hebrew words for the main parts of the Bible, which are: Torah (Teaching), Nevi'im (Prophets) and Ketuvim (Writings).

The well-known novelist Herman Wouk Herman vividly describes the Torah – understood as the Five Books of Moses:

'One starts in Genesis with a powerful vision of the birth of the universe. Mystic tales follow: a serpent speaks, the fruit of a tree can bestow knowledge or immortality, men live nine hundred years. The climax is a world deluge, ridden out by one six-hundred- year-old man and his family in an ark filled with beasts for repopulating the earth. After the deluge and a thousand years of genealogy we start breathing our own air, the men are like us, and we recognise the landscape. Hebrew history starts with a tale of Abraham, the father of the nation…

In Exodus, the story of Moses begins, and the Torah tells of the escape of Israel from Egypt and the blazing sun at Sinai. Then, just when the plot is getting really good, as it were, one runs into a stone wall; civil and criminal legislation, the construction of a tabernacle hook by hook and curtain by curtain, and a handbook of rules for priests.

Here and there all through Leviticus and Numbers, a patch of shining narrative emerges from the densely packed legal part, but then the law closes in again. Last comes Deuteronomy, the farewell address of Moses.[170]

Writings Of The First Century

The canon of the Hebrew Bible was closed in the second century BCE. The book of Daniel is probably the latest book. The Jewish religious literature of the following years and of the first century CE is extensive and of considerable value. Some additional books, written in Greek, were included in the Septuagint, which was the standard Greek translation of the Hebrew Bible. They are not in the Hebrew Bible. St Jerome included these books in his translation of the Bible into Latin, which is known as the Vulgate. Many Protestant Christian Bibles exclude these books and in some Bibles they appear in what is called the 'Apocrypha' - an appendix between the Old and New Testaments'

Other surviving Jewish books of this period, which are not included in the Bible or the Apocrypha, are known as 'pseudepigripha,' because the authors used a pseudonym, perhaps of a well-known Biblical figure.

In addition, during the last century, the Dead Sea or Qumran Scrolls, were found in caves near the ruins of Khirbet Qumran, close to the Dead Sea. Besides Biblical scrolls, numerous sectarian writings were also found, usually thought to be by members of the very ascetic community of the Essenes.

As well as religious texts, the writings of two first century Jewish authors are also important. Philo (c.20 BCE-50 CE), who was much influenced by the philosophy of the Stoics and of Plato, composed a large number of Biblical commentaries and books, which explained and defended Judaism.

Flavius Josephus Flavius (1st century CE), who is often regarded as a traitor because as a commander of Jewish rebels in Galilee he surrendered to the Romans in 67 CE, wrote a *History of the Jewish War* and the *Antiquities of the Jews.*

The first century was also the time in which the books in what Christians call the New Testament were written. Most of the authors were Jewish. (It is perhaps worth noting again that some Jews dislike the terms 'Old' and 'New Testament' as it may wrongly suggest that the Hebrews Bible has been superseded by the 'Greek scriptures. It is also important to recognise, as we shall see in the last chapter, that the New Testament picture of 'Pharisees' is unfair and unhistorical.)

The terms 'apocrypha', 'pseudepigrapha' and 'Qumran scrolls' are, however misleading. These labels are used by historians looking back: the actual authors would not have known what they meant any more than most people today. 'A more proper literary categorization of these writings would divide them into genres: apocalypses (which warn of impending doom), narrative fiction, testaments, history and the like.'[172]

The Beginnings Of Rabbinic Judaism

The fall of Jerusalem and the destruction of the Temple

in 70 CE by the Romans brought about far reaching changes in Jewish life and religion. That Judaism and the Jewish people survived the onslaught of the Romans is due, under God, primarily to Johanan ben Zakkai and Rabban Gamaliel II and their fellow rabbis.

In 66 CE, as has been said, some Jews revolted against the Romans, who eventually inflicted a devastating defeat on the rebels. In 70 CE Jerusalem was totally destroyed. The Temple was razed to the ground and the population massacred or exiled and the Sadducees lost their political and religious authority. Soon afterwards the Essene retreat at Qumran was destroyed. Many of the surviving Zealots took their own lives at the Dead Sea fortress of Masada rather than surrender to the Romans. Others escaped to North Africa or went underground. The Jewish Christian community and some Pharisees opposed the rebellion.

Rabbi Johanan (or Yohanan) ben Zakkai, a leading Pharisee, was one of those who opposed the rebellion. It is said that Johanan had been a student of the famous Rabbi Hillel (late first century BCE to early first century CE) and that he had spent eighteen years in the Lower Galilee. When he moved to Jerusalem, his school became so famous that students would go to great lengths to be admitted to it. Later generations would speak of his prodigious knowledge. He seems to have been a humane and moderate figure. For example, he stopped the practice of a woman suspected of adultery being made to drink 'bitter water.'

It is not known whether Johanan was a pacifist or whether he realized that the rebellion could only end in disaster. The ruins of his 'Burnt House' in Jerusalem have been excavated. It is said that he was smuggled out of the city, before its capture, in a coffin. Johanan said to the chief of the Zealots, who was his nephew, 'Find some sort of remedy for me to get me out of here, maybe there will be a possibility of saving something.' His nephew replied, 'Pretend to be sick and have everybody come and ask about you; have something bad smelling and put it by you, so people will think you're dead. Then let your disciples carry you out, but nobody else – so that no one will feel that you're still light, since people know that a living being is lighter than a corpse.'[222]

Having escaped, Rabbi Johanan went to the Roman camp and apparently obtained permission to set up an academy in Jamnia (Jabneh or Yavneh), near the Mediterranean coast between Jaffa and Ashdod.

Here, building on Pharisaic learning, he laid the foundations for Rabbinic Judaism. 'When the sages entered the vineyard at Yavneh, they said, "A time will come when a man will seek a Torah teaching and will not find it, a ruling of the scribes and will not find it... so that one precept of Torah will not be like another." Hence, they declared, "Let us begin with Shammai and Hillel."'[223]

Rabbi Johanan saw that nothing was gained by antagonizing the Romans. 'Do not rush to destroy the altars of the Gentiles, lest you will have to rebuild them yourselves.'

He was sceptical of Messianic groups, saying, 'If you have a plant in your hand and someone says, "The Messiah has come", go and complete the planting and afterwards go out and receive [the Messiah].' He was also realistic in his reaction to the destruction of the Temple.

This tragedy had left some people in deep gloom, as these verses from the Syriac apocalypse of 2 Baruch indicate.

Blessed is he who was not born,
Or who was born and died.

But we, the living, woe to us,
Because we have seen those afflictions of Zion,
And that which has befallen Jerusalem.

Others indulged in vain apocalyptic speculation that God would act to revenge his people. Johanan acknowledged the distress but encouraged people to make what life they could. One of his disciples expressed his Master's views, saying,

'My sons, mourning too much is undesirable and not to mourn at all is undesirable. Rather, our sages have said, "A person should plaster his house and leave a small portion [un-plastered] as a memory of Jerusalem. A person should make all preparations for a meal and leave a little bit [unfinished] in memory of Jerusalem. A woman should make jewellery for herself and leave a little [of herself unornamented] as a memory of Jerusalem."' [175]

Rabbi Johanan, therefore, set about restoring what he could of Jewish life. Clearly the sacrificial system of the Temple was at an end, but some of the practices could be transferred to the worship of the synagogue. For example, before 70, the shofar or ram's horn, used at New Year, (Rosh Hashanah) could only be blown in the Temple. Johanan said it could be blown anywhere. When Johanan was asked, 'Now that there are no sacrifices, how can we seek atonement?' he replied that good deeds (literally acts of loving kindness) will atone as sacrifices once did. [176]

Johanan ben Zakkai's work was continued by his successor, Rabban Gamaliel II (c.90-115). Gamaliel II belonged to a well-known Pharisaic family. His great grandfather was Hillel, a very distinguished rabbi, who was once was asked to recite the whole of Torah while standing on one leg. He replied, 'What is hateful to you, do not do to others. That is the whole of Torah; the rest is commentary on it.' His grandfather, Gamaliel the Elder (early first century CE), was also a much respected scholar. When some of his colleagues wanted to persecute members of the early church, he advised them to leave the followers of Jesus alone, saying 'If this enterprise... is of human origin, it will break up of its own accord, but if it does in fact come from God you will be unable to destroy them. Take care not to find yourselves fighting against God.' [177]

Despite Gamaliel II's youth, his leadership was acknowledged by other rabbis. Nearly 100 rabbis congregated at Yavneh. Legal questions were brought there from all parts of the country and the rabbis themselves travelled to neighbouring towns and cities.

Under Gamaliel II, Rabbinic Judaism was given a shape that has influenced it ever since. It became an obligation for all Jews to offer daily prayer, either privately or in a synagogue. Decisions were made which helped to decide which books should be included in the canon of the Hebrew Bible.

Much time was devoted to clarifying and codifying the Law. Shammai and Hillel were the two most influential rabbis at the beginning of the first century CE. Rabbi Shammai (c.50 BCE-c.30 CE) was known for his strict interpretation of the Torah.

Rabbi Hillel, (late 1st century BCE to early 1st century CE), mentioned above, who was born in Babylon, was more liberal in his interpretation. Both schools were recognised as authoritative, but priority was given to Hillel's more liberal interpretations. A leading scholar of the next generation was Rabbi Akiva (c.50-135 CE)., who is credited with systematizing the   various teachings in the Midrash (see below). He recognised Simon bar Kokhba as the Messiah in his revolt against Rome. This led to Rabbi Akiva suffering a martyr's death, being flayed alive by the Romans.

New liturgies were created for the observance of the High Holy Days. Passover was now to be at home - there was no Temple. An order of service – described earlier - known as *Haggadah*, was developed. It has continued to evolve over the centuries.

The Rabbis at Yavneh sought rapprochement with the Roman authorities and Gamaliel II received recognition from them as the spokesperson for the Jewish community. It is said that he went to Syria 'to be granted authority by the Roman governor.'[178]

Other Jews, however, still harboured hopes of revenge and the second rebellion, led by Bar-Kokhba, broke out in 132 CE, which was eventually crushed by the Romans. Afterwards, the name of the province was changed to Syria-Palestinia – instead of Judea - and a new pagan city, Aelia Capitolina, was built on the site of Jerusalem.

Nonetheless Judaism survived, largely thanks to the foresight and work of Johanan ben Zakkai and Gamaliel II. Their importance, however, is not confined to the Jewish world.

After centuries of antagonism and persecution at the hands of Christians, it is increasingly recognised that Christianity did not replace Judaism. Rather, in the second century two new religious movements emerged. One was Rabbinic Judaism: the other was the Christian Church, most of whose members were by then Gentiles. But both grew from the same Hebrew and Biblical roots. Moreover, the 'Parting of the Ways', as it is often called, was as much caused by historical events - not least the destruction of Jerusalem – as by theological disagreement. Even more important, the early Rabbis preserved the best traditions of first century Judaism and handed them on to future generations.

Midrash And Mishnah

The teachings of these early rabbis are preserved in the *Midrash* and the *Mishnah.* They are regarded as part of the oral tradition, which Orthodox Jews believe was given by God to Moses.

There are two main kinds of tradition: *Halakah*, which means 'walking' or instructions on how to live and *Aggadah*, 'God-talk which includes poetry and legendary and historical writing.

Another distinction is made between Midrash and Mishnah. An example of each is given below. The Midrash is a verse by verse commentary on scripture. The aim is to find a moral or theological teaching from scripture (aggadic Midrashim), at other times the aim is to explain the meaning of Biblical law (halakhic Midrashim). The Mishnah is a topic by topic discussion of the Law. This material dates from the first century BCE to the second century CE, in what is known as the Age of the Tannaim. In around 200 C.E., Judah Ha-Nasi recognised that the time had come to commit to writing, the halakhic traditions, which up to that point, had been memorised.

Different teachers have often emphasised the importance of *Halakah* or *Aggadah* at the expense of the other. This is one reason for the great variety of ways in which the Jewish faith has been expressed and lived. The twentieth century scholar Abraham Joshua Heschel insisted that this was a mistake. He wrote 'to maintain that the essence of Judaism consists exclusively of Halakhah is as erroneous as to maintain that the essence of Judaism consists exclusively of Aggadah.' He also explained the importance of both and memorably described how 'Halakhah – the law conserved in Mishnah - and Aggadah – the commentaries on scripture to be found in Midrash – complement each other: 'Halakhah represents the strength to shape one's life according to a fixed pattern; it is a form-giving force. Aggadah is the expression of man's ceaseless striving, which often defies all limitations. Halakhah is the rationalisation and schematisation of living ... placing life into an exact system. Aggadah deals with man's ineffable relations with God, to other men, and to the world...To maintain that the essence of Judaism consists exclusively of Halakhah is as erroneous as to maintain that the essence of Judaism consists exclusively of Aggadah. The interrelationship of Halakah and Aggadah is the very heart of Judaism.'

The Talmud

The Mishnah subsequently itself became the subject of study and interpretation. These discussions, known as the Gemara, date from the age of the Amoraim, which lasted from about 200-500 CE. They, together with the Mishnah, were collected in the Talmud. There are two versions of the Talmud. One is known as the Palestinian or Jerusalem Talmud, which was completed about 400 CE. The other, which is much more extensive, is the Babylonian Talmud or *Bavli*, completed in about 500 CE. The English translation of the Babylonian Talmud, published by the Soncino Press, takes up about 15,000 pages. So there is plenty of material for a lifetime devoted to its study.

Rabbi Jonathan Romain says, 'although the Talmud derives from scripture, it is the 'oral Torah' or commentary that has been central to Judaism rather than the Hebrew Bible. Effectively by "shutting down" the biblical record, by freezing the "Five Books" and then the rest of the Hebrew Bible as unchangeable "Scripture", the door has been opened to interpretation, and it is evident that the Judaism of the past two thousand years is that which was built up painstakingly by successive generations in quite clear contradiction to the biblical text.'[179]

In rather the same way, the Canon of books to be included in the New Testament were fixed by the middle of the second century. The commentaries on those books fill many libraries. The literature of the Tannaim and Amoraim preserves the discussions of the rabbis, so it reflects various points of view.

At the traditional *yeshivas*, where Ultra-Orthodox rabbis are trained, the Talmud and 'oral Torah' are the main subject of study rather than the scriptures, which receive greater attention at the training colleges of Progressive rabbis.

Here is an example of a Mishnah discussion: about the grounds on which a man could divorce his wife.

'The School of Shammai say, A man is not to divorce his wife unless he has found in her some indecency, as it is said (Deuteronomy 24, 1), "Because he found some indecency in her." But the school of Hillel say, Even if she spoiled the cooking, as it is said, "Because he has found some indecency in her." Rabbi Akiva says, Even if he has found another more beautiful than she is, as it is said (Deuteronomy 24, 1) "And it shall come to pass, if she does not find favour in his eyes."'[180]

A further discussion of this passage in the Mishnah

is recorded in the Talmud. It ends with a saying of Rabbi Johanan that 'he who sends away his wife is hated' (based on Malachi, 2, 16) and a saying of Rabbi Elazar that 'If a man divorces his first wife, even the altar sheds tears.'[181] Such remarks prevent divorces and remarriage becoming the norm, even if the Law made it easy for a man to divorce his wife.

Here now is an example of a passage from the Midrash. It is a commentary on Deuteronomy 15, 11:

'Thou shalt open wide your hand to your brother' This is explained to mean that you should give according to particular needs. To him for whom bread is suitable, give bread... to him for whom it is fitting to put food into his mouth, put food.

The House Of Assembly – Bet Ha-Kneset
The Rabbi

The synagogue is also a focal point for the community. The leader of the community is the rabbi, but his or her role has changed very considerably in the modern world. The term is probably derived from rav, which means 'great man' or 'teacher.' The suffix 'i' means my – so the term means 'my teacher.' The title 'Rabbi' seems to have been first used in the time of Hillel in the first century CE. The title is used of Jesus in both St Matthew's and St John's gospels, which were written in the latter part of the first century. The term 'Rabbuni,' which Mary Magdalene used to greet the Risen Lord, is early Aramaic.[183]

Traditionally the Rabbi was an ordained scholar-saint. He would usually have had a secular job, but devoted every available minute to the study of Torah. He guided the community in spiritual affairs and acted as judge in civil cases and matters of religious law. Ordination by the laying on of hands derives from a verse in the Book of Numbers, which says that Moses 'took Joshua and made him stand before Eleazar the priest and the whole assembly. Then he laid his hands on him and commissioned him, as the Lord instructed through Moses.'[184] In the early Rabbinic period only scholars who had received ordination in the chain reaching back to Joshua could act as judges. They also had to be resident in the land of Israel – not in the Diaspora.

After the close of the Talmud, ordination in this full sense came to end, although the term *semikhah*, continued to be used when a scholar was appointed a rabbi by a proper Halakhic authority and allowed to make legal decisions. This legal function is continued in the Bet Din or 'House of Law' which is composed of three judges, usually rabbis, who are learned in law. A Bet Din today is mainly concerned with marriage and divorce, conversions to Judaism and supervision of the rules of kosher. The fact that not every Bet Din recognises the decisions of another Bet Din can cause complications for those involved.

After the Emancipation, expectations of a Rabbi changed and grew. They were expected to be knowledgeable in modern thought as well as Jewish law. Candidates were encouraged to study for a university degree as well as training at a Rabbinical College, where the curriculum might include homiletics, philosophy and psychology as well as the study of Torah. Jews College was established in London in 1855 to train rabbis who would be at home in Victorian England. (Rabbis from the continent who came to Britain had been trained in yeshivas). Jews College, renamed as the London School of Jewish Studies (LSJS) is now 'the home of modern Orthodox Jewish learning in London.' It offers a wide variety of courses to all who are interested and is not confined to the training of rabbis.

In 1929, Gateshead Talmudical College, popularly known as the Gateshead Yeshiva, was established by Reb Dovid Dryanis. It is the largest Yeshiva in Europe and renowned as a deeply Haredi ultra-orthodox institution. Jonathan Arkush, former President of the Board of Deputies of British Jews, has called Gateshead "a unique university town for the very devout and a citadel of Orthodox intellectualism".

The Leo Baeck College for training Reform and Lberal rabbis was established in 1956 and has both men and women who are studying for the Rabbinate. The College is now at the Sternberg Centre, which is named after the philanthropist and interfaith activist, Sir Sigmund Sternberg.

The Rabbi

The role of the modern Rabbi is similar to that of a Christian clergyman. Indeed for a time rabbis started to wear clerical collars and used the title Reverend. Rabbis, however, have no priestly functions – the Jewish priesthood came to an end with the destruction of the Temple by the Romans. The five year post-graduate training at Leo Baeck College combines scholarly study and preparation for pastoral work. Expectations of a rabbi are impossible to fulfil. In his lively account of the search for a new rabbi for an important American synagogue, Stephen Fried, says that all congregations want 'the Perfect Rabbi,' who attends every meeting and is at his desk working until midnight, someone who is twenty-eight years old but has preached for thirty years, someone who has a burning desire to work with teenagers but spends all his time with senior citizens. One could add that the rabbi is expected to be a 'pastor, counsellor, fund-raiser and popular after dinner speaker.'[275] Increasingly also the rabbi will seek to be involved in the life of the community and in showing school parties round the synagogue

Care Of The Community

The Jewish community is remarkable for the varied provision for its members. The petition to Oliver Cromwell to allow Jews to return to Britain included the request for a place of burial, which was opened in Mile End Road, London, in 1657. The different Jewish traditions now have their own cemeteries and burial societies. Jewish funerals, as already mentioned, are supposed to take place within twenty-four hours.

Provision for the needs of the living is equally well organised. A Jew's Hospital for 'the reception and support of the aged poor and the education and industrial employment of the youth of both sexes' was opened in 1807 in what was described as 'an elegant modern edifice in Mile End Road.' The first of many Jewish benevolent societies was established in 1819. Jewish Care, which specialises in provision for the elderly, is the largest charity. Others deal with care for those suffering from cancer, mental needs, or special education. The cost to the community is very considerable and sadly increased by the need to ensure security.

There are a variety of Jewish schools. In the nineteenth century at Clifton College in Bristol, Polack's House was established for Jewish boys. Today, there are 120 Jewish schools - primary and secondary state schools and fee-paying schools – in the UK, ranging from ultra-orthodox same-sex schools to the more secular mixed schools.[186] Many Jewish children, of course, attend non-religious state schools. There are numerous adult educational bodies. The Association of Jewish Women's Organisations links together the many and varied provision for Jewish women.

Many Jews are active in dialogue with Christians and Muslims and members of other faiths through the Council of Christians and Jews, the Faith and Belief Forum and the World Congress of Faiths, as well as supporting a wide range of community work, public charities and cultural activities.

8. THE HIGH HOLY DAYS

Members of a faith community often learn as much about its beliefs and traditions from sharing in special days – some joyful, some sad – which re-enact the story of the community. Quite often, members of other faiths are invited to join them. As we follow the Jewish calendar, we shall also learn more about the history of the Jewish people.

Rosh Hashanah

The Jewish Year begins by celebrating the birthday of the world at Rosh Hashanah, which means 'Head of the Year.' Rosh Hashanah introduces ten days of remembering and retrospection, which reach their climax on the Day of Atonement or Yom Kippur. The Days of Awe are soon followed by the festival of Tabernacles or Sukkot. The emphasis is on judgement and repentance.

Jews prepare for Rosh Hashanah by saying special prayers of penitence during the month of Elul, in the days leading up to the New Year. Rosh Hashanah is welcomed with the blast of the shofar. Just as a trumpet proclaims the coming of a king, so the shofar heralds the King of Kings [196] The shofar is usually a ram's horn, which is a reminder that Abraham was provided with a ram to sacrifice in the place of his son Isaac.[197] No reason is given in the Torah for the blowing of the horn. In the Talmud, when someone asks, 'Why do we sound the shofar on Rosh Hashana?' the answer is, 'We blow because the All-Merciful has told us to blow.' [187]

A Shofar

The blowing of the shofar is an awesome moment. As Rav Amnon said, 'A great shofar is blown and a silent whisper is heard. And the Angels quake, and fear seizes them... And all earthly beings pass before You like sheep. Just as a shepherd counts his flock, so will You count every living being and assign a judgment for all.'[188] Rosh Hashana is regarded as the day on which all people are judged. 'Today is the birthday of the world; today God will sit in judgment over all the world's creations.' [188]

It is, therefore, more appropriate to wish friends 'a good New Year' rather than 'a Happy New Year.' On this day, the righteous and the wicked are judged – others are given a ten-day reprieve. It is a time to ask forgiveness of anyone whom one has wronged. This is necessary before God will pardon their sins.

Rosh Hashana is a solemn day - but it is also the day to

remember the dramatic time when some of those who had been exiled in Babylon, led by Nehemiah, were allowed to return to Jerusalem. There they renewed their covenant with God. After Ezra had read from the Torah – 'from daybreak to noon' - the people were much distressed at hearing the demands of the law and were conscious of their wrong-doing. To cheer them up, Nehemiah told them, 'Go on your way, eat the fat, and drink the sweet and send portions unto him for whom nothing is prepared; for this day is holy unto our Lord: neither be you grieved for the joy of the Lord is yours. The first meal of Rosh Hashana usually begins with apples dipped in honey. Sometimes in the afternoon some people may congregate by a riverside, symbolically to throw their sins in the river.

Yom Kippur

Yom Kippur, the Day of Atonement, is the most solemn day of the Jewish year. Although it is a day of fasting and self-denial, it is also a day of rejoicing, because sin is pardoned and reconciliation with God made possible. The synagogues are crowded for the service, which starts as night falls. The men wear their prayer shawls. The cantor begins the service by chanting the Kol Nidre, which is repeated three times.

'May we be absolved from all the vows and obligations we make to God in vain, from this Yom Kippur to the next – may it come to us for good; the duties and promises we cannot keep, the commitments and undertakings which should never have been made. We ask to be forgiven and released from our failings. Though all the promises of our fellow men stand, may God annul the empty promises we made in our foolishness to God alone, and shield us from their consequences. Do not hold us to vows like these! Do not hold us to obligations like these! Do not hold us to such empty oaths!'[191]

These opening words signify absolution from vows to God,

which have not been kept, as well as the intention to avoid future failure.

The evening service is lengthy. The congregation returns in the morning, staying throughout the day, until nightfall. The morning service is followed by a series of reflections on passages from Leviticus in which God gave instructions to Aaron, the High Priest, who was told, after he had discarded his garments of splendour, to approach the Holy of Holies wearing only a plain linen tunic, breeches, girdle, and turban of an ordinary priest. On entering the Holy of Holies, the most sacred place in the Sanctuary, Aaron was to atone for his own sins, the sins of his household and for the sins of the whole community of Israel. Two goats were then taken. One of which was chosen for the sacrifice. The chief priest then confessed the sins and rebellion of the Israelites and laying his hands on the other goat's head put these sins on to the scapegoat. Then the scapegoat 'carrying on itself all their sins' was driven into the desert to a solitary place.[192]

Yom Kippur is a day of fasting. It is a penance and an exercise in self- discipline. It also focusses the mind on spiritual matters and encourages compassion for the suffering.

> Is not this the kind of fasting I have chosen:
> To lose the chains of injustice
> and untie the cords of the yoke,
> To set the oppressed free and to break every yoke?
> Is it not to share your food with the hungry?
> And to provide the poor wanderer with shelter –
> When you see the naked, to clothe him
> And not to turn away from your own flesh and blood? [194]

Besides fasting, the Mishnah says a person should avoid bathin and not put on sandals It is inappropriate on this day when God's mercy is remembered, to use material taken from an animal that has been killed.

The universal message enshrined in the particular tradition is reflected in words that may be used at the end of the Yom Kippur service:

All the world shall come to serve you
and bless your glorious name.
And your righteousness, triumphant,
the islands shall proclaim
And the people shall go seeking,
who knew you not before,
And the ends of the Earth exalt you,
Praising evermore.[196]

'The God of Abraham could not abandon me.'
By Rabbi Hugo Gryn,
at that time he was a teenager in a concentration camp.

'Two contradictory emotions governed much of my inner life. That I was innocent and that I was abandoned. They came to a head … on Yom Kippur, the Day of Atonement. A day we had spent in the synagogue as far back as I could remember.

We knew the date. On that day in 1944, I was at my place of work. Like many others, I fasted and cleared a little hiding place for myself amongst the stack of insulation board. I spent most of the usual working day there, not even emerging for the thin soup given to us at midday. I tried to remember as many of the prayers as I could and recited them, even singing the Kol Nidre, asking God's forgiveness for promises made and not kept. But eventually I dissolved in crying.

I must have sobbed for hours. Never before or since have I cried with such intensity and then I seemed to be granted a curious inner peace. Something of it is still with me. I believe God was also crying. And I understood a bit of the revelation that is implicit in Auschwitz. It is about man and his idols. God, the God of Abraham, could not abandon me, only I could abandon God.'[197]

Sukkot

Maybe, as you looked around your friend's house, you saw a sort of awning or a tool shed without a roof. This is transformed into a temporary place for the family to eat during the festival of Sukkot, which recalls the long years that the Israelites spent in the wilderness, without proper houses, before they reached the land of Canaan. The forty years in the wilderness was God's response to people grumbling and saying, 'If only we had died in Egypt.' They talked about stoning Moses and his brother Aaron, so God threatened to send a plague and destroy the people: but in response to Moses' pleading for them, God forgave them

God, however, was determined that none of those whom he rescued from Egypt were to enter the Promised Land.' Even Moses was only allowed to see the Promised Land from Mount Nebo, where one gets a splendid view of the Jordan valley. Sukkot recalls these events and still today, Jews observe the command that 'All native-born Israelites are to live in booths so that your descendants will know that I made the Israelites live in booths when I brought them out of Egypt. I am the Lord your God.' Sukkot is also a harvest festival.[198]The joy of the season is symbolised by four species:

The fruit of a goodly tree or citron, known as the *etrog*.
A palm branch, known as the *lulav*
Some myrtle called the *hadas*
Some willow known as the *arava*

The four species are bound together and held during the reciting of the appropriate blessing. The festival is followed by Simchat Torah, or Rejoicing in the Law. The day marks the completion of the cycle of readings from the Five Books of Moses. Having reached the end of Deuteronomy, one starts again at the beginning of Genesis. It is a night for dancing and rejoicing.

> Rejoice and be happy on Simchat Torah
> And give honour to the Torah.
> For its merchandise is better that any other.
> It is more precious than fine gold or pearls.
> Let us exalt and rejoice in this Torah,
> For it is for us strength and light.[199]

Hanukkah

Hanukkah, which is another eight day festival, falls in December. The Maccabean rebellion, like the Warsaw Ghetto Uprising in 1944, shows that Jews have at times successfully resisted oppression. It is this that is celebrated at Hanukkah. Looking round at your friend's home, you may have noticed a nine-branched candle-stick. This is to be distinguished from the menorah, which is first mentioned in the book of Exodus.[158] The menorah has seven branches as a reminder of the seven days of creation and is sometimes used as a symbol for Judaism.

The festival of Hanukkah recalls events that took place in the second century BCE. In 336, Alexander the Great, as we have seen, conquered the Persian Empire, which included Judea. When the Seleucids of Syria took control of the area, they put pressure on the Jews to abandon their traditions and adapt to Hellenistic ways of life. Antiochus IV known as Epiphanes or Madman went much further. He came to Jerusalem in 168 BCE, supposedly in peace. In fact, he plundered the Temple and took 10,000 captives – mostly women and children – to sell into slavery. Worst of all, he desecrated the Temple by erecting a statue of Zeus Olympus, sacrificing a pig – splattering the animal's blood in the Holy of Holies and demanding Jews to make sacrifices to the pagan gods.

Some Jews, inspired by Mattathias, refused to take part in the sacrifices which the king had ordered. His sons, known as the Maccabees or 'hammers', lead a rebellion and eventually recaptured Jerusalem in 165 BCE. The Temple was restored and three years after it had been defiled, it was rededicated on the twenty-fifth of the month of Kislev in 164 BCE. But when the time came to light the temple Menorah, only one small jar of olive oil, which had not been defiled, could be found. To get new oil would take eight days, but the High Priest went ahead and lit the Menorah. Miraculously the small jar of oil lasted for eight days until the new supply arrived. Ever since, Jews have remembered this event at the festival of Hanukkah – a word which means dedication. One candle is lit on the first night and another candle each night thereafter for eight nights in all. The ninth candle is the servant candle (*shamash*), which is used to light the other candles.[200] The evening is given over to games and fun – one of which makes use of a dreidel, which is a four-sided top, with the Hebrew letters, *nun*, *gimel*, *hay* and *shin* on it. It is customary to eat foods friend in oil, especially potato latkes.

Purim

The mood in the synagogue at Purim is a complete contrast to that at Yom Kippur. Purim is a minor festival on which work is permitted. The events remembered are told in the book of Esther. In the reign of King Ahasuerus.[208] who is usually identified as King Xerxes I of Persia (486-465 BCE), Mordecai, who was one of the Jews who was captured by Nebuchadnezzar and taken captive to Babylon (near modern Baghdad). One night, Mordecai had a dream. This was a warning of a plot to kill the king. When Mordecai told the King of this, he was rewarded with a position at court. However, Haman, who enjoyed the king's favour, hated Mordecai. He schemed to kill all the Jews in Babylon. Mordecai, however, pleaded with Queen Esther, who was Jewish, to intercede with the king for her people's safety. But the danger was that anyone who appeared before the king without having been summoned would incur the penalty of death, unless the king extended his golden sceptre.

After a three day fast, Esther, wearing her most beautiful royal garments, risked her life by entering the inner court, uninvited. The King extended his golden sceptre and he and Haman accepted Esther's invitation to a banquet. When Haman went home, at his wife's suggestion, he erected a gallows fifty cubits high, upon which to hang Mordecai. That same night, however, King Ahasuerus could not sleep and so he asked his servants to read from the chronicles. As he listened he realised that Mordecai had not been adequately rewarded for revealing the plot on the king's life. So in the morning, the King asked Haman, 'What should be done for the man the King wishes to reward?' Haman, thinking he was the one to be honoured, said the man should be dressed in royal clothing and be led through the city, riding on a royal horse. It was, however, Mordecai who was to be rewarded and soon afterwards Haman was hanged.

The story is of the triumph of good over evil. Surprisingly, God is not mentioned even once during the reading of the *Megillah*, or scroll of Esther but whenever Haman's name is mentioned during the reading of the *Megillah*, children jeer and stamp their feet. Jews at Purim are expected to give food to the poor. They are also told to enjoy a festive meal, at which the Talmud says that a person should drink so much that he cannot tell the difference between 'cursed is Haman' and 'blessed is Mordechai.'[206] Children add to the festive event by dressing up, often as characters in the story.

Pesach – Passover

Sukkot, as we have seen, recalls the forty years that the children of Israel wandered in the wilderness. Passover recalls the night before the Israelites fled from captivity in Egypt.[207]

But to discover why they were in Egypt, we need to go back in history to the arrival of Abraham in the Promised Land. In Genesis, the first book of the Bible, we are told that, Abraham's father, Terah with his whole family, left the city of Ur, which was on the Euphrates in what is now Southern Iraq.

They travelled north-west, along the river, as far as Haran, which is now in South East Turkey. When he was seventy-five, Abraham was told by God to go to the land of Canaan.

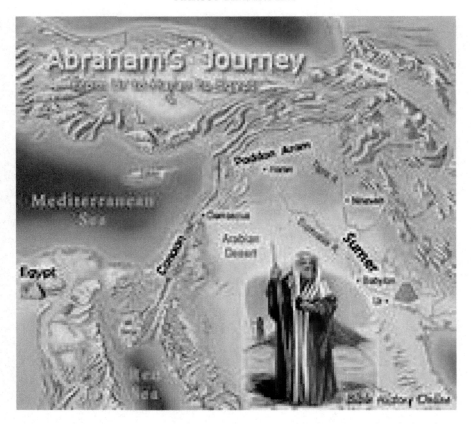

Abraham's son Isaac - whom his father had been willing to kill as a sacrifice to God - had two sons, Esau and Jacob. Jacob, the younger son, tricked his brother out of his birth-right and also stole his father's blessing. Jacob then fled to Haran, (although later he was reconciled with his brother Esau). In Haran, Jacob took refuge with a relation called Laban. Eventually he married his two daughters, Leah and Rachel. Jacob had twelve sons. Two of them, Joseph and Benjamin, were children of his favourite wife Rachel - whose tomb is next to the check-point through the wall into Bethlehem.

Joseph - famous for his 'coat of many colours' or 'decorated tunic' (as the Jerusalem Bible pedantically calls it) - was sold by his jealous brothers and taken as a slave to Egypt. There Joseph won favour with Pharaoh. When a prolonged famine spread across the area, his brothers, who eventually discovered the identity of Pharaoh's right had man, brought their father and their families and animals to settle in Egypt.

Time passed and Joseph was forgotten. The Hebrews became slaves, labouring to build pyramids and other monumental buildings demanded by the Pharaoh, who was probably Rameses II (c.1303-1213, BCE).[208] Despite the slavery, the Hebrew population increased so much that their growing numbers were felt by the Egyptians to be a threat to their security. Pharaoh, therefore, ordered that any Hebrew male baby was to be put to death.

Moses, however, thanks to his mother's care, survived and was brought up at the Egyptian court. As a young man, Moses saw an Egyptian beating a Hebrew. 'Then glancing this way and that and seeing no one,' he killed the Egyptian.[209] But next day he discovered that what he had done was known, so he fled to Midian, which is close to the Gulf of Aqaba. There, Moses worked as a shepherd for Jethro, who became his father-in-law, when Moses married Zipporah, who was Jethro's daughter.

One day, as Moses was looking after the flock, God spoke to him from the burning bush. 'I have indeed seen the misery of my people in Egypt. I have heard them crying out because of their slave drivers, and I am concerned about their suffering. So I have come down to rescue them from for the hand of the Egyptians and to bring them up out of that land into a good and spacious land flowing with milk and honey (Canaan)... I am sending you to Pharaoh to bring my people out of Egypt.'[210]

Reluctantly, Moses was talked into leading the Hebrews out of Egypt – but, first, Pharaoh had to be persuaded to let the people go. That was no easy task and it took ten plagues before Pharaoh gave in.

The final plague brought death to every first-born son in Egypt. As the plagues are remembered at the Seder (meal), a drop of wine is spilt in compassion for the Egyptians. The Ten Plagues are: Frogs; Vermin; Flies; Cattle; Disease; Boils; Hail; Locusts; Darkness; and Slaying of the First Born. On the same night that 'the Lord smote all the firstborn in the land of Egypt, 'the Israelites were told to kill a lamb for each family.'[211]They were to use some of the blood to mark their homes so that the Lord would 'pass over' that house and no one there would die. They were also told only to eat bread without yeast – unleavened bread – for seven days and to do so in perpetuity as a reminder of God's great act of deliverance.

That same night, urged on by the Egyptians, the Israelites fled. Pharaoh had told them to go, but he changed his mind and chased after the Israelites. With sea in front of them and the enemy approaching from the rear, standing on the shore, the Israelites were terrified and complained bitterly to Moses. But the Lord told Moses to raise his staff. Then the waters of Red or Reed Sea parted to allow the Israelites to cross over on dry land – the exact route is much debated. When the Egyptians followed the water ceased to part. The tide turned and they were all drowned.

It is these momentous events that are remembered at Passover or Pesach, which was probably originally a Spring Harvest festival. A festive meal and service is held in the evening, which is known as the Seder (Order). This usually takes place at home.[212]

The events are more than remembered, they are re-enacted, so that participants recall 'what the Lord did for me, when I went forth from Egypt.' As Rabbi Luzzato Moshe Chaim Luzatto (1707-1746) said, 'In the night of Passover all that happened in Egypt renews and bestirs itself; and this helps to bring the ultimate redemption.[213] This is sometimes spoken of as 'contemporaneity' or the capacity to think oneself into past or future situations in such a way that one speaks as if one had been actually present. The people of Israel have celebrated God's merciful rescue ever since.[214]

The Seder

Traditions, which date back to different periods of Jewish history, vary. Here is an outline of what you might expect if you are a guest.

Early on in thee Seder, the youngest child asks,

> *Why is this night different from all other nights?*
> *On all other nights, we can eat bread or matzo:*
> *Why tonight only matzo?*
> *On all other nights we can eat any kind of herbs:*
> *Why tonight, bitter herbs?*
> *On all other nights, we don't dip the herbs into anything:*
> *Why tonight, do we dip them twice?*
> *On all other nights, we can eat either*
>   *sitting up straight or reclining:*
> *Why tonight do we all recline?*

The leader will probably answer like this – it doesn't matter if the children know the answers – everyone else at the Seder will know the answers as well

'Our ancestors were slaves to Pharaoh in Egypt, but God brought us out from there, "with a strong hand and outstretched arm."

If the Holy One, Blessed be He, had not brought our ancestors out of Egypt, we, and our children, and our children's children would still be slaves to Pharaoh in Egypt.

So even if we were all wise and clever and old and learned in the Torah, it would still be our duty to tell the story of the Exodus. The more one talks about the Exodus, the more praiseworthy it is.'

The special Passover foods are reminders of what happened. At the beginning the father raises one of the matzot or pieces

of unleavened bread, saying, 'This is the bread of affliction …
This year we are free men.' During the meal four cups of wine
are drunk to recall the four stages of the exodus: freedom,
deliverance, redemption and release. The cups are often made
of silver, engraved with suitable blessings or quotations from
the scripture. There is also a particularly elegant cup, which
is the cup of Elijah, whom Jews await as the herald of the
messianic future. Indeed a chair is kept for him and at the end
of the Seder the door is flung open in the hope that he is about
to come. Because Passover is the festival of freedom, everyone,
as was customary for freemen in the ancient world, reclines as
they eat

At the centre of the table is the Seder dish. On the Seder dish,
there are five symbolic foods. There are Bitter Herbs – usually
horseradish– to indicate the bitter affliction of the Hebrews.
There is also a sweet herb or Carpas – usually parsley - which
signifies the hyssop, which the Israelites used to smear blood

on their door posts. The herb is dipped in salt water, which recalls the people's tears as well as the salt water of the Red Sea. Thirdly there is Charoset, which is a mixture of crushed apples and almonds mixed with cinnamon and wine. It is a reminder of the clay bricks, which the Israelites had to make and also symbolises the fruits of the Promised Land. You will also see a shank bone, which is a reminder of the Paschal offering that used to be made each year while the Temple was still standing and a roast egg, which represents the festival meal offering. Sometimes the plate also includes lettuce - perhaps as a reminder of persecution under Roman rule.

Passover is more than just the Seder. It lasts for seven or eight days, with services at the beginning and end. It was one of the three pilgrim feasts, (we will look at others later) when, in Biblical times, people from all over the Land and from the Diaspora went up to Jerusalem. It links together key moments of the continuing historical journey of the Jewish people from leaving slavery, receiving the Torah at Sinai, and travelling through the wilderness to the Promised Land. – carrying the Torah with them.

Rabbi Leon Klenicki Leon in his introduction to *The Passover Celebration* highlights what he calls 'the main concepts of Judaism' which are expounded and discussed during the Passover celebration. It may be helpful to follow his headings.

The concept of call and election. The blessing over the first cup of wine reminds everyone of God's call and the election of Israel. 'Praised are you, Lord our God, Ruler of the universe, who has chosen us among all peoples and sanctified us with your commandments...'

Solidarity with the poor. At the beginning of the Seder the leader lifts up the *matzot* or 'Bread of Affliction' as a reminder of the days of slavery and pain, endured by Israel in the land of Egypt.' 'It is a symbol' in Klenick's words, 'of the centuries of sufferings of the Jewish people for centuries and also of the slavery and pain of so many people in the world today. Our hope that next year we will be free, and that humankind will be free of all oppressions.'

God in history. The God 'who brought us out of Egypt with a mighty hand and an outstretched arm' is active in history. The obligation on Jews, 'even though all were wise,' is to teach future generations the story of God's great act of rescue. Children have an active role in the Seder and much of the story is told in answer to their questions.

The actuality of oppression. 'The story of the Exodus has given to us and to all humanity the courage to face oppression.' The Warsaw Uprising against the Nazis began during the Passover of 1943. Anne Frank in hiding, found hope in the celebration. Liberation theologians look back to the Exodus and echo the cry, 'Let my people go.'

Messianic Hope. There is a rabbinic tradition that the prophet Elijah never died but that he ascended into heaven in a fiery chariot and will return as a forerunner of the Kingdom of God – hence the references to Elijah already noted. The hope that, however much delayed, the Messiah will come can inspire hope in life's darkest moments. Persecution and expulsion has been the experience of the Jewish people in many countries over the centuries. Yet the hope of return has never been extinguished. Indeed the Passover evening ends with the song, 'Next year in Jerusalem.'[215] Rabbi Klenickic's *Passover Celebration* ends with a grace praising God for freedom and for 'the Torah which you have taught us.'[216]

What perhaps is missing from Rabbi Klenickie's list is the powerful way that the Passover, with its ritual, with its meal and its songs, bonds all generations together. A song by Ree Goodman Ree expresses this beautifully:

Family group at table changes year to year
Some born some gone, different faces here
But the blessings never change,
No the blessings never change
I hear my father's voice;
Family roles at service shift;
Time moves up the stairs to another generation.
Other members lead the prayers,
But the blessings never change,
No the blessings never change;
I feel my father's melody
and with each ringing memory of syllable and song
I taste my father's music. [217]

Guests At A Passover Seder

Shavuot

Seven weeks later, the 'Feast of Weeks' or Shavuot is celebrated. This is both a harvest festival and a solemn commemorates of the giving of the Torah on Mount Sinai. But before we join in the celebrations, we need again to catch up on the history.

What route the Israelites travelled through the wilderness to the land of Canaan is still a matter of keen debate. For us, it is enough to know that they made their way through the wilderness to Mount Sinai. Again there is debate about which mountain is referred to, but having twice climbed Mount Sinai, I am happy to accept the traditional identification and even the site of the burning bush at the lonely monastery of St Catherine.

In the wilderness, the children of Israel soon started grumbling because they were thirsty. They travelled for three days without finding water. When they came to Marah, the water was so bitter that they could not drink it. But Moses threw a piece of wood into the water and it became sweet – perhaps it was wood of an oak, which contains tannin and can help to purify water. One rabbi said that it was not the water which was bitter, but that the Israelites were bitter so that it tasted bitter to them.[218]

Then the Israelites started complaining that they were starving and longed for the 'flesh pots' of Egypt. The Lord fed them with manna –'bread from heaven' – and with quails. Again a natural explanation may be given and the manna may have been an exudation of the tamarisk tree – which Bedouins still collect.

Whatever the explanation, the food in the wilderness was remembered as a sign of God's care for his people, although the Lord was angry at the people's grumbling and lack of trust in his power to help.

> He commanded the clouds above:
> and opened the doors of heaven.
> He rained down manna also upon them for to eat:
> and gave them food from heaven.
> So man did eat angels' food:
> for he sent them meat enough...
> He rained flesh upon them as thick as dust.
> and feathered fowls like as the sand of the sea.[151]

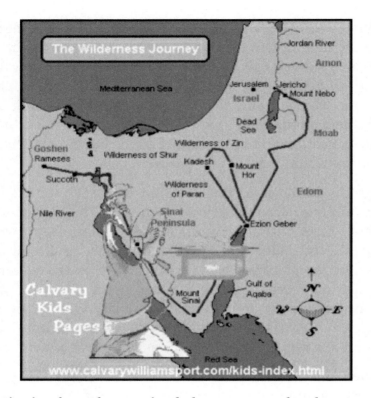

Sinai, when they arrived there, was to be the mount of revelation. Having purified the people, the Lord called Moses to climb to the top of the where he received the Torah. Moses is then pictured coming down carrying the Ten Commandments on tablets of stone. Torah, literally means 'Teaching' but 'Way of Life', rather like the Hindu *dharma*, might be a better translation of the word. The Torah, for Orthodox Jews, includes all the teaching and instruction that Moses received – both what was written down and what was passed on aurally. Torah, therefore, comes to mean the Five Books of Moses, with which the Bible begins, and indeed the whole Hebrew Bible.[220]

Shavuot is also the day on which a young child is often introduced to Torah study, as it was the day on which the Torah was received.

There is a story that on the morning when God was to reveal the Commandments, the people of Israel overslept. Jews, therefore, keep a vigil on the eve of Shavuot and spend the time studying the Torah and the Talmud. It is also customary to eat dairy foods. Some people relate this to the promise that the people would eat milk and honey in the Promised Land. Others say that among the instructions Moses received were the dietary rules (Kashrut). As they were not equipped to provide kosher meat, they had to eat dairy foods, which today include blintzes - thin, folded pancakes filled with cream cheese – and cheese cake.

By custom, perhaps because the origin of Shavuot was a harvest festival, the Biblical book of Ruth is read. The book tells the story of a man from Bethlehem, Elimelech, who went with his wife Naomi and two sons to live in Moab. The sons both married local girls, Orpah and Ruth. When Naomi's husband and both her sons died, she decided to go back to Bethlehem. She thought her daughters-in-law would stay in Moab, but Ruth, in well known words, insisted, 'Where you go I will go and where you stay I will stay. Your people will be my people and your God my God.' When Naomi and Ruth arrived back in Bethlehem, it was harvest time. The story goes on to tell how Ruth married Boaz, a leading member of the town. The vivid story has real importance because Ruth, a Moabite woman by birth, was the Great Grandmother of King David and, therefore, an ancestor of the Messiah.

Tisha be-av and the Destruction of the Temple

There are fasts as well as feasts. The fast of Tisha be-av recalls the destruction of the Temple in Jerusalem in 586 BCE and again in 70 CE. Some people, in addition, also remember the victims of the Holocaust'

It is a jump of several hundred years from the giving of the Torah at Sinai to the destruction of the Temple. Very briefly, after Moses' death, his appointed successor Joshua led the Israelites across the river Jordan into Canaan. Gradually the Israelites, after a protracted struggle with the land's existing inhabitants, came to occupy much of the land. There was, however, continuing conflict with the Philistines, who settled on the coastal plain. At first, the Israelites' leaders were Judges and Seers.[221]

Eventually Samuel was reluctantly persuaded to appoint the Israelites' first king - King Saul. After Saul's death in battle against the Philistines, he was succeeded by David, who had killed the Giant Goliath. David has been looked back to through the centuries as a model ruler and to whom the writing of the Psalms is traditionally attributed.

David's son Solomon was renowned for building the Temple, for his wisdom, and for his many wives. After Solomon's death, the kingdom split in two: Israel in the north and Judah in the south. In 722 BCE the Northern Kingdom's capital Samaria was captured by the Assyrians.

Most of the people were deported. The Southern kingdom survived for more than a century. In 586 BCE Nebuchadnezzar seized the city of Jerusalem and its Temple was destroyed. Most of the inhabitants were sent into exile in Babylon, but forty years later they were allowed back by Cyrus the Great, the Persian ruler who had destroyed the power of Babylon, and who is called 'the Lord's anointed' by Isaiah.[222]

For the next five hundred years or so, Judah – a tiny state – struggled to maintain its autonomy, although it was under constant pressure from the Super-Powers. Following the conquests and death of Alexander the Great (d.323), Palestine initially came under the suzerainty of the Ptolemies of Egypt and then of the Seleucid Empire. As we have seen at Hanukkah, the oppressive action of Antiochus IV, known as Epiphanes or 'Madman' triggered an uprising led by the Maccabeans. This regained for Judea its independence, which it maintained until 63 BCE. In that year the Roman general Pompey, after a brutal siege, captured Jerusalem.

As a client state of the Romans, Judea had some autonomy and the priests continued to control the Temple. Under the energetic rule of Herod the Great (37-4 BCE), there was much construction work, including the rebuilding of the Temple on Temple Mount, which is now dominated by the golden Dome of the Rock. Roman rule, however, was resented by many Jews and after periodic unrest a full-scale rebellion broke out in 66 CE. Jerusalem was eventually captured by the Romans and the Temple, for the second time, was destroyed. The isolated and impressive fortress of Masada, overlooking the Dead Sea, was captured three years later – after the Jews inside chose to commit suicide rather than be killed or taken into slavery.

It is these two disastrous destructions of the Temple that are recalled on Tisha be-av. Other tragic events such as the expulsion of the Jews from England in 1290 and from Spain in 1492 and the horrors of the Holocaust may also be remembered. Orthodox Jews observe the tenth day of the month of Tevet, when Nebuchadnezzar laid siege to Jerusalem.

Days To Remember The Holocaust

There has been some question among Jews whether there should be a special day to remeber the Shoah or   whether a new dimension should be added to some existing observances.

Yom Ha'Shoah

In 1951, Israel's Knesset proclaimed that Yom Ha' Shoah, Holocaust Memorial Day should be on the 27th day of the month of Nisan, which is the first month of the year in the Jewish calendar. The date was chosen as it was close to the end of the Warsaw Ghetto Uprising and because it occurs during a traditional period of mourning. Holocaust Memorial Day is observed in Britain since 2001on 27th January - the day Russian troops entered Auschwitz. [223]

Holocaust Memorial Services

Some Churches in the USA, from the early 1970s, started holding a 'Holocaust Memorial Service.' It has now become quite common in Britain.[224] If Jews and Christians arrange a 'Holocaust Memorial Service' together but the cautionary note of Rabbi Albert Friedlander is still relevant. He said, 'It must be remembered that the Holocaust continues to be the most sensitive area of contact between Jews and their neighbours. The local rabbi and members of the Jewish community must be included in the first planning session. This should start many months in advance – some problem always emerges which needs time to be resolved.'[225] Friedlander added, however, the hope is that: 'Remembering the past and praying for each other, we come to pray together. In that encounter, we encounter God.[226]

Those who plan such services should take note of the Holocaust scholar, Alice Eckardt who emphasised the many perpetrators were Christian and warned against 'Christianizing the Holocaust.

Do not turn the Holocaust experience into a triumphalist demonstration of the truth of the Christian gospel.

Do not use readings from Jewish sources and then criticise or reinterpret them to fit Christian views.

Do not attempt to strip the Holocaust of its terrifying and awesome character.

Remember the total abandonment Jews experienced.

Do not allow a Yom Hashoah service to become a one-time occurrence. [226]

There is a good example of a service in *The Six Days of Destruction* edited by Elie Wiesel and Albert Friedlander. [227]

Tu Bishvat

To end this chapter on a more hopeful note: the festival of Tu Bishvat, marks the season (February) in which the earliest-blooming trees in the Land of Israel emerge from their winter sleep and begin a new fruit-bearing cycle It is also called *Rosh HaShanah La'Ilanot* and celebrated as an ecological awareness day, and is often marked by the planting of trees.

TU BISHVAT

9. A LIVING RELIGION

The wealth of Jewish literature stretching back for some three thousand years may obscure the continuing creative spiritual and intellectual activity of Jews. A helpful picture is of the children of Israel journeying toward the Promised Land with the Torah in a portable ark. The Torah stretches back to Sinai, but every generation carries it forward, adding commentaries, interpretations and their learning – and this is still true today.

Many of the outstanding Jewish thinkers of the last Millennium, but not all, were Rabbis. Jewish scholars have made important contributions to many fields of learning in academia as well as in the Synagogue.

Commentaries And Other Mediaeval Literature

The discussions of the Talmud engendered further discussions. Numerous scholars wrote commentaries on the Torah. Perhaps the best known are the commentaries written by Rashi - Rabbi Shlomo Yitzhaki (1040-1105), who lived in France. He wrote one on many of the books of the Bible and on some of the Babylonian Talmud. Some of them are, often, printed alongside the text of scripture. Rashi's commentary on the Pentateuch may have been first printed Hebrew book (in 1475).

Rashbam, Rabbi Shemuel ben Mei (c.1080-c.1174), who also lived in France, was another famous commentator. Rashbam said that Rashi had told him that if he had his time over again, he would have put more emphasis on the plain meaning of the text, which is what Rashbam tried to do. Judah Halevi (d.1141), who lived in Spain, where there was a vibrant Jewish community, was known for his beautiful religious and secular poetry.

Because Jews were widely scattered, there was at times the need for translations of scripture as well as commentaries. The Aramaic translation by Onkelos, which is known as the Targum Onkelos, was regarded as an authority next only to the Hebrew text. With the invention of printing, prayer books with a translation into the local language on the opposite page were also published. Collections of Responsa or answers to legal questions by famous scholars were also collected and printed.

Maimonides

The most important Mediaeval Jewish philosopher was Maimonides, whose 'Thirteen Principles of Faith' were discussed above. He influenced some Christian scholars. Moses Maimonides is his Greek name. He was also known as Rambam, 'Rabbi Moshe Ben Maimon' He was born in Cordova in 1135, seven years after the birth there of the great Muslim philosopher Averroes. Maimonides' early years were spent in Muslim Cordova were Jews were given full religious freedom. He engaged with Islamic scholarship and helped to pass on knowledge of Aristotle's philosophy to Christendom.

The situation changed dramatically when the city was captured in 1148 by the intolerant Almohad rulers. Jews now had the choice of converting to Islam or being expelled from the city. Maimonides' family stayed for a time and then went to Fez in Morocco.

Maimonides eventually settled near Cairo, where Muslims and Jews lived fairly amiably together. There was quite a large Jewish community there, including some Karaites, who were members of a Jewish sect that relied only on scripture and rejected subsequent interpretation. In Egypt, Maimonides felt safe from persecution, but family problems soon assailed him. Shortly after he got there, his father died. Then his brother David Maimonides, who was a jewellery merchant, died in a shipwreck – taking the family fortune with him. Maimonides had been dependent on his brother's wealth, but now had to find work.

Maimonides, who insisted that a rabbi should earn his own living, turned to medicine and was soon so successful that he became court physician to the Sultan Saladin. There was an Arabic saying at the time that 'Galen's medicine is only for the body, but that of [Maimonides] is for both body and soul.' Maimonides also had a private practice and lectured to other doctors. Besides all this, he played a leading part in Jewish communal life, of which he twice held the position of 'Head.' It is no wonder that Maimonides complained that the pressures of his many duties deprived him of peace of mind and undermined his health. Two years before Maimonides died in 1204 there had been a devastating famine, followed by a plague

Maimonides' writings were of two kinds: a systematic summary of Jewish law and works of philosophical speculation. The Talmud, as we have seen, records the fascinating rabbinical debates about the Torah. This, however, made it difficult for those Jews who were not scholars to know what God's law required of them. In his Introduction to the Mishneh Torah, Maimonides recognised the difficulties. 'In our days, severe dangers prevail, and all feel the pressure of hard times. The wisdom of our wise men has disappeared; the understanding of our prudent men is hidden.' His aim was to ensure that 'the entire Oral Law might become systematically known to all without citing difficulties and solutions of differences of view...but consisting of statements clear and convincing, that have appeared from the time of Moses to the present, so that all rules shall be accessible to young and old.'[232]

Maimonides' major philosophical work was the *Guide of the Perplexed*. Maimonides' purpose was to explain in a logical and ordered way all that can be known about metaphysical problems. Maimonides, however, is perhaps best known for his 'Thirteen Principles of Faith', which has been discussed above.

Kabbalah

There is also a wealth of Jewish mystical teaching, which has come to be known as Kabbalah. A mystical strand of Judaism stretches back at least as far as the visions of the prophet Ezekiel and the apocalyptic material in the Book of Enoch and in IV Ezra. A similar mystical approach is also to be found in the Merkaba and the Heichalot literature. Merkaba (Chariot) dates back to the first century CE and perhaps to the Dead Sea Scrolls. Heichalot (The Palaces) refers to a collection of Jewish literature, which dates from Talmudic times or earlier. Many motifs found in these writings recur later in Kabbalah.

The authoritative Kabbalah text is the Zohar or 'Book of Splendour,' which is a collection of several books, which give a mystical commentary on the Pentateuch. The Zohar first appeared in the late thirteenth century in Spain, where many of the practitioners of Kabbalah lived until all Jews were expelled in 1492. Safed, a small town in the hills above the Sea of Galilee with several historic synagogues, then became the centre of the movement. The most famous Kabbalist was Isaac ben Solomon Luria (1534-72), who taught that the world came into being by God's act of contraction, *zimzum*. The world, however, seeks to overcome its separation from God. This can be achieved through the super soul, *neshamah*, which is an emanation of the deity lodged in the human body. In so far as the soul unites itself with God by keeping the commandments, it helps to unite the world with God. It is striking that the community which produced Lurianic Kabbala were survivors of the Spanish disaster. It seeks to find God in the midst of suffering. Evil is recognised as real, but not as of God's creation.

Spinoza

It is a moot point whether Baruch Spinoza (1632-77), who grew up in Amsterdam, should be mentioned here.

In his *Tractatus Theologico-Politicus* (1670), which was a work of Biblical criticism, Spinoza questioned revealed religion, voiced his opposition to persecution by the churches and argued for religious freedom. He questioned the traditional picture of God and challenged the classical views that both the written and the oral Torah were the very words of God.

Spinoza was a very significant figure in general philosophy, but his radical views were rejected by the Jewish community in Amsterdam, who placed him under the ban (*herem*). From time to time attempts have been made to reclaim him for Judaism: but Rabbi Louis Jacobs said, 'If this means that Spinoza was a Jew and an admirable person who did not deserve to have been placed under the ban, many Jews would go along with it. But if it means that Spinoza's philosophy is compatible with Judaism, Spinoza himself would have rejected totally such a claim.'[232] Rabbi Jonathan Sacks is even more blunt, saying, 'No one could follow Spinoza and remain a Jew.'[232]

Rabbi Tony Bayfield, however, recognising that it is understandable that this is the position of Orthodox Jews, asks why Spinoza is still largely disregarded by Progressive Jews. Rabbi Bayfield writes that there is a religious quality to Spinoza's pantheism and this explains Spinoza's fierce denial of atheism...Spinoza challenged traditional understandings and dogma in a way that was necessary before Judaism could engage further and more creatively with both the Torah and the modern world. Our pariah treatment of him delayed that progress and left us (Jews) behind the curve. The Synagogue has treated Spinoza in a manner reminiscent of the Church's rejection of Galileo; repentance and rehabilitation are called for.'[233]

The Eighteenth Century

Although the eighteenth century was a time of continuing isolation for Jews in Eastern Europe, in some countries restrictions were beginning to be relaxed.

Three outstanding eighteenth century figures, Elijah ben Solomon, Ba'al Shem Tov and Moses Mendelsohn, have had a lasting influence on Judaism. Rabbi Elijah ben Solomon Zalman (1720-97), a man of prodigious learning - known as the Vilna Gaon - led a revival of Talmudic study. Rabbi Israel ben Eliezer (c.1700-60) - better known as Ba'al Shem Tov or by the acronym Besht – was the founding figure of a populist movement.[235] They both lived in the closed world of Eastern Europe. Moses Mendelssohn (1729-1786), who lived in Germany, was a founding figure of the Jewish response to the Enlightenment and has been described as the first modern Jew.

Elijah Ben Solomon

The most authoritative opponent of Hasidism was Elijah ben Solomon (1720-1797), who led a movement to intensify Talmudic study. Elijah ben Solomon was *gaon* or leader of the Jewish community in Vilna, in Lithuania. He was an infant prodigy, delivering a homily in the synagogue at Vilna at the age of six. He was not against the Kabbalah or mystical tradition, as such, but insisted that everything should be subordinate to *Halakha*. Elijah ben Solomon regarded the Hasidic claims to ecstasy and miracles as a sham and would not accept that prayer was a substitute for scholarship.

Elijah ben Solomon wrote more than seventy commentaries on the scriptures and Talmud and other Jewish writings. He believed in the eternity of the Torah and declared, 'Everything that was, is and will be is included in the Torah. And not only principles, but even the details of each species, the minutest details of every human being, as well as every creature, plant and mineral – all are included in the Torah.'237

Ba'al Shem Tov

Ba'al Shem Tov had a profound influence on the growth of Hasidism, in which mysticism became part of daily life and joy became a part of religion. Hasidism's pietism captured the imagination and loyalty of large numbers of Eastern European Jews in the nineteenth and twentieth centuries. Many Hasidic communities were destroyed in the horrors of the Holocaust, but today Hasidic groups are growing fast in Israel, America and Europe.

By the time that the Ba'al Shem Tov was born, Eastern Europe had become home to a considerable number of Jews and an important centre of rabbinic scholarship. In the later Middle Ages, as we have seen, Jews had been expelled from some countries in Western Europe, including England in 1290 and Spain in 1492. During the sixteenth century the Jewish population in Poland grew rapidly from about 10,000 at the beginning to more than 150,000 by 1648. In that year, however, Bogdan Chmielnicki led a nationalist revolt of Ukranian Cossacks. For two months the Cossacks, who were Greek Orthodox Christians, moved from town to town, slaughtering Jews. The attacks, during the period known as 'the Deluge,' lasted till 1667. As a result, a few Jews fled to the Austro-Hungarian Empire or to Holland. Those who stayed were scattered across the Polish countryside.

Rabbi Israel Eliezer

Rabbi Israel ben Eliezer (c.1700-60), as mentioned above, is usually known by the acronym Besht or as Ba'al Shem Tov. This is a title probably meaning 'Master of the Good Name.' A ba'al shem was a sort of 'shaman', who was a healer and a charismatic spiritual leader, who might write out charms and amulets and do some healing work. Israel ben-Eliezer became a *ba'al shem* at the age of thirty-six. His importance, however, rests not on his work as a ba'al shem, but on his original religious teaching, which was recorded by his favourite disciple, Yacob Yosef – although we do not know how accurately.

At the time, the emphasis in Judaism was on scholarship and learning. To some, preoccupied with the difficulties of daily life, this seemed rather distant. Ba'al Shem Tov wanted to experience the joy of God's presence in daily life. Kabbalah, Jewish mystical teaching, which was well known in eighteenth century Poland, said such union was possible. As a teenager, Ba'al Shem Tov became acquainted with Luria's teaching and was influenced by Kabbalah, but his main emphasis was on individual salvation through which the world would be redeemed and he did not share Luria's emphasis on asceticism. 'Before one prays for general redemption, one must pray for the personal salvation of one's own soul.' Taking literally the verse 'the whole earth is full of the Glory of God', he believed that God's presence could be found wherever one looks for it. The world, he said, is the garment of God.' Faith involved 'cleaving' to God 'in all daily affairs.'[236]

Ba'al Shem Tov insisted that religious observances required total concentration or *kavvanah*. He encouraged the study of Torah, which should not only be understood 'for its own sake', but also by contemplating the significance of each individual letter – a Kabbalist practice - which 'will make a man wise and radiate much light and true eternal life.' Ba'al Shem Tov, however, was uneasy with the stern discipline often demanded by teachers. He spoke of God's love and emphasised the need to rejoice in God. Religion should be a cheerful not a mournful business, although he and his followers were criticised by some rabbis for 'dancing, drinking and making merry all their lives.'

To gain the necessary emotional enthusiasm to experience a sense of oneness with God in prayer, Ba'al Shem Tov would stimulate the emotions by shaking, singing and shouting. Prayer was not a matter of asking God for something, but the means by which a person communes with God. 'Prayer, as it were, touches the Holy One, blessed be He.'

Moses Mendelssohn

Moses Mendelssohn (1729-1786), by contrast, was a child of the Enlightenment. He was born in Dessau in Germany and was a younger contemporary of Ba'al Shem Tov and Elijah ben Solomon, whose followers despite their own bitter disagreements, were to unite in opposition to the Jewish enlightenment or *Haskalah*, to which Mendelssohn made a vital contribution. Moses Mendelssohn, spent most of his life in Berlin, which, under Frederick the Great, was a lively place to be. Jews were still required to live apart in ghettos, to which Jewish doctors or businessmen, who had to mix with Gentiles during the day, would return at night, but Mendelsshon was exempted from this rule. He was much admired for his conversation and became a welcome guest in Berlin society.

Paul Johnson describes the attitude of many Christians in the eighteenth century towards Jews in these words: 'Jews at that time were figures of contempt and derision, dressed in funny clothes, imprisoned in ancient and ludicrous superstitions, as remote and isolated from modern society as one of their lost tribes. The gentiles knew nothing, and cared less, about Jewish scholarship.'[238] Added to this Christians, wrongly, continued to blame the Jews for killing Jesus Christ.[239]

Mendelssohn dedicated the latter part of his life to the benefit of his children and 'a goodly portion of my nation.' He sought to bring the Jews closer to 'culture, from which my nation, alas! is kept in such a distance that one might well despair of ever overcoming it.' At the time German Jews mostly spoke Yiddish – which, as already explained, is a mixture of German, Hebrew and Slavonic languages, written in Hebrew characters. Mendelssohn, however, encouraged Jews to speak German fluently and arranged for the Hebrew Bible to be translated into High German and transliterated into Hebrew letters. Accompanying this was a Hebrew commentary, which highlighted the literary and moral qualities of the Bible.

Mendelssohn himself did some of the translation and wrote much of the commentary. Traditional rabbis, however, reacted angrily to the news of this intended publication. They saw it as a threat to the primacy of Talmudic study and a way of seducing readers to become interested in secular learning.

Mendelssohn also tried to persuade the majority population to accept Jews and allow them greater rights. His *On the Civil Amelioration of the Condition of the Jews* was published in 1781 and helped to promote tolerance. He followed this up by his book *Jerusalem* (1783), which argued that the state had no right to interfere with the religion of its subjects. This emphasis on tolerance was in tune with the time. For example, the American Declaration of Independence (July 4, 1776) had stated that it was 'self-evident that all men are created equal' and had guaranteed freedom of religion.

Mendelssohn, personally and in his writings, anticipated the emancipated Jew of the nineteenth century. In keeping with much Enlightenment thought, Mendelssohn upheld the rationality of religion and belief in God. Mendelssohn, in *Jerusalem*, suggested that Judaism was essentially a natural religion, containing no revealed truths, which were not available to unaided reason. The distinctiveness of Judaism, together with the belief that the Jews are God's chosen people, lay in the way of life commanded at Sinai. 'Judaism boasts of no exclusive revelation of eternal truths that are indispensable to salvation, of no revealed religion in the sense in which that term is usually understood. Revealed religion is one thing, revealed legislation another.'[240] The distinction is still often made between Christianity. with its emphasis on right beliefs (orthodoxy) and Judaism, which stresses obedience to the Torah as the right way of life (orthopraxy). Mendelssohn insisted that the Jewish way of life was of benefit to all people. His *Jerusalem* ends with a reference to the Messianic prophecy of Zechariah that in the last days, 'many peoples and powerful nations will come to Jerusalem to seek the Lord Almighty and to entreat him,'[241] and the words, 'Love truth, love peace.'

Mendelssohn's final years were overshadowed by a controversy about pantheism, which is the doctrine that God is, or is in, everything. Friedrich Heinrich Jacobi, claimed publicly that the German poet and essayist Gotthold Ephraim Lessing (1729- 81), who had been a great friend of endelssohn, was a pantheist and linked him with Spinoza. Others joined in the attack. Mendelssohn hastily composed a defence of his friend, entitled *To the Friends of Lessing: an Appendix to Mr Jacobi's Correspondence on the Teaching of Spinoza*. It is said that Mendelssohn was in such a hurry to deliver the manuscript to the publisher that he forgot to put on his coat before setting out on foot on a freezing New Year's Eve. He caught a cold from which he died four days later on January 4th, 1786.

Mendelssohn was to be a role model for many Jews, as at last emancipated from the discrimination from which they had suffered for many centuries, they began to play a full part in

European life. To do so, some Jews, who came to belong to Reform or Progressive Jewish movements, initiated reform in Jewish worship and ways of life and insisted that they could hold together fundamental Jewish belief with contemporary ways of thinking. The constant danger, however, was of assimilation. Of Mendelssohn's own children, only two out of six, retained their Jewish faith. His son Abraham (1776-1835), for example, brought up his children as Protestants in order to improve their social opportunities. Later, he and his wife embraced Christianity 'because it is the religious form acceptable to the majority of civilized human beings.'[242] His grandson Felix (1809-1847) converted to Christianity. By the end of the nineteenth century, however, it was becoming clear that full participation in the life of Europe was no protection against anti-Semitism, which, under the Nazis was to claim millions of innocent lives and to destroy much of the rich cultural heritage of European Jewry.

The Nineteenth Century

How to be Jewish in the modern world is still a vital question for members of the faith. In the nineteenth century the three best-known Jews were Karl Marx, Sigmund Freud and Albert Einstein. None of them were traditionally observant, but each of them have had a lasting influence on the world.

Karl Marx

Karl Marx (1818-83) was born to Jewish parents, although his father, a man of the Enlightenment, was baptised – probably to advance his career. He also arranged for Karl to be baptised when he was six. Marx regarded religion as the opium of the people. Ironically, his masterpiece *Das Kapital*, was described by the International Working Men's Association as 'the Bible of the Working class.' It is sometimes suggested that the book is a secular version of the Jewish Messianic hope.

Sigmund Freud

Sigmund Freud was born in 1856 in Freiberg, in what was then Moravia (now Pribor in the Czech Republic). His parents were Jewish. One memory that haunted him was of his father telling how his new fur hat had been knocked off by a Gentile who shouted at him, 'Jew - get off the pavement.' The twelve-year old Sigmund asked his father how he had reacted. He replied, 'I stepped into the gutter and picked up my hat.' This permanently damaged Sigmund's respect for his father.

Although he did not practise the faith, Freud believed that his 'Jewish nature' was responsible for his intellectual curiosity and willingness to advocate unpopular opinions. Freud's psychoanalytic hypothesis suggested that human identity is made out of three components, known as the id, the ego, and the superego. He believed the distinctiveness of the Jewish people was explained in terms of secular, not religious, values.[244]

Religion, for Freud, was a collective expression of neurosis. It was used, he said, by individuals to escape from the realities of a hostile and indifferent universe. Relying on an attitude of *als-ob*, 'as if', people create an illusory world of make-believe, in a heaven and in a God, which they project. In a long correspondence with Oskar Pfister Oskar Freud constantly reviewed his estimate of religion, but continued to maintain its essentially neurotic character. His views have not gained wide acceptance but have increased awareness that some manifestations of religion are unhealthy.

In an earlier work *Totem and Taboo* (1913), Freud had argued that religious solidarity and restraints begin in a primaeval rebellion of the sons against the father. In his *Moses and Monotheism* (1939) he suggested that Moses wanted the Hebrews to accept the ethical monotheism of Pharaoh

Akhenaten, but that they preferred the magic they were accustomed to and killed Moses. The Mosaic monotheism, however, Freud held, did eventually reassert itself. Again, these views have found little scholarly support.[245]

Freud believed that just as Copernicus (1473-1543) showed that the Earth moved round the sun and had displaced humanity from the centre of the universe and that Darwin (1809-1892), with his theory of evolution, had taken away the idea than humans were different to animals, so he, Freud, had shown that the mind is not subject to human control, but is the product of unconscious forces. Freud also treated religion from the standpoint of human behaviour, so helped to prepare the way for sociological and phenomenological approaches to the study of religion, which focus on the role of religion in society and in the life of the believer, but make no assumptions as to whether or not there is a Divine or metaphysical Reality.

Albert Einstein (1879-1955)

Albert Einstein, who was one of the greatest physicists of all time, a Nobel Prize winner and discoverer of the special and general theory of relativity, was born on March 14, 1879, in Ulm in Germany, of secular Ashkenazi parents.Einstein was observant for a time, but he never had a *bar-mitzvah*.

A Jewish medical stuent and family friend — ironically named Max Talmud — introduced Einstein to science books, which Einstein saw as contradicting religious teachings. Einstein did not believe in the commonly accepted anthropomorphic conception of God. "I believe in Spinoza's God who reveals himself in the harmony of all being, not in a God who concerns himself with the fate and actions of men," he wrote to a rabbi in 1929.

As his fame spread, Einstein travelled widely, but in Germany he was increasingly attacked not only for his work but also for his pacifist politics, which aroused violent animosity. During the Third Reich, Einstein's name could no longer be mentioned in lectures or scholarly papers, though his relativity theory was still taught. At first Einstein was hesitant to support Zionism, but the ant-Semitism he faced in Europe convinced him of the need for a Jewish state. In 1921, he went on a fundraising tour of the United States.

In the following year, he stopped in Palestine for 12 days on the way back from to Asia and gave the first-ever scientific lecture at the Hebrew University. Einstein said he was proud of how Jews were becoming "a force in the world," but never visited again.

Four years after the creation of Israel, Einstein was offered the Presidency of Israel by Prime Minister David Ben-Gurion. Though moved by the offer, Einstein declined. He explained: 'I am deeply moved by the offer from our State of Israel [to serve as President], and at once saddened and ashamed that I cannot accept it. All my life I have dealt with objective matters, hence I lack both the natural aptitude and the experience to deal properly with people and to exercise official functions. For these reasons alone I should be unsuited to fulfil the duties of that high office, even if advancing age was not making increasing inroads on my strength. I am the more distressed over these circumstances because my relationship to the Jewish people has become my strongest human bond, ever since I became fully aware of our precarious situation among the nations of the world.'[246]

His simplicity, benevolence and good humour as well as his scientific genius gave Einstein a unique fame and prestige among physicists, even though after the mid-1920s he diverged from the main trends in the field, especially disliking the probabilistic interpretation of the universe associated with quantum theory.

The Twentieth Century

In the twentieth century three of the most influential German Jewish religious thinkers were Franz Rosenzweig (1886-1929), Martin Buber (1878-1965) and Abraham Joshua Heschel (1907-72).

Franz Rosenzweig

Franz Rosenzweig's family were assimilated Jews with little attachment to Judaism or Jewish life. Rosenzweig nearly converted to Christianity, but while he was thinking about this he attended a Yom Kippur service in Berlin. He was so impressed by the devotion of those attending the Day of Atonement services that he realised that he could find salvation in his ancestral faith and declared, 'I shall therefore remain a Jew.'[246] As he put it later, the Christian claim that no one can come to the Father except through Jesus was true for all others but not for the Jew, since Jews, being already with the Father, had no need to 'come' to him. Rosenzweig shared with of many of his generation the disillusionment caused by the butchery of the First World War and the political intrigue of the fledgling Weimar Republic.

Rosenzweig's major work, *The Star of Redemption*, published in 1921, was, in part, written on postcards sent back from the trenches during World War 1. The book is a masterly fusion of the Western philosophical tradition and Jewish learning. Rosenzweig, however, did not pursue an academic career, but concentrated on encouraging Jewish learning in the community.

Martin Buber

Martin Buber (1878-1965) has been described as 'one of the most influential figures in twentieth century spiritual and intellectual life' and as 'one of the last great figures of German Jewry.'[249] His writings have had a lasting impact on Christian as well as Jewish thought.

Martin Buber, whose Hebrew name was Mordechai, was born on February 8th, 1878 in Vienna, Austria. His mother left home when he was a child and he was mainly brought up by his grandparents, who lived in Lemberg - now Lviv - in the Ukraine. His grandfather Solomon Buber (1827-1906) was a wealthy philanthropist and scholar. His grandmother was more in tune with the Enlightenment. Martin spoke the local languages – Hebrew, Yiddish, Polish and German – and learned Greek, Latin, French, Italian and English. When in 1892, he returned to his father's house, he gave up observing Jewish festivals. Instead he started reading philosophical works. He became interested in Zionism. He also took up the study of Hasidism and his books, especially his *Tales of Rabbi Nachman, Tales of the Hasidim* and *The Legend of Baal Shem*[250] helped to make this movement more widely known.

In 1937, he left Germany to settle in Jerusalem, where he lived, teaching and writing until his death on June 13,1965. His *Ich und Du (I and Thou)* was very influential, especially on some Christian writers, such as Bishop John Robinson, who wrote *Honest to God.*[251]

He distinguished two patterns of relationship: 'I-Thou' and 'I-It.' The 'I-Thou' relationship between human beings, in which both parties enter into the fullness of their being, is rare, but may occur in great love or an ideal friendship. Much of the time, as humans, we only share part of our self with others. In our relationship with the material world we adopt an objective or an 'I-It' relationship, which Buber acknowledged was necessary for scholarly work and scientific research. It is in our meeting with God, Buber maintained that a true 'I-Thou' relationship is possible. Indeed it is God, 'the Great Thou' who makes personal relationships possible. Often, however, we treat God as an object, either by concentrating on dogmas or teaching about God, or by making God a lawgiver or by focusing on religious organizations.

Buber applied his distinctive approach to the Bible, which with Rosenzweig he translated into German and on which he wrote a number of commentaries. He saw the Bible as originating in the ever-renewed encounter between God and his people. This meeting, he said, could give rise to a tradition, which authentically reflected this experience and another that distorted the encounter to serve later ideological aims. He dismissed most of the legal prescriptions of the Talmud as 'spurious' and obscuring a living relationship with God. Orthodox Jews, not surprisingly, viewed his teaching with suspicion. Buber's *Good and Evil* (1952) is less well known than his *I and Thou*, but is an important study of the subject.

Buber was an early supporter of Zionism, although he did not settle in Jerusalem until the late nineteen thirties. Already in the nineteen-twenties, he advocated a bi-national Jewish-Arab state. The Jewish people, he said, should make clear their 'desire to live in peace and brotherhood with the Arab people and to develop the common homeland into a republic in which both peoples will have the possibility of free development.'[252] Buber, going beyond nationalist sentiment, looked for the creation of an exemplary society in which Jews and Arabs could live together. In 1925, he shared in the Creation of 'Brit Shalom' (Covenant of Peace), which advocated a bi-national state and maintained this hope until the end of his life. At the time of violent riots in 1928 and 1929, he opposed the arming of Jewish settlers and opted for the minority pacifist position. In debates about immigration quotas, Buber argued for parity rather than the attempt to achieve a Jewish majority.

Buber took a particular interest in the kibbutz movement and wrote about it in his *Paths in Utopia*. Living through the early and dangerous years of the newly born state of Israel, Buber was conscious that his continuing hope for a bi-national state was a minority view, but he held to his convictions, insisting that a person should be true to his or her beliefs, whether or not they were popular. It was fitting that, at his state funeral in Jerusalem in 1965, a delegation of the Arab Students' Organization placed a wreath on the grave of 'one who had striven for peace between Israelis and Palestinians.'

Abraham Joshua Heschel

Abraham Joshua Heschel, in David Novak's words, was 'in a significant sense Buber's pupil... While retaining much of Buber's theological vocabulary, Heschel's theory of revelation developed it in a different direction, under the influence of Kabbalah and Hasidism.'[253]

Heschel (1907-72) grew up in Poland. He was descended on both his father and his mother's side from Hasidic Zaddikim or charismatic leaders. Heschel, however, decided to study modern philosophy and scholarship and made his way to Berlin. He escaped from the Nazis to London and then moved to America, where he became a professor at the Reform Hebrew Union College in Cincinnati and subsequently at the Conservative Jewish Theological Seminary in New York.

His prolific writings show the influence of the Hasidic mystical tradition. Accepting Buber's teaching that God can only be addressed as 'Thou', Heschel argued in his book *Man Is Not Alone*, that God's address to humans precedes the human address to God. Prayer is subsequent to Torah, which is God's revelation to us.

Rejecting the view that Torah was literally given to God by Moses, Heschel held that God speaks through scripture. In a striking sentence, he wrote, 'As a report about revelation, the Bible itself is a Midrash.'[254] By this he implied that the words of Torah are an interpretation of something deeper than the words – namely, the divine-human encounter, which we call revelation. Unlike Buber and Rosenzweig, who seem to affirm the absolute priority of language in human experience, Heschel, who was also a poet, knew that words point beyond themselves. He said, drawing on the negative theology of Maimonides, 'in the beginning was not the word.'[255] Nonetheless, much of his life was devoted to the study of Torah and he said of the Bible that 'it surpasses everything created by man.'[256]

Heschel was appreciative of Christianity and other religions. 'The issue I am called upon to respond to,' he said, 'is not the truth of dogma, but the faith and spiritual power of the commitment of Christians.'[257] He was also deeply committed to the search for peace and justice and marched with Martin Luther King.

Feminist Writing

There are many other Jews who by art and music have had a wide influence, but before leaving the house of study, attention should be drawn to the growing importance of Jewish feminist writers, both in the interpretation of Torah and in philosophical discussion. It has been claimed that 'the question of Women and Judaism is more crucial than all the political problems.'[258] The key issue is whether 'the common status of women is not only sanctioned but, in fact, divinely ordained.' Tamar Ross argues that Halakah contains within itself the wherewithal to counteract the centuries of patriarchy and affirms that 'the Jewish tradition provides ways and means of dealing with the challenges.'[259] Even so, the importance of the growing feminist movement in Judaism is as yet not fully appreciated. It expressed itself at first as a demand for equality. By the early twentieth century women were allowed to sit with men in Liberal and Reform synagogues.

The first woman to be ordained as a rabbi in the USA was

Sally Priesand in 1972. In 1976, Jackie Tabick became the first woman in Great Britain to become a rabbi. Reform and Liberal Synagogues now use inclusive language in their worship. At that time women were expected to imitate the role of male rabbis. Susan Grossman recalls that when she was interviewed for entrance into the first class to accept women at the Jewish Theological Seminary Rabbinical School, she was told that this meant she would have to accept all *mitzvoth* (commands), even those which she had not as a woman been previously expected to observe. 'The morning after my interview, I took down my husband's *teffillin* and a book explaining how to put them on. ... Everything felt strange and constricting until I began wrapping my fingers with the straps of the *yad*. As I wound them around my second and ring fingers, I read from the prayer book this excerpt from the prophet Hosea: (2, 19-20)

I will betroth you to Myself for ever,
I will betroth you to Myself
In righteousness and in justice,
In kindness and mercy
I will betroth you to Myself in faithfulness
And you shall know the Lord.'

As a woman, because she was aware of the ring finger, she had found a new significance in traditional ritual.[260] Increasingly the influence of women is finding new significance and meaning in Torah but at the same time questioning the authority of Halakhah. Indeed the question is asked whether 'gender justice is possible within Halakhah.'[261]

According to Halakhah, there are no differences between the ethical obligations of men and women, but women are exempt from many of the ritual requirements - partly because of their family responsibilities - and from the obligation to study Torah. The discussions in the law, for example, about marriage and divorce, are entirely from the man's point of view. Women rabbis, however, are adding new insights.

A Prayer for Healing after a Miscarriage

Nothing helps
I taste ashes in my mouth,
My eyes are flat, dead, I want no platitudes,
* no stupid shallow comfort.*
What is my supplication?
Stupid people and new mothers, Leave me alone.
Deliver me, Lord, of this bitter afterbirth.
Open my heart to my husband-lover-friend
That we may comfort each other.
Open my womb that it may yet bear living fruit.

Practical issues reflect underlying theological presuppositions. As Rabbi Wright Alexandra says, 'it is an illusion to suggest Jews have no theology and that the human task is simply to be decent to each other.'[262]

Rachel Montagu likewise refers to Judith Plaskow, who said that 'the right question is theological.' Rachel Montagu continues, 'While the first serious Jewish feminist studies were often focussed on issues of Halakhah, Plaskow says that one has to look at the framework of meaning behind the Halakhah to make sense of these issues – and that is theology.[264]

Our picture of God is coloured by the language that we use of God. 'King' or 'Judge' may suggest a remote figure of whom one is in awe. 'Mother' may suggest a God who cares for us and consoles us. Some of recent Progressive Prayer Books try to use gender-neutral language, such as 'The Eternal' or 'Our Rock', but this may obscure our personal relationship with the Holy One. It has also been pointed out that male imagery for God implies that it is only men who are made in the image and likeness of God.

Re-Visioning Sarah: A Midrash On Genesis 22

It was morning. Sarah had just awakened and reached over to touch her husband, Abraham to caress him, but Abraham wasn't there. Neither, she discovered, was Isaac, her only son, Isaac, whom she loved more than anyone or anything in the world. She quickly dressed and went outside, hoping they'd be nearby. But they were gone … And so she waited, and wept, and screamed…And then she saw them… Abraham walking with his ass and servants and Isaac, far behind, walking slowly, his head turning from side to side… Sarah knew in an instant where Abraham and Isaac had been and why they had gone. Though she could barely make out the features of Isaac's face, she could tell from his movements and his gestures that he was angry, that he wanted nothing to do with his father who had tried to kill him…

Abraham would try to make her understand his side of the story… She was tired of hearing Abraham's excuses and even more tired of hearing what he thought God demanded. And so Sarah turned and went inside and prayed that if only for one night, Abraham would leave her alone.265

10. THE SHADOW
OF THE SHOAH

The Evil

'One Must Speak'

The event took place
One must speak.
The event defies description.
One cannot speak.
The event suggests an alternative.
One could choose silence.
The event precludes silence.
One must become a messenger.

Words of Elie Wiesel, a survivor and well-known novelist

When more than sixty years ago, I went into the Chamber of the Holocaust – a small museum on Mount Zion – I was silent. I was totally unprepared for what I saw and read there – although at school one of my main subjects was Modern European History. I have never forgotten seeing the bars of soap, said to have be made from human flesh.[279]

Subsequent visits to Auschwitz and other sites of concentration camps or to Yad Vashem or other Holocaust museums, still leave me speechless. I cannot imagine the feelings of those whose family members were among those who perished. Yet the unspeakable crime in which some six million Jews were murdered must not be forgotten and indeed the literature on the Shoah is enormous. The horror raises especially difficult questions for all who believe in a Righteous God.

Silence

"The first time it was reported that our friends were being butchered there was a cry of horror. Then a hundred were butchered. But when a thousand were butchered and there was no end to the butchery, a blanket of silence spread. When evil-doing comes like falling rain, nobody calls out 'stop!'"

Bertolt Brecht (Washington Post (29.12.2021)

For twenty years there was silence. 'Our catastrophe is beyond belief.[280] The survivors hesitated to say what they had endured and what haunted them in their nightmares – they feared no one would listen. They wanted to try to rebuild their lives. Jews wanted to ensure the survival of the new-born state of Israel. Others did not wish to enquire. Christians could not face their guilt.

Arthur Waskow wrote: 'We are the generation that stands between the fire behind us and the smoke and flame that rose from Auschwitz: before us the nightmare of the flood and fire and smoke that could turn our planet into Auschwitz. We come, like Abram, in an agony of fear for us - for all of us – there may be no next generation.[281]

The novelist Eva Figes, who as a child fled with her family to Britain in the spring of 1939 remembered, 'For something like twenty years a veil of silence existed in families like mine. It was part guilt, part fear at what we might find if we dared to look.[282] For a family like ours... the challenges were specific: to build a future in a new country and forget the old. There was no going back and there was nobody to go back to. A few of our relatives were scattered across the world, the rest were dead. There were no graves, no death certificates, but we knew. An unspoken rule in our household was silence.'[283]

Mimi Schwartz, whose family escaped to America, has said the same. 'No one in the early 50s, Jew or German talked much about what had happened, especially not to parents starting again.'[284]

Both the well-known authors Elie Wiesel and Primo Levi found it difficult to get a publisher for their first writings.

Gradually, survivors began to speak and Christians began to recognise that centuries of anti-Jewish teaching had been exploited by anti-Semites. It was not until 1961 that the World Council of Churches repudiated accusations of 'deicide' (killing the Son of God). The Vatican Council's Decree, *Nostra Aetate*, which repudiated much traditional anti-Jewish teaching was not issued until 1965.

The mood changed in the aftermath of the Six Day War. Israel's allies were silent when Israel's future hung in the balance. This awoke many Jews to the terrible possibility of another massacre and led a younger generation to ask what had happened under the Nazis.

One of the first to speak was Elie Weisel, whom I once had the honour of meeting. The driving force for Wiesel - the compulsion that made him put pen to paper - was the need to record the story for posterity. As a survivor, he felt he had to tell the story. He had no choice. The story had to be remembered for three reasons.

The dead are owed a debt by the living and deserve to be remembered. Those whose names are not known must also be remembered. Secondly, by never forgetting we will never allow it to happen again. Thirdly, in remembering the past, it is re-created. Then it is possible to mourn the dead properly.

Scrolls
A poem by Lotte Kramer

If in two thousand years a stumbling boy
Picks up some scrolls in Poland's fleshless plains
And if efficiency failed to destroy
One charcoaled vest and skirt with needled names;
A handbag with a bracelet or a purse,
A private letter laced with someone's blood:
A picture of a child, some scraps of verse –
All those embalmed in sarcophagal mud:
Someone will write a book of dredged-up tears,
Clutter with sores an exhibition room;
Queues of bright people will poach hunch-backed fears
Chasing the boredom from their Sunday gloom:
Then useless rebels burn as victims fall
Blazing moon-deserts from their wailing-wall. 286

One cannot come close to the Jewish people without a painful and wounding encounter with the Shoah – even though Jews may hesitate to speak about it. The use of the word 'Shoah' raises the question of what name to give to the horrendous murder of six million Jews. The word Holocaust comes through Latin from the Greek word *ólokauston*, which derives from the words for 'whole' and 'burnt.' Holocaust was used in the Septuagint (the Greek translation of the Hebrew Bible) to translate the Hebrew word *olah*, which is used in the Hebrew Bible of a sacrificial offering burnt whole before the Lord. It was already in use by the mid nineteen-twenties, although a rare word, for 'a complete or thorough destruction, especially by fire, as of large numbers of human beings.'[287]

'Genocide' was not a word then in use. It is not known who first used the word 'Holocaust' of the destruction of the Jews by the Nazis, but it was presumably because their bodies were burnt in the crematoria. Some people dislike the word as it imposes a religious meaning of 'sacrifice' on the horror. They prefer the

Hebrew term Shoah or 'Catastrophe.' Others use the Hebrew and Yiddish word *Churban*, (Destruction). Churban was used in some rabbinic literature of the destruction of the first and second Temples. Does it, therefore, mask the uniqueness of the Nazi attack on Jews and Judaism?

This uniqueness of the attempted annihilation of the Jews may also be masked by the word 'Holocaust', which, like the word 'Genocide' has come to be used of any horrific massacre. Even when applied to the Nazi killings, it is not always clear whether those who speak of the Holocaust are referring to the destruction of some six million Jews by the Nazis or to the Nazi's systematic murder of more than eleven million people - gypsies, homosexuals, the mentally ill, Jehovah's Witnesses and opponents of the Third Reich as well as Jews. This was an issue debated in relation to how Holocaust Day should be observed in Britain.

Simon Wiesenthal, who brought many perpetrators to justice, argued that by referring to eleven million you broadened support for their remembrance Elie Wiesel said the word should be confined to the six million Jews, as the attack on them was *sui generis*. 'Not all the victims were Jews, but all Jews were victims' - the accident of birth. As Paul Johnson wrote, 'No Jew was spared in Hitler's apocalypse... No Jew was too old to be murdered... No Jew was too young to die.'[289]

The Holocaust was unique in the fact that Jews were attacked not because of anything they had done, but just because they were Jewish. Conversion to Christianity or joining the National Socialist party allowed no escape. Other than plundering Jewish wealth, there was no obvious advantage to the German nation in the destruction of the Jews – indeed the intellectual life of the country was severely damaged. The destruction of the Jews served no military purpose and diverted resources from the war. It was not in 'hot blood', but coolly and systematically planned. The modern scientific and technological resources of an industrial country were used to perpetrate mass murder.

Yehuda Bauer, (b. 1926) who was Professor of Hebrew Studies at the Hebrew University in Jerusalem, suggested that although the Holocaust had many features in common with other acts of genocide, it differed in this way: 'The Holocaust is the attempted total annihilation of all people defined as Jews by their perpetrators, everywhere on the globe, for ideological reasons that have, in their basis, little to do with economic or pragmatic considerations... I fail to see any other genocides, except perhaps the destruction of small groups or tribes especially in the Americas that have the same characteristics. You can add what most people add, namely that this particular genocide happened at the centre of a civilization that has spread... all over the world.'[290]

Winston Churchill said the Holocaust was 'the greatest and most horrible crime ever committed.'

What happened?

The exact number of Jews killed in the Holocaust will probably never be known. At the Nuremberg trials of Nazi war criminals in 1945, the figure was estimated to be 5.7 million. Others put it higher and the figure 'six million' is often quoted – that is one-third of the Jewish population in the world at that time. Of the six million, about one million were children under the age of 15. About 3.5 million people were killed in concentration camps by gassing – others were victims of medical experiments. 1.3 million People were shot by Einsatzgruppen, which were mobile killing battalions. These were used especially in Eastern Europe or at other public shootings. Another 800,000 were lost by disease, starvation, - caused by forced labour - and ghettoization.[292]

A Dead Child Speaks
My mother held me by my hand.
Then someone raised the knife of parting:
So that it should not strike me,
My mother loosed her hands from mine.
But she lightly touched my thighs once more
And her hand was bleeding…
As I was led to death,
I still felt in the last moment
The unsheathing of the great knife of parting.[293]
Nelly Sachs

'Herded to Death' by Helen Hobin.

Holocaust Denial

In 2016, the International Holocaust Remembrance Alliance (IHRA), at its meeting in Bucharest, adopted this non-legally binding working definition of anti-Semitism: 'Anti-Semitism is a certain perception of Jews, which may be expressed as hatred toward Jews. Rhetorical and physical manifestations of anti-Semitism are directed toward Jewish or non-Jewish individuals and/or their property, toward Jewish community institutions and religious facilities.'

The IHRA gave a number of examples of different forms of Holocaust Denial, which sometimes, it said is masked by targeting of the state of Israel, conceived as a Jewish collectivity. However, criticism of Israel similar to that levelled against any other country cannot be regarded as anti-Semitic. Anti-Semitism frequently charges Jews with conspiring to harm humanity, and it is often used to blame Jews for "why things go wrong." It is expressed in speech, writing, visual forms and action, and employs sinister stereotypes and negative character traits. Contemporary examples of anti-Semitism in public life, the media, schools, the workplace, and in the religious sphere could, taking into account the overall context, include, but are not limited to:

. Calling for, aiding, or justifying the killing or harming of Jews in the name of a radical ideology or an extremist view of religion.

. Making mendacious, dehumanizing, demonizing, or stereotypical allegations about Jews as such or the power of Jews as collective – such as, especially but not exclusively, the myth about a world Jewish conspiracy or of Jews controlling the media, economy, government or other societal institutions.

. Accusing Jews as a people of being responsible for real or imagined wrongdoing committed by a single Jewish person or group, or even for acts committed by non-Jews.

. Denying the fact, scope, mechanisms (e.g. gas chambers) or intentionality of the genocide of the Jewish people at the hands of National Socialist Germany and its supporters and accomplices during World War II (the Holocaust).

. Accusing the Jews as a people, or Israel as a state, of inventing or exaggerating the Holocaust.

. Accusing Jewish citizens of being more loyal to Israel, or to the alleged priorities of Jews worldwide, than to the interests of their own nations.

. Denying the Jewish people their right to self-determination, e.g., by claiming that the existence of a State of Israel is a racist endeavor.

. Applying double standards by requiring of it a behaviour not expected or demanded of any other democratic nation.

. Using the symbols and images associated with classic anti-Semitism (e.g., claims of Jews killing Jesus or blood libel) to characterize Israel or Israelis.

. Drawing comparisons of contemporary Israeli policy to that of the Nazis. Holding Jews collectively responsible for actions of the state of Israel.

. Anti-Semitic acts are criminal when they are so defined by law (for example, denial of the Holocaust or distribution of anti-Semitic materials in some countries.

. Criminal acts are anti-Semitic when the targets of attacks, whether they are people or property – such as buildings, schools, places of worship and cemeteries.

In 2019, there was much criticism of Labour party leaders for not accepting this statement in full. The current leader (2022) Keir Starmer has expressed his determination to purge antisemitism in the party. [294]

Why Did It Happen?

The causes of the Holocaust were complex and this book is not the place to explain why it happened. Even so, it is useful to outline some of the factors, although each has been the subject of many books.

The Political And Economic Situation After World War I

The Balfour Declaration

In 1917, in the Balfour Declaration, the British Government expressed itself in favour of 'the establishment in Palestine of a national home for the Jewish people' with the proviso that 'nothing shall be done which may prejudice the civil and religious rights of existing non-Jewish communities in Palestine.' The inherent contradiction in this Declaration has bedevilled the situation in Palestine for over a century. In 1923, Britain was given the mandate by the League of Nations to govern Palestine. The period between the wars was one of growing strife as British policies veered backwards and forwards from pro-Jewish to pro-Arab. The growing number of Jewish settlers in Palestine aggravated the tensions. Their arrival provoked a violent reaction from some Arabs. The British administration's concern not to upset the Arab world was the main reason why Jewish emigration to Palestine in the thirties was much restricted.

The Versailles Treaty, at the end of the First World War, redrew the map of Europe and imposed new solutions on ancient quarrels, but without providing the physical means to effect these changes. Moreover, in Eastern Europe, after the Bolshevik overthrow of the Russian Tsar, violence continued for some time. Many at the time were more afraid of Communism than of Fascism. Germans, some of whom regarded the war as part of a Jewish conspiracy to establish world control, much resented the harsh treatment they received after their defeat. Moreover the war accustomed people to violence and it was from the background of radical ex-servicemen's violence that Adolf Hitler emerged.

A world-wide economic Depression - sometimes blamed on 'the Jews' - caused misery to millions of people, including many Germans. The various democratic governments of the Weimar Republic were short-lived and often ineffective. As a result, many Germans who did not support the National Socialist party, at first, welcomed the firm government that it promised.

The Racist Theory of Anti-Semitism [295]

The term Anti-Semitism is thought to have been coined by August Ludwig von Scholzer, but was brought into general usage by Wilhelm Marr (1819-1904), who was a journalist. Marr was the founder of the League of anti- Semites. His pamphlet 'The Victory of Judaism over Germanism' was printed twelve times between 1873-1879.

The word derives from the eighteenth century etymological

analysis that differentiated between languages with 'Aryan' roots and those with 'Semitic' ones. The distinction led to the false assumption that there are corresponding racial groups. This led to Jews being labelled 'Semites.' Marr could have used the word for 'Jew-hatred', *Judenhass*, but he avoided this because it had religious overtones. He wanted, using bogus evolutionary arguments, to emphasise the racial superiority of Aryan people. Anti-Semitism is one particularly vicious form of the racism, which was so prevalent in nineteenth and twentieth centuries and expressed itself in imperialist attitudes, racial segregation and apartheid.

Bismarck, the imperial chancellor, gave tacit support to anti-Semitic propaganda, as a weapon against liberal opponents – some of whom were Jewish. The court chaplain to the Kaiser, Adolf Stöcker, denounced the sinister conspiracy of Jewish 'international capitalism' from the pulpit. Wagner helped to popularise Anti-Semitism - both because of his personal standing and because he claimed that Jews were taking over the citadel of German culture, especially music. 'I regard the Jews', he said, 'as the born enemy of pure humanity and everything that is noble in it.' He wrote this in *Religion and Art*, which was published in 1881, the year of the Russian pogroms. Wagner's music was often played in the concentration camps.

Hitler's Hatred of Jews

Paul Johnson has given a good summary of Hitler's Anti-Semitism:

It 'was composed of all the conventional elements, from the Christian Judensau, (or repulsive iconography) to pseudo-scientific race theory...But it was distinctive in two respects. First, it was to him a complete explanation of the world, a *Weltanschauung*, a world outlook.

Second, Hitler was an Austrian by birth but a pan-German by choice. He joined the German, not the Austrian army in 1914. His Anti-Semitism was a marriage of the German and Austrian models. From Germany, he took the huge and growing fear of 'Jewish – Bolshevist Russia' and the proliferating mythology of the Protocols of Zion [a forgery which purported to unveil a Jewish plot to establish world dominance]...

He blended it with the kind of Anti-Semitism he had absorbed in Vienna. This concentrated on the fear of the *Ostjuden*, a dark and inferior race corrupting Germanic blood... Hitler believed and taught that there was not only a direct political and military threat to Germany from Jewish Bolshevism but a deeper biological threat from any contact, but especially sexual congress, with members of the Jewish race. The sexual-medical aspect of Hitler's Anti-Semitism was probably the most important, especially among his own followers. It turned the merely prejudiced into fanatics, capable of any course of action, however, irrational and cruel.' [297]

Shortly before he took his own life, Hitler dictated a last political testament in which he said, 'But before everything else I call upon the leadership of the nation and those who follow it to observe the racial laws most carefully, to fight mercilessly against the poisoners of all the peoples of the world, international Jewry.'[298]

The Horror

However familiar one is with the facts, the sheer horror and cruelty of the mass murder, on an industrial scale, of those killed in the Holocaust is always a shock. Even though I have visited the sites of several camps and also intensely moving Holocaust Museums, it is still hard to realise such cruelty was possible.

People talk of 'the six million', but numbers can blind us to the suffering of each individual. Each person had a family he or she loved and who was loved, as was brought home to me when I visited Auschwitz. With me was a survivor, who although she lived less than twenty miles away, never had been back before. It is important, I think, to remember this before discussing some of the many questions relating the Shoah'

Arriving at Auschwitz

An extract from Night by Elise Wiesel in which he describes the train journey and arrival at Auschwitz-Birkenau in 1944:

"Jews, look! Look at the fire! Look at the flames!"

And as the train stopped, this time we saw flames rising from a tall chimney into a black sky. Mrs. Schachter had fallen silent on her own. Mute again, indifferent, absent, she had returned to her corner.

We stared at the flames in the darkness. A wretched stench floated in the air. Abruptly, our doors opened. Strange-looking creatures, dressed in striped jackets and black pants, jumped into the wagon. Holding flashlights and sticks, they began to strike at us left and right, shouting: "Everybody out! Leave everything inside. Hurry up!"

We jumped out. I glanced at Mrs. Schachter. Her little boy was still holding her hand. In front of us, those flames. In the air, the smell of burning flesh. It must have been around midnight. We had arrived. In Birkenau.

Holocaust Gas Chambers

The Nazis started their use of poison gas in 1939, as a tool for killing mentally and physically disabled patients in hospitals.

In 1941, Germany invaded the Soviet Union and developed the mobile killing unit known as the *Einsatzgruppe*, which was focused on mass shootings of civilians.

At this time, they also started experimenting with the possibility of using killing vans for mass gassing, which allowed them to kill large numbers of women and children without the mental anguish and at a lower cost.
Later that year, they decided that shipping Jews to concentration camps or extermination camps would be more effective, both time and cost wise, and started building gas chambers in various camps where they would go on to kill millions of Jews and other 'inferior' citizens.

Chelmno, a camp in Poland, was the first to use gas to kill people - using mobile van units initially. In 1942, the Nazis started using stationary gas chambers at Treblinka, Sobibor and Belzec, camps that were all located in Poland.

Victims would be unloaded from cattle cars and instructed to undress as they had to shower to be 'disinfected'. Some were beaten or yelled at along the way if they didn't comply. People were told to enter the room (what they thought was a shower) with their arms raised so that more people could fit in. This, also, increased efficiency, it also killed them faster because more people meant they suffocated faster because there was less oxygen to spare.

At Auschwitz, which was the largest extermination camp, the Nazis wanted a more efficient and effective way to use gas. They experimented with a known fumigation chemical, Zyklon B, which in pellet form became a lethal gas when it hit the open air. It was quick and effective and became the chosen method for use in gas chambers during the Holocaust in Auschwitz, where at the height of the transits, as many as 6,000 Jews were gassed every single day.

The Silence Or Indifference Of The Many

How much did the German people know?

The Nazis tried to hide their murderous policies and employed various 'euphemisms', but, writes Paul Johnson, 'The German people knew about and acquiesced in the genocide.' There were, he says, 900,000 Germans serving in the SS and over a million involved with the railways. Jewish forced labour was exploited by German industrialists. Daniel Jonah Goldhagen takes the same position in his controversial book, *Hitler's Willing Executioners: Ordinary Germans and the Holocaust.*

Mimi Schwartz's *Good Neighbours, Bad Times*, gives a more balanced picture of the complexities of human behaviour. Her book was inspired by the discovery that, in the German village where her parents lived, the Torah scroll had been rescued from the synagogue by a Gentile.

Some SS guards were loving parents. A passage in *The Librarian of Auschwitz* illustrates this ambiguity.

'Did you hear about Lederer's escape with a first officer of the SS, who didn't want to be a Nazi anymore?'

'Yes. It was that Nazi who used to look at you.' Renée nods her head very slowly.

'It turns out he wasn't a bad person.' Renée tells them, 'He really didn't like what was going on in here. That's why he deserted.'

To a Jew, a Nazi SS officer who acts as an executioner in an extermination camp ... can it really be that he's not a bad person? It's hard to accept... But when they look into his eyes, they don't see an executioner or a guard; they see a young man.[290]

The Failure Of The Churches

To these reasons must be added the failure of the Churches,

which many Christian churches have confessed and deeply regret.

In the year 2000, Pope John Paul II said 'sorry' for the sins of Christians towards the Jews. At Yad Vashem, the memorial in Jerusalem to the victims of the Holocaust, the Pope said, 'I assure the Jewish people that the Catholic Church … is deeply saddened by the hatred, acts of persecution and displays of Anti-Semitism directed against the Jews by Christians at any time and place.' Later the Pope visited the Western Wall, pressed his lips to the wall and, following Jewish tradition, left a piece of paper bearing a prayer for the forgiveness of the sins of Christians towards Jews.

There are two main reasons for the Church to say 'sorry' to the Jewish people. First, Christians did too little to oppose the Nazis or to protect the Jews. Secondly, Centuries of anti-Jewish preaching provided the soil in which 'the evil weed of Nazism was able to take root and spread.'[300]

We shall consider the legacy of anti-Jewish teaching in a subsequent chapter. Still today many Jews, more especially those who have had little recent contact with Christians, feel that the Holocaust was an outcome of Christian hostility. It is true that the Shoah happened at the heart of what had been traditionally Christian Europe. It is not clear, however, in what sense twentieth century Germany should be described as a Christian country. The Nazis were anti-Christian as well as anti-Jewish. Moreover many people from other Christian countries lost their lives fighting against Hitler's regime.

' I said nothing.'
First they came for the Communists:
But I was not a Communist, So I said nothing.
Then they came for the Social Democrats,
But I was not a Social Democrat, So I did nothing.
Then they came for the Trade Unionists
But I was not a Trade Unionist. So I did not speak out

And then they came for the Jews,
But I was not a Jew, So I did little.
Then they came for me,
There was no one left to stand up for me.
Martin Niemoller 301

More Questions

The literature on many aspects of the Shoah is very large. There are many more questions which cannot be discussed in detail here.

One, particularly addressed to Christians is 'Could local populations have done more to oppose the Nazis and to protect Jewish citizens?' Studies of different European countries, some of which are mentioned below, have indicated that determined opposition by the churches to the Nazis helped to save Jewish lives. At Yad Vashem, which is the memorial in Jerusalem to the victims of the Holocaust, there is an Avenue of Righteous Gentiles in which those Gentiles who risked their lives to save Jews are remembered.

'Should or could Pope Pius XII have done more to oppose the Nazis?' The question is still hotly debated.

Why was not Hitler excommunicated? Only now are the Vatican records to be made available to scholars to study

'Why did the allies not bomb the railway lines leading to Auschwitz?' 'Why were allied governments so reluctant to take seriously reports of the atrocities that the Jews in central Europe were suffering?'

The situation was different in each country.

Germany

Germany seized, annexed or absorbed the following countries Austria & Czechoslovakia Germany Poland, Denmark, Norway, Netherlands, Belgium, Luxemburg, France, the Channel Islands, Yugoslavia, Greece, Egypt (a colony of Great Britain) and the Soviet Union.

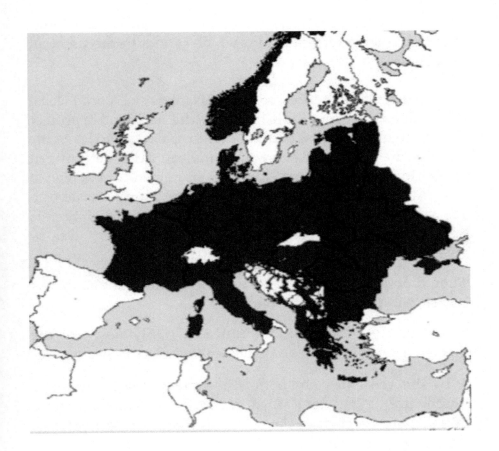

In Germany, both Roman Catholic and Protestant churches received money from state taxes. The Lutheran Church respected St Paul's teaching that the 'powers that be are ordained by God.' (See Romans, 13, 1-7) The Catholic Church entered into a Concordat, which Cardinal Pacelli, (later Pope Pius XII) signed with Hitler.

Protestant Sympathizers

Some Christians embraced Nazism.

Ludwig Müller, while he was still a naval chaplain, joined the Nazi party and had a personal meeting with Hitler.[302]

Muller became head of the German Christian Movement which advocated an integration of Nazi ideology and Protestant religion, a purging of the Church of all Jewish components and the introduction of the Hitler cult and romantic nationalism into Protestant religious practices. 'We must emphasize with all decisiveness,' he said in 1934 'that Christianity did not grow out of Judaism but developed in opposition to Judaism. When we speak of Christianity and Judaism today, the two, in their most fundamental essence, stand in glaring contrast to one another. There is no bond between them, rather the sharpest opposition.'[302] Some Christians even denied that Jesus was Jewish by birth: most ignored this fact.

Germany's twenty-nine regional Protestant churches were unified into the so-called 'Reich Church' and Müller was nominated as Reich Bishop of the so-called 'German Christians.' His position, however, was undermined when Hitler appointed a Minister for Church Affairs.

Protestant Opponents

Some Protestants opposed Hitler. Martin Niemöller strongly

objected to the 'German Christian' movement's plan to exclude non-Aryans from the clergy – the so called Aryan paragraph. Karl Barth (1886–1968), a very influential theologian, was also a vigorous opponent of both National Socialism and the 'German Christians.' Together Barth and Niemöller, both of whom rejected the state's attempt to control the church, organised the Synod of Barmen (May 1934), which issued the *Barmen Declaration* - drafted by Karl Barth. This led to the creation of the Confessing Church, which claimed to be the true evangelical church in Germany, as distinct from the established church, which did not oppose National Socialism.

Karl Barth refused to take an unconditional oath of obedience to Hitler. As a result, he was suspended from his post at Bonn. Soon afterwards he was offered a chair of theology at Basle in Switzerland, where by his writing he continued to oppose Hitler and encouraged those who resisted him. Initially, the Confessing Church gained quite a lot of support. When, however, church affairs came under the minister of church affairs, Hans Kerrl (1887-1941), the approach was less doctrinaire. This led to a split in the Confessing Church.

Some were prepared to co-operate with the government: others, led by Martin Niemöller, refused because the church's independence was threatened. After a meeting with Hitler, at which Niemöller was outspoken in his criticism, he was watched by the Gestapo and eventually arrested in 1937. He was sent to Sachsenhausen concentration camp and then to Dachau until the camp was liberated in 1945. After the war, he became a pacifist and a leading member of the World Council of Churches.

As Nazi power increased, the government strengthened its control of the churches. Some Church leaders, such as Bishop Theophil Wurm of Württemberg, continued to protest about government policies, especially against medical experiments on the mentally ill and the murder of the handicapped. Others helped to rescue some Jews.

Dietrich Bonhoeffer

Best known of the opponents was Dietrich Bonhoeffer (1906-45). In 1931, he was appointed a lecturer in systematic theology in Berlin. From the first he opposed National Socialism, including its persecution of the Jews. From 1935 he headed a secret seminary of the Confessing Church. Some of his best-known books, such as The Cost of Discipleship (1937), date from this period, although English versions were not published until after the war. In 1939, he considered taking refuge in America, but soon returned to Germany, writing to his sponsor Reinhold Niebuhr, that 'I will have no right to participate in the reconstruction of Christian life in Germany if I do not share the trials of this time with my people.'[305]

His brother-in-law introduced him to a group which was seeking Hitler's overthrow. In May 1942 he flew to Sweden to meet Bishop Bell and asked him to convey to the British government the group's proposal for a negotiated peace. The Allies, however, were committed to a policy of 'unconditional surrender.' Bonhoeffer was arrested in 1943 and imprisoned in Berlin. Following the failure of an attempt on Hitler's life on July 20th 1944, papers were found linking Bonhoeffer to the conspirators and this led to his execution on April 9th, 1945. During his time in prison, he wrote his well-known Letters and Papers from Prison, which was published in 1951 and in an English translation in 1955.

Roman Catholics

The German Roman Catholic Church's reaction to Hitler was mixed. Many bishops warned Catholics not to join or vote for the National Socialist party because of its racism. In 1933, after Hitler had come to power, the Reich Concordat was signed defining the relationship between the German government and the Church. The chief Catholic negotiator was Eugenio Pacelli, who Papal Nuncio in Germany. By 1933 he was the Vatican Secretary of State. Later, Cardinal Pacelli was to become Pope as Pius XII.

The Concordat was meant to preserve the liberties of the Church, but it also inhibited church leaders from voicing their opposition to many of Hitler's policies, although some spoke out against the 'euthanasia' of mentally handicapped people. During the war, the bishops avoided appearing unpatriotic by opposing the war effort. Some Roman Catholics risked their lives to save Jews, but at the time of the Second Vatican Council, the German bishops apologised for the 'inhumane extermination of the Jewish people.'

Some German Christians, therefore, actively allied themselves with National Socialism, some opposed it and a few either risked their lives or paid with their lives for trying to undermine the regime or for rescuing Jews. The majority did not get involved politically and continued to practise their religion. Standing orders for Germans working at the concentration camps often included the times of Catholic and Protestant services. Hitler and other leading Nazis were never excommunicated or denied the sacraments.

Smaller Religious Groups.

Members of the Seventh Day Adventists, Jehovah's Witnesses and some Quakers and Christian Scientists and other groups which opposed the government or rescued Jews were sent to concentration camps. 306

Jehovah's Witnesses at an early date decided to continue their missionary work. They refused to join Hitler's army or offer the Hitler salute. In their literature they publicly identified the evils of the regime, including what was happening to the Jews. By 1935 they were among the first Germans to be thrown into labour camps and were, throughout the Nazi regime, subjected to special tortures and humiliation.

Other Countries

It is important to reflect on the varying responses of Christians to the Nazi onslaught. According to the sociologist Helen Fein in *Accounting for Genocide*, two factors were largely responsible for the higher or lower victimization of the Jews. First, it is clear that where the Church was vocal in its opposition, this did restrain Nazi persecution of the Jews. Secondly, the existing pattern of relationships between Jewish and non-Jewish communities was important. Here are some samples of the different responses in some countries.

Poland

In Poland, which had the largest number of Jews, Anti-Semitism was strong. It was there that the largest concentration camps were sited. Not one of the three Councils held by Bishops during the German occupation mentioned the mass murder of the Jews. Many Poles were victims of Nazi terror. Others assisted the Nazis. A few Poles helped to rescue Jews, especially Polish nuns and members of Zegota, which was an underground movement to help Jews in Nazi occupied Poland. Zegota was founded by Zofia Kossak-Szczuka. She was a Polish writer and devout Catholic, who despite her anti-Jewish feelings condemned their murder. 'The silence can no longer be tolerated,' she wrote in 1942 in an illegal leaflet called 'Protest."

Denmark

By contrast in Denmark, which Nazi Germany invaded in 1940, the Danish Government insisted that there was no Jewish problem. Jews were Danish citizens and would not be treated differently. They were not forced to wear a yellow star nor were they banned from public places. When in September 1943 it became clear that German Aktion against the Jews was imminent, protests were read in churches. Most Danes combined to protect the Jews and many of them – nearly 8,000 – were saved.

The Netherlands

There was a long established and well integrated Jewish community in the Netherlands – made famous, of course, in *Diaries of Anne Frank*. One of my special memories is of meeting Otto Frank, when he visited Britain. This was before the diaries were published. I was greatly impressed by his concern to bring together young Dutch people when and young Germans.

Britain.

In Britain, as we shall see in more detail in the section on Jewish-Christian relations, dialogue, on a very limited scale, had begun well before the outbreak of the Second World War. Already James Parkes (1896-1981) had condemned the Anti-Semitism of the Church. Both Christian and Jewish leaders denounced Nazi action and help was provided for refugees

Help To Refugees

As refugees from Germany began in the thirties to make their way to Britain, various groups tried to offer them help. In 1936, an Inter-Aid Committee was formed, which was affiliated to the Save the Children Fund, which included Jewish and Christian caring agencies. Following *Kristallnacht* (1938), as the situation deteriorated, the number of refugees increased. A Refugee Children's Movement was formed and also a Christian Council for Refugees. W.W.('Bill') Simpson, who devoted his life to building good relations between Christians and Jews and whowas later to be for many years Secretary of the Council of Christians and Jews (CCJ), was appointed to be secretary A number of unaccompanied Jewish children were sent from Germany to Britain in what was known as the Kindertransport.

'Nobody to go back to'

One day one of the teachers walked into our class. She said something to our teacher who then announced that the war had come to an end. I was so excited, I just shouted '"Hurray" at the top of my voice because now I would be able to go home. I was sent out of the room for creating too much noise.

It took me a little time to realise that I would not be going home. Gradually I learned that everybody was dead: my parents, my grandmother, my aunts, my uncles. There was nobody to go back to. This was terrible.[308]

The Council of Christians and Jews

In 1942, the Council of Christians and Jews was formed to combat religious and racial intolerance, to promote mutual understanding between Christians and Jews and to affirm the ethical principles shared by both religions. Archbishop Temple and Dr George Bell, Bishop of Chichester, were outspoken in expressing outrage at Nazi atrocities and pressed the government to make it easier for refugees from the Nazis to be admitted to Britain. It was to Bell also, as mentioned above, that Bonhoeffer, in a secret meeting in Sweden, revealed the plot to kill Hitler. He asked Bell to sound out whether the allies would consider a negotiated settlement with the leaders of the German opposition, if the plot were to be successful.

Righteous Gentiles.

The Avenue of Righteous Gentiles at Yad Vashem - the memorial in Jerusalem to victims of the Holocaust – honours those brave Christians who did risk their lives to save Jews from the Nazis. By 2019, Yad Vashem has recognized over 28,000 Righteous Among the Nations from nearly 60 countries.[309]

A study of Dutch rescuers suggests that nearly half were in the resistance. 'Saving Jews was sanctioned by the political authority of the resistance even if one had no particular religious or social feeling for Jews.'[310]

It is tempting to tell the stories of many of these courageous and righteous people. Let the bravery of Pastor Andre Trocmé and his wife Magda of the French village of Le Chambon serves as an example. In the winter of 1940-41, a Jewish woman from Germany asked Magda for help. She consulted her husband, whose initial response was that the woman should be sent away. But, realizing that the persecution was contrary to God's will and the Christian faith, Pastor Andre Trocmé persuaded the villagers to shelter fugitive Jews, who were then taken on dangerous treks to the Swiss border. When the Vichy authorities demanded an end to these rescues, Pastor Trocmé replied: 'These people came here for help and shelter. I am their shepherd. A shepherd does not forsake his flock... I do not know what a Jew is. I know only human beings.'[311]

There were probably many more rescuers whose names have not been recorded. Few of the rescuers seem to have had a particular concern for Jews. Many of them said that they did nothing special. It was how they would behave to anyone they saw who needed help.

Besides the Rescuers, there were many others who tried in small ways to help Jews. Books, such as Goldhanger's *Hitler's Willing Executioners*, which has already been mentioned, needs to be balanced by the sort of stories collected by Mimi Schwartz. She was told of the shopkeeper who gave Jews food over the back fence at night and of the barber who cut Jewish hair under the sign

'No Jews Allowed Here.' There was a farmer's wife who said, 'Law or no law, I will not force Jews to work for me on the Sabbath'.[313]

Reflecting On The Shoah

Many Jews after the Holocaust concentrated their energies on rebuilding their lives and that of the community. To what extent they reflected on why it happened we do not know. Some Jewish leaders, such as former Chief Rabbi, Lord Jakobovits, questions 'the sanctification of the Holocaust as a cardinal doctrine of contemporary Jewish thought and teaching.' He recalls that there have been previous disasters and warns that it would be a catastrophic perversion of the Jewish spirit if brooding were to become ... an essential incentive to Jewish action. 'We must shift the current emphasis on the survival of Jews to the survival of Judaism. For without Judaism, Jewish survival is both questionable and meaning less. To me the meaning of being a Jew has not changed with Auschwitz.'[314]

The technical name for this discussion is theodicy. One dictionary definition of 'theodicy' is: 'a vindication of divine justice in the face of the paradox that God is both omnipotent and benevolent and yet permits evil to exist?[315] You could put the question in other words, 'Why if God is all powerful and all loving does God allow so much evil and suffering?' The question is not new and one that all believers have to wrestle with, but the scale of the suffering in the camps posed it in the most agonizing and acute form.

My teachers, you heard that God destroys His people from the face of the earth because of their sins. Isn't it foolish to believe that? If this were a punishment from heaven because of our sins, why did all the rabbis, the pure and holy *Tzadikim* (righteous ones) who were full of Torah and good deeds, why did they die?[317] *Reb Chaim*

There are some Jewish thinkers who believe that traditional answers are still relevant. Others say that traditional answers, after Auschwitz, are no longer adequate. Indeed, perhaps the horror was so great, that the very attempt to give some theological explanation is impossible, but it may be helpful to Christians to listen to how some Jewish teachers some have struggled with the question.

Traditional Answers.

Several ideas about evil emerge from Jewish scriptures:

Evil Is God's Punishment For Sin.

In the book of Deuteronomy we read that God will bless those who obey Him and curse those who disobey Him. Punishment will automatically follow disobedience. In Exodus we see punishment extending into succeeding generations, although the prophets taught that only the individual who was responsible was punished.[318] It follows, then, that the Holocaust was God's punishment for wrongdoing. The Holocaust was just another, if perhaps the most painful, tragedy to befall the Jewish people. It does not contribute anything new to our understanding of God.

Divine punishment is, of course, linked to a keen sense of guilt and of Israel's faithlessness. Elchanan Wasserman (1875-1941) was a leading pre- war Orthodox rabbi. He visited the United States in 1938 and was dismayed by the lack of Torah learning and observance. In his pamphlet

Iqvata di-Meschicha, he predicted that dire destruction would come upon the Jewish people on account of its lack of faith and laxity in observance of God's commandments. [319]

Rabbi Dr Norman Solomon quotes Gershon Greenberg, who said Wasserman's brother-in-law, Chayyim Ozar Grodzinski of Vilna, blamed the Reform movement for its denial of Torah. 'Wasserman blames religious and cultural assimilation and nationalism as an act of normalization and defiance of religion and God.' The required response was to turn to God through Torah.

Solomon adds, 'similar views are nowadays commonplace in orthodox writing,' - for example in *With God's Fury Poured Out* by Benjamin Maza or *Thy Brother's Blood* by David Krantzler. [32]

Evil Is A Human Failing And Responsibility

Evil is part of being human. Each human has the freedom to express evil if he so desires. [321] Thus, the Holocaust was just another example of human wickedness. To some, the Holocaust was the greatest manifestation of human evil. Evil is the price mankind has to pay for human freedom. The Holocaust reflects humankind's behaviour. It does not touch upon God's existence or His perfection.

God Is The Creator Of Both Good And Evil

It is clear from Jewish scriptures that God is omnipotent and as such everything emanates from Him, both good and evil. The best example is the story of Job where God allows Satan to test Job over and over again, to prove a point. [322] Lurianic Kabbalah teachers, as we have seen, struggled with this. The Holocaust, then, is an example of evil.

Suffering Is An Inexplicable Mystery

Human beings, as Job learned, are too small to understand the ways of God. It is arrogant of them to think they can understand His ways. All humans can do is have faith in God. The Holocaust is a mystery that no one can explain.

The Holocaust Is An Example Of Hester Panim.

Several examples of God 'hiding His face' exist in the scriptures. God is unable to look upon wickedness.[323] The Holocaust was such a dreadful crime that even God was forced to look away. There are times when God is inexplicably absent in history. We cannot explain it.

The Holocaust Is An Example Of Wrestling With God

Several examples exist where men argue with God in the face of suffering. Abraham asked God whether if there were fifty righteous people in Sodom and Gomorrah, would not God spare the cities from destruction?[324] Moses argued with God when the children of Israel constructed the Golden Calf and worshiped it and God planned to punish them.[325]

The Evils Of This World Will Be Redressed In Heaven

Some people emphasize 'Divine punishment,' and express also belief in life after death where the evil will be punished and the righteous rewarded. Dan Cohn-Sherbok has complained that many post-Holocaust attempts to explain Jewish suffering make no reference to the Hereafter.

Other Responses

These traditional biblical responses do not satisfy all Jews. Some argue that there is a need for a unique response because the Holocaust was a unique event. The theologian Steven Katz, who has studied the writings of post-Holocaust theologians, has usefully added their responses to the list above.

The Holocaust: A Modern "Akedah"

The first Akedah was when Abraham took his only son Isaac on the trek to the mountaintop, fully prepared to sacrifice him if God so commanded. But the point of the story is that God did not require Isaac's sacrifice. He required only Abraham's commitment. The Holocaust was different in this respect. God accepted the sacrifice of the six million.

Holocaust: A Call For Jews To Survive

The Holocaust is a revelation calling for Jewish affirmation. 'Jews, survive!' Emil Fackenheim (1916-2003) is famous for saying that after the Holocaust there is a new commandment: that 'Jews are forbidden to hand Hitler posthumous victories.' By this he meant, that if Jews gave up on God and their Jewish identity, they would have done Hitler's work for him.

Israel

For some Jews the creation of the state of Israel is evidence that God had not abandoned his people. The Journal of Babylonian Jewry, The Scribe, has said, 'The Holocaust did not mark the end of the Jewish people. Indeed it was followed by the establishment of the State of Israel.'[331] In Emil Fackenheim's words 'Israel is indispensable to a future Judaism.[332] Jews have seen building and defending the State of Israel as their only protection .

God Is Dead

For some Jews, their faith in God was destroyed Jewish responses is that 'God is dead,' If there is a God, God surely would have prevented the Holocaust. If God did not, then God does not exist. This view was expressed forcefully in the early writings of the philosopher Richard Rubenstein.[333] 'No man can really say that God is dead... Nevertheless, I am compelled to say that we live in the time of the "death of God." This is more a statement about man and his culture than about God man, heaven and earth, has been broken. We stand in a cold, silent, unfeeling cosmos, unaided. The death of God is cultural fact... When I say we live in the time of the death of God, I mean that the thread uniting God and by any by any purposeful power beyond ourselves. After Auschwitz, what else can a Jew say about God?'

Interestingly, this is not the response adopted by many of Holocaust survivors. Research shows that some came out of the camps with a stronger faith than before. It is important not to confuse Rubenstein's position with that of some Christian writers, who for other reason spoke of the 'death of God.'

A New Picture Of God.

'We must not fail God. If God is to be intelligible in some manner and to some extent (and to this we must hold), then His goodness must be compatible with the existence of evil, and this is only if God is not all-powerful.' 'We literally hold in our faltering hands the future of the divine adventure and we must not fail him, even if we would fail ourselves.' *Hans Jonas.*

If God is not dead, then our picture of God may have to change. Some thinkers such as Hans Jonas (1903-93), Arthur A Cohen (1928-86) and Jon Levenson have pictured a limited God, whose creation is not yet complete. God's self-limitation means that the future is genuinely open and this requires human beings to take responsibility for the healing of the world - *Tikun Olam.*

This I a view that I personally have found helpful and my contribution to *Dialogue with a Difference* was entitled

'The Power of Suffering Love.'334

Justice.

As news of the mass murder of Jews became known outside Germany, the Allied leaders of Great Britain, the United States and the Soviet Union, in December 1942 resolved to prosecute those responsible for violence against civilian populations. It seems that Joseph Stalin, the Soviet leader, proposed the execution of 50,000 to 100,000 German staff officers.

British Prime Minister Winston Churchill discussed the possibility of summary execution, without a trial, of high-ranking Nazis He was, however, persuaded by American leaders that a criminal trial would be more effective. Among other advantages, criminal proceedings would require documentation of the crimes charged against the defendants and prevent later accusations that the defendants had been condemned without evidence.

Although there had been prosecutions for war crimes in the USA and Turkey, there was no precedent for an international trial of war criminals. Indeed, when Lord Justice Lawrence opened the proceedings at the Nuremberg trials, he began by saying that the trial was 'unique in history of the jurisprudence of the world.' There had been considerable debate about what the charges should be. The Allies eventually agreed that the prisoners should be accused of waging wars of aggression in violation of international agreements, war crimes and crimes against humanity.

In a historical coincidence, two of the prosecutors, Hersch Lauterpachtt and Rafael Lemkin, unbeknown to each other, had lived for a time in the same city of Lviv (Lemberg) in Latvia, They had disagreed on whether or not beside crimes against humanity there should be specific reference to genocide. It is thought that Hans Frank, one of the criminals being prosecuted who had been Hitler's personal lawyer and Governor-General of Poland, may have been responsible for the murder of both of their families. [335]

The best-known of the Nuremberg trials was the Trial of Major War Criminals, held from November 20, 1945, to October 1, 1946. Twenty-four individuals were indicted, along with six Nazi organizations determined to be criminal (such as the "Gestapo," or secret state police).Hitler and two of his top associates, Heinrich Himmler and Joseph Goebbels had committed suicide in the spring of 1945 before they could be brought to trial and Hermann Gōring committed suicide before he was sentenced. Those found guilty were sentenced to 'death by hanging.' Some others Nazis, most notably Adolf Eichman, were later condemned as criminals, but others adopted a new identity and escaped to different parts of the world.

The Nuremberg trials were controversial even among those who wanted the major criminals punished. Nonetheless, they were an important step forward for the establishment of international law. The findings at Nuremberg led directly to the United Nations Genocide Convention (1948) and Universal Declaration of Human Rights (1948), as well as the Geneva Convention on the Laws and Customs of War (1949). In addition, the International Military Tribunal supplied a useful precedent for the trials of Japanese war criminals in Tokyo (1946- 48); the 1961 trial of Nazi leader Adolf Eichmann (1906- 62); and the establishment of tribunals for war crimes committed in the former Yugoslavia (1993) and in Rwanda (1994).

Forgiveness And Reconciliation

To survive, many other Germans had acquiesced in the Nazi regime. How were those Jews and others who survived to relate to them? I once was an observer of a meeting of some people whose parents had worked for the SS. and others whose parents had perished at Auschwitz.

Is forgiveness possible? Questions about the possibility of forgiveness and reconciliation are another subject over which Jewish and Christian thinkers have agonised. Some Christians were shocked by a report that Elie Wiesel, prayed at an unofficial ceremony to mark an anniversary of the liberation of the camps that there would be no forgiveness of those who perpetrated the crimes there. On the other hand, here is an anonymous modern prayer written by someone who lived in Tel Aviv:

I forgive you for what you have said and done.
I forgive you for what you believe to be true.
I forgive you for making light of the hurt
  you have caused
I forgive you for not saying sorry.
I do not withhold my love
If I ever do so, please forgive me. [336]

Sometimes unfairly Christians accuse Jews of being unforgiving and quote the verse 'An eye for an eye' – although the verse was a limitation on revenge and from early days was met by financial compensation.

Even so, Solomon Schimmel rightly says that there are differences between the Jewish and Christian approach to the subject of forgiveness, although similar differences are found within each religion. It is also clear that people use the word 'forgiveness' in different senses.

It is helpful to distinguish between 'private' and 'interpersonal' forgiveness. Private forgiveness relates to the internal feelings of the victim. Interpersonal forgiveness deals with the relationship of the victim to the perpetrator. It is possible for the one to exist apart from the other, although they may overlap. Jews', often say that only the victim can forgive.

Rabbi Dr Albert Friedlander, who was attending a Kirchentag or Church Conference in Nuremberg, wrote, 'I talked about the Anguish of Auschwitz', he wrote. 'A young girl rushed up to me after the lecture, "Rabbi", she said, "I wasn't there, but can you forgive me?" We embraced and cried together. Then an older man approached me. "Rabbi", he said, "I was a guard at a concentration camp. Can you forgive me?" I looked at him. "No", I said, "I cannot forgive". It is not the function of rabbis to give absolution, to be pardoners. In Judaism, there is a ten day period between the New Year and the Day of Atonement, when we try to go to any person whom we have wronged and ask for forgiveness. But you cannot go to the six million. They are dead and I cannot speak for them. Nor can I speak for God. But you are here at a church conference. God's forgiving grace may touch you: but I am not a mediator or spokesman for God.'[338]

The passage highlights the fact that whereas in some Christian traditions priests claim to speak for God and to offer absolution in God's name, Rabbis – who are not priests - claim no such authority. Only the person who has been injured can forgive, but if they are dead no one can speak for them.

A memorial at Yad Vashem
to the children, who died at Auschwitz

Words written on a cellar wall in Cologne, Germany,
where some Jews hid from the Nazis

I believe in the sun when it is not shining
I believe in love even when feeling it not,
*I believe in God even when God is silent.*347

We remember those we knew, and those
whose very name is lost.
We mourn for all that died with them; their
goodness and their wisdom, which could have
saved the world and healed so many wounds.
We mourn for the genius and the wit that died, the
learning and the laughter that were lost. The world has
become a poorer place and our hearts became cold as
we think of the splendour that might have been.
We stand in gratitude for their example of decency
and goodness. They are like candles, which shine
out from the darkness of those years, and in their
light we know what goodness is – and evil.
We salute those men and women who were
not Jews, who had the courage to stand outside
the mob and suffer with us. They, too, are Your
witnesses, a source of hope when we despair.
Because of our people's suffering, may such times never

come again, and may their sacrifice not be in vain.In our daily fight against cruelty and prejudice, against tyranny and persecution, their memory gives us strength and leads us on.

In silence we remember
those who sanctified His name on earth.[348]

11. ISRAEL - THE HISTORY

Everyone has a city called Jerusalem

A city he or she dreams about
Nathan Yonatan

Why Is Israel So Important?

It is hard to be objective about Israel/Palestine. Indeed, when I studied at the Ecumenical Institute at Tantur, near Jerusalem, in 1978, a wise Benedictine monk asked me, 'How long are you staying?' 'Three months,' I replied. 'A pity,' he said, 'anyone who stays more than three weeks never writes about the situation.'

I am no expert, but relying much on the meticulous works of Martin Gilbert, I take the risk because Christian pilgrims, who come to the Land for perhaps ten days, often rush to judgment. The more one is aware of the tragic complexity of the history and politics of the Land, which is holy to members of three religions, the harder it is to make constructive suggestions. Nevertheless, Christians cannot come close to Jews until they appreciate why Israel is so important to most Jews. This we shall seek to do first and then try to unravel the tangled history before considering Christian responses.

Those who wish to balance this with a Palestinian perspective would do well to read books by Kenneth Cragg or Naim Ateek or Justin Butcher [349] The *Lemon Tree*, which is both a book and a film, is a moving human narrative gives a great deal of historical background as it tells the story of the friendship of Dalia, a Jewish refugee from Bulgaria, and Bashi, who is a young Palestinian refugee.[350]

No one should forget the lives cut short by terrorist and military action or the lives stunted by deprivation and humiliation as well as those whose consciences have been coarsened by security requirements.[351] Israelis and Palestinians alike have seen relatives and friends killed before their eyes and have attended funerals unable to look into the eyes of parents and orphans.[352]

Most Jews have an affinity with Israel, although the nature of this attachment, even amongst those Jews who live there, is very varied. The state of Israel offers protection and hope for the Jewish people: but tragically its creation came too late for six million people. Besides the survivors of the Holocaust, Israel has offered a home to Jews from Arab countries, from the Soviet Union and Eastern Europe, from Ethiopia and many other parts of the world. With the ever-present threat of anti-Semitism and fears of renewed persecution, Israel offers to Jews everywhere a safe haven in times of trouble.

'As a twelve year old in 1948, the founding of the state of Israel meant to me what it meant to almost every American Jewish child: redemption after the Shoah – hope for our own lives and the lives of our grandchildren. It meant that while you might destroy Jews by the millions, the Jewish nation was itself indestructible... it was also bittersweet, this birth of a Jewish state. It had come too late. This nation would have protected Jewish life, taken in Jewish refugees.'[354]
Moreover, as a nation state, with considerable military power, Israel can speak for and protect Jews in an uncertain world. Zionism means controlling your destiny; it means achieving power, mastering the gun, and sometimes, tragically, misusing power. But this is far better than being powerless in a dangerous world.'[355]

A young Israeli, as he reluctantly packed his bag to return to reserve duty, said, 'We know that without the army, there wouldn't be an Israel. We can't afford to lose even one war or we'd lose our country.'[356] Another soldier said, 'If we put down our weapons today, there'd be no more Israel.'[357]

Some Facts And Figures

In March 2023 of a population of 9.73 million people, 73 per cent were Jewish, 21 per cent Arab and about 5 per cent belonged to other communities. When the state was established, there were only 806,000 residents and the total population reached its first and second millions in 1949 and 1958 respectively. Judging by current population trend data, experts predict that the population of Israel will reach 10 million by 2024. sooner. In addition to these numbers, there are approximately 170,000 people living in Israel who are neither citizens nor permanent residents. Out of the 14.7 million Jewish people in the world, 47% reside in Israel.

Israel Feels Like Home.'

For many Jews Israel is a place where they can be Jewish without apology. They can assume that the rhythm of public life accords with the Jewish calendar, that food will be kosher, they can wear what they like, and 'When I see a non-observant woman reflexively touch her hand to the mezuzah when she enters a room', writes David Raab, who settled in Israel from the USA in 1999, 'or I am wished Shabbat shalom by the checkout clerk at the supermarket, or I hear a Talmudic idiom inserted into a totally secular conversation on the radio or ... a mid-December business conference in Tel Aviv is suddenly halted to light Chanukah candles... I remind myself, "That's why I moved here."'[358]

Many of the first Jewish Zionist settlers – all escaping the persecution in Tsarist Russia - were inspired by socialist ideals which echoed the message of the prophets. Their pioneering work, living in communities in which everything was held in common (*kibbutzim*), cleared the valley of Harrod and other barren places. Like European colonists, the question of 'to whom the land belonged?' was not asked. For others the return to the Land was seen as a fulfilment of God's promises. The Covenant implies living as a holy people – and a people need a place to live. 'A third of the Mishna makes sense only in the context of the land of the Bible.[360]

'Without Israel we are a truncated, incomplete people,' writes the distinguished reporter Charles Fenyvesi. 'Jewish life cannot be sustained without Israel at its core... the Torah that spells out for us a way of life and a religious destiny also binds us to a land. Many Jews have chosen to continue to live in the Diaspora, yet even so they have close ties with Israel and many visit the country frequently. 'To me Israel is family,' 'Most of my relatives live in Israel, by now nearly all of them have been born and raised there... I am at home in their houses and apartments, and they feel the same way when they visit my nuclear family in the United States. Because Israel is like one big extended family, Jews will often be defensive when Israel is criticised. In a family, if someone from outside criticises our children, even if we also don't like the way they are behaving, we will stoutly defend them.' [361]

It is common to hear Jews point out that Israel is the only democracy in the Middle East. Many Jews both in Israel and in the Diaspora are critical of government policies, including the settlements in occupied teritory, but only the most extreme critics as well as some ultra-Orthodox Jews question Israel's right to exist, which was affirmed by the United Nations and guaranteed by International law. Israelis point out that none of the many critics of George Bush's 'War Against Terror', both inside or outside America, had any doubt about the USA's right to exist. Why, they ask, do non-Jewish critics of Israel, including some Arab nations, still question Israel's right to exist?

Considering how often Israel is in the news, it is a surprise for some people that geographically the country is so small – about the size of Wales - even if the landscape is very varied.

Is Criticism Of Israel Always Antisemitic?

Criticism of Israel's government or army may not be an expression of anti-Semitism, but may spring from a genuine love and concern for the country: but anti-Semites do exploit anti-Israel feelings. Even well-meant criticism is often heard as anti-Semitism by some Jews in Israel and abroad. This is why Christians have to earn the right to be listened to and intemperate denunciations are counter-productive. To equate the harsh treatment of Palestinians with the extermination of Jews perpetrated by the Nazis is gratuitously offensive and historically misleading.

Besides my real sympathy and concern for the Palestinian people, I am, like many Jews, sad, that the struggle for survival has meant that some of the hopes that the rebirth of a Jewish nation aroused have been disappointed. The actor Theodore Bikel, who many times played Tovey in 'Fiddler on the Roof,' in his criticism of settlements and growing rift between religious and secular Jews, says his words of anguish are driven 'by a passion for Israel's survival; not mere physical survival, but for the continued existence of an Israel as a moral force rooted both in history and modernity.'[363]

In my first visits to Israel over sixty years ago, I shared these hopes, but like many of my youthful hopes - for example, for an effective United Nations - they have been disappointed. It was perhaps unrealistic to hope that Israel, surrounded by enemies, would behave differently than any other government. A government's first responsibility is the safety of its people. Susannah Heschel is right to say that it is unreasonable to expect the state of Israel to behave better than other states. Yet perhaps it is a compliment to the embodied in Torah that non-Jews as well as Jews such as Rabbi Michael Lerner still hope that Israel can be a light to the nations.[364]

Aloni Shulamit (1928-2014), who grew up during the British Mandate and who founded the Ratz party (a Civil Rights Movement) and later was a Leader of the Opposition from 1988 to 1990 and Minister of Education from 1992-3, wrote; 'It is difficult for us today to talk about "Jewish ethics", about Jewish values of justice and the law, not only because they have been trampled underfoot, but because fewer and fewer citizens of Israel know what democracy and human rights mean… I do not wish to leave this world with the feeling that the entire Zionist revolution, all our efforts to gain sovereignty, all my friends and comrades and schoolmates who were killed or wounded and fought for Israel sacrificed themselves for the existence of a violent, occupying, and rapacious state. It's just not fair. Ben-Gurion spoke of a "treasured people", and the treasure is ethics, knowledge, culture, art, science, literature, openness, and listening to and respecting every single person, man, woman and child as freeborn human beings, created in the image of God, regardless of their faith, race, religion and ethnic origins.'[365]

Ze'ev Sternell, a leading intellectual in the Peace Movement voiced the same concern, 'We didn't save Israel in time. This is why I am now racked by anxiety. Israel is my life, but I see Israel fading away. I see a terminal illness consuming the nation I love.'[366]

Sixty Years Ago

My first visit to the Land was in 1958, when, during National Service, I with a friend had a week's leave from Cyprus. We stayed in Tel Aviv and I remember one day crowds of people were hurrying past the window. Was it an alarm or a demonstration? No, it was the opening of the country's first Supermarket! In Tel Aviv I sensed, in the words of Ari Shavit in his book *My Promised Land*: 'the triumph and the tragedy of Israel... the energetic, exuberant and hopeful young Israel,' but later, I also sensed his feeling that 'beyond the well-to-do houses and upper-middle-class lawns of his hometown, lay a dark ocean that would sweep Israel away soon like a tsunami. As we approached Jerusalem, my thoughts were of the hymn, 'Jerusalm the Golden' which I had known, from childhood: but soon discovered that, as most of the city was ruled by Jordan, we could only go the Church of the Dormition. As we approached it, Jordanian soldiers had us in the sights of their rifles. Our guide was armed when we went to Galilee and to the part of the Dead Sea to which Israel at the time had access. The hope and the fear are still there beneath the surface, as I have sensed on subsequent visits.[367]

Historical Flash Back
The Destruction Of Jerusalem

In the first century, Palestine was part of the Roman Empire – either ruled indirectly by King Herod and his descendants, who are mentioned in the New Testament, or ruled directly by Roman governors such as Pontius Pilate. In 66 CE, as mentioned, above, some Jews, although opposed by some religious leaders, rebelled against the Romans. Titus, later the Emperor, crushed the First Revolt and destroyed the Temple in 70 CE. The Zealots took refuge at the mountain-top fortress of Masada, where they held out against the besieging Roman army until 74 CE.

Sixty years later, after another uprising led by Simon Bar Kochba was crushed, Jerusalem was then given the new name of Aelia Capitolina. Jews were forbidden to live in or visit the city. The Temple, which had been so central to Jewish life that some scholars estimate that more than half the *mitzvot* had to be carried out there was destroyed. Nonetheless, miraculously, two new religious movements emerged from the wreckage, Rabbinic Judaism and the Christian Church.

From Constantine To The Capture Of Jerusalem By The British

When the Emperor Constantine 'converted' to Christianity in 313 Palestine acquired a new importance. His mother Helena identified the most important sites associated with the life of Jesus. The building of the Church of the Nativity at Bethlehem was commissioned in 326. The building of the Church of the Holy Sepulchre, which marks the traditional and probable site of the Crucifixion and the Resurrection, was started in 335.

Palestine, although briefly captured by the Persians in 617, remained part of the Byzantine Empire until 638. In that year, Jerusalem was captured by the Muslim Caliph Omar. For Muslims, Jerusalem is Islam's third most holy city, as it is believed that it was from there that the Prophet Muhammad, set out on his night journey to heaven. Omar promised security to the Christians in the city and small Christian and Jewish communities survived in Palestine throughout most of the Middle Ages.

In 661 CE, Muawiyah I founded the Umayyad Caliphate in Jerusalem. His successors built the Dome of the Rock - the world's first great work of Islamic architecture - and the al-Aqsa Mosque. The Abbasids replaced them in 750, until the Fatimids conquered the region in 969 and ruled it for the most of the period up to the city's capture by the Crusaders, but, for a time, lost it to the Great Seljuk Empire in 1071.

The new Seljuk Turkish rulers stopped Christian pilgrims from coming to the city. This was the pretext for Pope Urban II, in 1095, to call for a Crusade to recapture the place of Jesus' passion for Christendom. In fact by that time the Fatimid dynasty, which had recaptured the city fromthe Seljuk Turks, were happy to reopen the pilgrimage routes: but the Crusaders were on their way.

The Crusaders captured Jerusalem in 1099 and massacred many Muslims. Christian Kings ruled the city for nearly one hundred years, until the Muslim sultan and hero Saladin (1137-1193), after defeating King Guy at the Battle of the Horns of Hattin in Galilee, recaptured Jerusalem in 1187 – sparing the lives of the Christians. For another hundred years the Crusaders held on to some of northern Palestine, but finally left after the fall of Acre in 1291. Even so, various European rulers, until the nineteenth century, continued to claim to be 'King of Jerusalem.'

The area was now under Muslim rule. In 1516 The Ottoman Turks captured Palestine and Syria. Their rule of the country lasted without interruption for three centuries, until its conquest by Egypt in 1832. The United

Kingdom quickly intervened and returned control of the Levant to the Ottomans in return for extraterritorial rights for Europeans living in Palestine. Throughout this period there was a sizeable Jewish community in .

By the middle of the nineteenth century there was growing interest in Jerusalem in England. The English Jewish philanthropist Sir Moses Montefiore did much to try to help the Jews who lived there - often in great poverty. He visited the land seven times in the middle of the nineteenth century. He built some houses to reduce the overcrowding and a windmill, which, he hoped, would be the basis for a flour industry. At the same time some Christians began to make pilgrimages to the Holy Land. One of them was Phillips Brooks, an Episcopalian priest, who wrote the hymn 'O Little Town of Bethlehem.'

Throughout the centuries, Jews never forgot the holy city. The Passover meal traditionally ends with words 'Next Year in Jerusalem. In 1471, Judah Halevi, a Spanish philosopher and poet, reached Palestine, although he may have failed in his attempt to get to Jerusalem. Earlier, he had written, 'My heart is in the East, and I in the depths of the West ... It will be nothing to me to leave all the goodness of Spain. So rich will it be to see the dust of the ruined sanctuary.'

Despite the dangers, other Jews were more successful. By the late nineteenth century, as we have seen, some Jews, who were fleeing persecution in Eastern Europe, made their way to Palestine – in what is known as the First *Alayah.*

The Balfour Declaration

In 1917, as we have see, the British Cabinet issued what is known as the Balfour Declaration.

The Declaration said: 'His Majesty's Government view with favour the e tablishment in Palestine of a national home for the Jewish People and will use their best endeavours to facilitate the achievement of this object, it being clearly understood that nothing shall bedone that may prejudice the civil and religious rights of existing non-Jewish communities in Palestine, or the rights and political status enjoyed by Jews in any other country.

Caim Weizmann, a leading Zionist, had lobbied for this for some time. As he waited outside the cabinet room, one of the emerging officials told him, 'Itis aboy.' Five weeks after the Balfour Declaration was published, Jerusalem was captured by the British. General Allenby issued a proclamation, in seven languages, telling the people that the city was now under martial law and that they were to pursue their lawful occupations. He added that 'Now the Crusades are over.' Incidentally, Allenby insisted on entering Jerusalem on foot and not on a horse, saying that he would not ride into the city, which his Master had entered on a donkey. Earlier, in 1898, some of the old city wall had been demolished to allow the German Emperor William II to ride in on a white charger.

Following the First World War, Britain was given a Mandate by the League of Nations to govern Palestine. Ben Gurion, who was in the USA at the time, hailed the Declaration as a 'magnificent gesture' but warned that 'only the Hebrew people can transform this right into tangible fact, only they, with body and soul, with their strength and capital, must build their National Home and bring about their national redemption. 366

Between The World Wars: The British Mandate

The military government was superseded by a civil administration, entrusted to Britain by a Mandate of the League of Nations. Sir Herbert Samuel, the first Jewish ruler since the time of the Maccabees, was appointed governor.

The period between the wars was one of constant strife and disturbances. Arabs resented the influx of Jews. British governments changed; some were 'pro-Arab' and some 'pro-Jewish,' Initial hopes of those, wh, like Martin Buber, dreamed that Jews and Arabs might live together in one state, soon faded. The Peel Commission of 1937 recommended partition, but the Foreign Office persuaded

Prime Minister Neville Chamberlain, to reject this. Instead a White Paper in 1939 proposed that within ten years a supposedly secular state with an Arab majority should be established and Jewish immigration restricted. All the surviving members of the Peel Commission wrote to *The Times* stating that the 'cessation of immigration' would 'not eliminate the fear of domination; it only transfers it from Arab minds to Jewish.' Winston Churchill described it as 'a mortal blow.'[368]

Just before the start of the Second World War, a pact was signed between Hitler's Germany and Stalin's Soviet Union to divide Poland, where many Jews lived. On 1 September 1939, Germany invaded Poland and on 3 September 1939, Britain and France declared war on Germany. The Jewish community in Palestine supported the British war effort although the para-military Haganah movement built up its weaponry to defend themselves against the Palestinians. The Grand Mufti of Jerusalem sided with Hitler.

Despite the war and growing knowledge of the German plans to eliminate its Jewish population, boats 'illegally' bringing Jewish refugees to Palestine continued to be intercepted. The British government refused an offer from the Italian government to facilitate the passage of German Jewish refugees through Italian ports. It was not until the late summer of 1943, at Churchill's insistence, that the rules were relaxed so that any Jewish refugee who reached Palestine was allowed to enter, regardless of quotas.

In January 1944, Irgun, a militant Zionist underground movement led by Menachem Begin - later to be Prime Minister of Israel – which was responsible for the bombing of the King David Hotel, called for the immediate transfer of power to a Provisional Hebrew government. Ben-Gurion, however, insisted that Allied victory over the

Nazis was of overriding importance.

From The End Of The Second World War To Independence

The end of the Second World War by no means heralded the coming of peace to Palestine. The British government stuck to the position outlined in the 1939 White Paper and, despite protests from President Truman, continued to enforce the ban on illegal Jewish immigrants, who, if intercepted, were sent to Cyprus. In the notorious case of the ship Exodus, Ernest Bevin ordered that all on board, including survivors of the Holocaust, should be made to return to displaced persons camps in Europe. In what Abba Eban described as 'a gruesome operation' these miserable people were forcibly transferred to another ship called the Empire Rival and many of them were eventually taken back to the British controlled zone in Germany. 'If anyone had wanted to know what Churchill meant by a "squalid war,"' Abba Eban (1915-2002) who was for a time Foreign Minister and the Israeli representative at the United Nations, recalled in his autobiography, 'he would have found out by watching British soldiers using rifle butts, hose pipes and tear gas against the survivors of the death camps. Men, women and children were forcibly taken off to prison ships, locked in cages below decks and sent out of Palestinian waters.'[371]

A clergyman, with whom I worked, was in the army at that time. He tried to object and felt ashamed of what happened until his dying day. Despite British efforts, about 40,000 Jews secretly made their way to Palestine between August 1945 and May 1948.

Attacked from both sides and unable to halt the mounting communal violence, the British government, in February 1947, handed the problem of Palestine over to the United Nations. The UN set up a Special Committee, known as UNSCOP,[372] which recommended the creation of two separate and independent states, with Jerusalem under UN control. The Arab Higher Committee rejected the proposals, whereas the Jewish Agency, with qualifications, accepted them. Ben-Gurion was preparing the Jewish community to fight for what was offered and to seize more if possible.

Israel is Born

The United Nations Vote

On November 29th, the General Assembly of the United Nations debated the proposals. Judy Feld Carr, who helped to rescue many of the Jews of Syria, recalls that on that cold November day, her grandmother – 'my Bubby' - gave her a pad of paper with two columns. One was headed 'Ya' and the other 'Nein.' Her grandmother turned on the radio and every time the speaker named a country, I had to write down its vote in the appropriate column. 'After a certain "Yes" had been announced, a roar of applause reverberated through the radio. My Bubby clapped her hands together and burst out crying. Her tears were tears of joy, as she exclaimed in Yiddish, "We have a Jewish state."'[373]

In a museum in Jerusalem, there was an old radio on which someone had listened to the debate. It reminded me of the old radio on which as a boy I tried, despite the atmospherics, to hear commentaries on test matches in Australia. I hope the reception was better in November 1947.

The surprise of the evening was the warm endorsement of a Jewish state by the Soviet representative, Andrei Gromyko, who later became Foreign Minister of Russia. Thirty-three nations voted for the partition proposal, thirteen against with ten abstentions – one of which was Britain. The American Zionist Emergency Council heralded the vote as 'a milestone in the history of the world,' which 'ended 2,000 years of homelessness for the Jewish people.[374]

The British government was still 'responsible for law and order', but as also happened in India, the country slid into civil war. Often the British were targets of attack from both sides. The British finally left at 9.30 a.m. on Friday May 14th, 1948.

The Inauguration Of The State Of Israel

At Tel Aviv Museum, a ceremony took place to inaugurate the State of Israel, although until the declaration few people knew what the name of the new state would be. Eleven minutes after the declaration, as previously, secretly, agreed with Weizmann, President Truman announced America's *de facto* recognition of the state of Israel. The British Foreign Office predicted that the new state would be wiped out. [375]

That same evening, Egyptian aircraft bombed Tel Aviv.

The Early Years To 1967

For the first two years of the new state, Israelis fought a desperate struggle for survival with much cruelty on both sides. When the armistice was signed in 1949, Israel had captured nearly a third more of the land than allowed for in the UN plan for partition. The gains included West Jerusalem, which became a divided city, with the old city under the control of Jordan. Israel also conquered the Negev and on the day that the cease-fire was signed, the Star of David the flag of Israel, was raised at what is now the holiday resort of Eilat. Israel had gained access to the Red Sea.

Large numbers of Arabs, in what they call *Al-Nakbah*, 'the Calamity,' fled from Israeli forces. Israel made clear it would not allow them to return – the right of return is still a contentious issue in current peace negotiations.[376] Once visiting a refugee camp in Bethlehem in 2008, we were button holed by a Palestinian woman who told us the tragic story of her whole life as a refugee – being moved from camp to camp.

At the start of the 1948 war, 940,000 Arabs lived in what became Israel, but by the end of the war the figure was about 150,000. Ben-Gurion, often said, 'Israel did not expel a single Arab', and it was said the Arab nations encouraged Palestinians to leave the area, bu, according to some new historians many were forced to leave by military units. This has been challenged by the so-called 'New Historians', who have had access Israeli government papers that were declassified thirty after the founding of Israel.

These scholars acknowledge that perhaps as many 60,000 Arabs were expelled from Lydda and Ramla.[377] A number of deserted Arab villages were obliterated. There were, of course, atrocities on both sides. Had the Arab armies triumphed it is unlikely that they would have been more merciful. Those Arabs who, after the armistice, found themselves in Israel were given full citizenship.

Others in the parts of Palestine not under Israeli control, came under Jordanian rule, as the territory was annexed by King Abdullah of Transjordan, who had thwarted the attempt of the Palestinian National Council to declare a state with an 'all-Palestinian government.'

During the early fifties terrorists or *fedayeen* attacks from Egypt claimed a number of lives. Israel saw its chance of hitting back during the Suez crisis in 1956, when Britain and France tried to regain control of the Suez Canal. America, however, insisted that land gained from Egypt had to be returned.

From The 1967 War To The First Intifada

In 1967, Israel faced growing threats from President Nasser of Egypt as well as constant bombardment from Syrian artillery.

In the weeks before the war, the United Nations withdrew. Rabbi Jonathan Magonet, who was in Jerusalem at the time, has written 'I remember the feeling of utter abandonment... and shared the feeling that the nations of the world were simply waiting to see Israel destroyed so that they could weep salt tears at the familiar sight of a Jewish tragedy. How far that was simply a paranoid delusional state, shared by many Israelis at the time, I cannot tell.'[378]

Many Israelis still doubt whether the nations of the world would have come to Israel's defence, if its security was at stake. They are convinced, therefore, that their only security is in their own strength. In fact, Israel launched a pre-emptive strike in what is known as the Six Days War. By the time the Israeli public were told of the war, the Israeli army had put some 400 Egyptian, Syrian and Jordanian aircraft out of action. Israel had mastery of the air from the Sinai border to the Golan Heights. 'The War was won in six days in early June'.

As a result of the war, Israel took control from Egypt of

the Sinai and the Gaza strip. Israel also captured the Golan Heights from Syria, - land which it still controls. From the Golan Heights one can look down onto Galilee and out towards Damascus, some sixty miles to the East. Israel also captured all the territory controlled by Jordan. East Jerusalem and the surrounding territory were annexed and Jerusalem once more became – at least politically– a single city, with Teddy Kollek as its enlightened mayor. The West Bank and Gaza became 'occupied' or 'administered territories.'

It is important to realise that the status of Arabs in the Israel of pre-1967 boundaries, where they are citizens, is different to that of those in the West Bank, where Arabs, for a time continued to hold Jordanian passports. Since 1995, the Palestinian National Authority has issued passports, which are recognized by practically all countries, including Israel. In 2012 Palestine got 'Non-Member Observer Status' at the United Nations. This has not made a significant difference, although the wording on the passport cover changed. To travel overseas, Palestinians in the West Bank have to make their way to Amman – getting permission to do so may be difficult – and several countries are reluctant to grant visas.

The Yom Kippur War (1973 Arab–Israeli War.)

In 1973, Syria and Egypt tried to avenge their defeat by launching a surprise attack on Yom Kippur, the Day of Atonement, the holiest day of the Jewish year. Israel was unprepared – although the fact that so many people were in the synagogues for Yom Kippur made mobilisation quicker. There was a moment when defeat seemed possible and indeed Arab leaders claimed victory. For many Jews this was a decisive moment when they realised again that the rest of world would not or could not protect them. The USA sent military supplies, although the British government, headed by Edward Heath, refused to allow these American planes to land and refuel at the British base at Akrotiri in Cyprus.

In fact, Israel struck back and even took control of some land on the west bank of the Suez Canal. Casualties on both sides were heavy. The Israelis lost 2,522 people – more than three times the casualties suffered in the Six Day War. Some leaders realised that military strength was not enough and there began to be talk of trading land for peace.

Likud Election Victory And The Camp David Agreement

The Israeli public was disillusioned with the Labour led coalition which had left Israel unprepared for the attack. The 1977 election brought the Likud party, headed by Menahem Begin, to power for the first time. The party had promised to hold on to 'Judea and Samaria.

In a surprise move – since Menahem Begin had been considered an extreme right-winger for all his political life - the Likud Prime Minister accepted the olive branch offered by Anwar Sadat, President of Egypt. In November 1977 in his historic visit to Jerusalem, The Egyptian President spent his morning reciting prayers at the Al-Aqsa Mosque in Jerusalem and visiting the Holocaust Memorial at Yad Vashem. Before entering the Knesset to deliver his address, Sadat placed a wreath at a memorial for Israel's fallen and then addressed a specially arranged sitting of the Knesset. Sadat opened his remarks by stating, "I come to you today on solid ground, to shape a new life, to establish peace. We all, on this land, the land of God; we all, Muslims, Christians and Jews, worship God and no one but God. God's teachings and commandments are love, sincerity, purity and peace." I watched Sadat's historic and lengthy address to the Kenesset, which was on television. Afterwards, I sent good wishes on behalf of the World Congress of Faiths to Prime Minister Begin. His reply was dated December 25th – not everyone observes Christmas.

In the following year, 1978, thanks to the persistence of President Carter, peace was agreed at Camp David and the Sinai peninsula - which I first visited when it was under Israeli control - was returned to Egypt.

The position of the Palestinians was not addressed and under the leadership of Yasser Arafat, the Palestinian Liberation Organisation, which was at the time committed to the destruction of the state of Israel, launched missile attacks from Lebanon. The Soviet Union was at the same time arming Syria with missiles.

In 1982, Israel entered Lebanon - the first time that Israel invaded another country, although originally Ariel Sharon, said the troops would advance no more than twenty-five miles. In fact, Israeli forces advanced on Beirut, intent on destroying the PLO headquarters there and driving the Palestinians out of the city. The siege and bombardment of the city, shown on television around the world, caused widespread shock and outrage. Yitzhak Rabin, an opponent of the war, was subsequently haunted by his agreement to Ariel Sharon's plan to cut off the city's water supplies. Eventually, protected by American Marines, the PLO left the city for Tunisia. Soon afterwards, the President-elect of Lebanon, Bashir Jemayel was assassinated. The Christian Maronites were incensed and blamed the Palestinian Muslims for his murder. Israeli troops moved into West Beirut, supposedly 'to protect the Muslims.' Many of the Muslims were in the Sabra and Chatila refugee camps, which Israeli forces had sealed off.

In early September Christian Phalangist forces entered the camps and massacred the Muslim refugees. The number of people who died is disputed, but probably over 2,300 Palestinian men, women and children had been slaughtered. The massacre shocked the world and was widely condemned. It was carried out by Christian Phalangists, but Israel was blamed for not protecting the refugees and maybe conniving at the slaughter, as the official inquiry acknowledged. There was widespread horror in Israel and over 400,000 people attended a Peace Rally in Tel Aviv. I was at the time Director of the Council of Christians and Jews. This was the moment when, in Britain, Christian sympathy for Israel began to ebb away and soon the ebb became a flood as Israel sought to suppress the 'Intifada,' which is Arabic for 'shaking off.' The well-known reporter Robert Fisk described the scene: 'I recall the old man in pyjamas lying on his back on the main street with his innocent walking stick beside him, the two women and a baby shot next to a dead horse, the private house in which I sheltered from the killers with my colleague Loren Jenkins of *The Washington Post* – only to find a dead young woman lying in the courtyard. Some of the women had been raped before their killing. The armies of flies, the smell of decomposition. These things one remembers.'[382]

Following the horrors of Sabra and Chatila, Israel withdrew its forces to a buffer zone along its northern border. Ariel Sharon resigned. A Government of so-called national unity - in fact divided much divided – was formed. The Likud party led by Yitzhak Shamir Yitzhak wanted to retain the West Bank, whereas Labour led by Shimon Peres was prepared to swap land for peace, but would not deal with the Palestinian Liberation Organisation as long as it was committed to the destruction of the state of Israel. There were divisions too among the Palestinians.

From The First Intifada To The Assassination Of Rabin

The first Intifada was initially a spontaneous eruption by frustrated Arab youths, who hurled stones and Molotov cocktails at Israeli soldiers. It was provoked by Ariel Sharon's visit to the Temple Mount – the site of the Golden Dome and El-Aqsa Mosque. He claimed the area was integral to the state of Israel, This provoked violent opposition from Palestinians. This became known as the *Intifada*, which is Arabic for 'shaking off.' The 'strong-arm' response of the Israeli military to the stone-throwing young Palestinians was widely condemned.

Soon Arafat took control and used the Intifada to keep world attention on the plight of the Palestinians. The harsh measures used by Israel to suppress the uprising further alienated world opinion. Schools and kindergartens were closed. Some Israelis protested. Stanley Cohen, a professor of criminology, said the action contravened the Fourth Geneva Convention and the Universal Declaration of Human Rights and effectively deprived 290,000 school-age children of education.[383]

The army was given permission to fire at masked youths even if they were not involved in stone throwing.[384] According to figures issued by the army in September 1991, 697 Arabs – 78 under the age of fourteen - had been killed by Israeli soldiers, while over five hundred Arabs had been killed by fellow Arabs.[385]

The conflict brutalized life in both the Palestinian and Israeli communities and further reduced human contact between the two communities. Jews no longer walked in the Old City. In August 1989 Yitzhak Rabin told officers that the uprising represented 'the will of small groups to discover their national identity and demand its realization.'³⁸⁶

By that time, Jordan had withdrawn its claim on the West Bank and the PLO had set up a government in exile. Labour leaders wanted to start talks with the Palestinians but were thwarted by Likud. Arafat's support for Saddam Hussein in the First Gulf War made him even more hated in Israel, especially as Scud missiles fell on Haifa and Tel Aviv.

Eventually, thanks to the patient efforts of James Baker, the American Secretary of State, Israelis and Palestinians were brought together at the Madrid Conference in October 1991, at which the opening speakers were Presidents Bush and Gorbachev. For the first time since the War of Independence forty-three years before, representatives of the belligerents were talking to each other.

When the following year Rabin, who had successfully challenged Peres for the leadership of the Labour Party, became Prime Minister, he made it clear that he believed peace was possible, ending his speech to the Knesset with the words, 'May the Lord give His people strength, may the Lord bless His people with peace.'³⁸⁷

In August 1993 the secretly agreed Oslo Accord was made public. Then in September on the lawn at the White House, the signing of the Declaration of Principles was followed, with President Clinton's encouragement, by Rabin's uneasy handshake with Arafat and his wry smile – watched by millions across the world.

Rabin, recognising that the ceremony had come too late for families in which mothers had wept for their sons, appealed to the Palestinians:

'We, the soldiers who have returned from battle stained with blood,
We who have seen our relatives and friends killed before our eyes,
We who have attended their funerals and cannot look into the eyes of parents and orphans...
We say to you today in a loud clear voice:
Enough of blood and tears...
We like you are a people who want to build a home, plant a tree, love, live side by side with you ...
Let's pray that a day will come when we will all say:
Farwell to arms.'[388]

The Agreement was finally signed – despite last minute prevarications – in Cairo on May 4th, 1994. Under the Cairo Agreement, the Palestinian (National) Authority, headed by Arafat, who now called himself President, was to be given 'legislative, executive, and judicial powers and responsibilities', including its own armed police force, and full control over internal security, education, health and welfare. Israel retained control of foreign affairs and defence.[389]

Within a fortnight, the Palestinian flag flew over Jericho and Gaza. It has black, white and green stripes and a red triangle.

Israeli extremists tried to derail the peace process. So also did Hamas, which was founded in 1987, soon after the First Intifada. Co-founder Sheik Ahmed Yassin stated in 1987, and the Hamas Charter affirmed in 1988, that Hamas was founded to liberate Palestine, including modern-day Israel, from Israeli occupation and to establish an Islamic state in the area that is now Israel, the West Bank and the Gaza Strip. Rabin insisted, 'We will continue the (peace) process as if there is no terror. And we will fight the terror as if there is no process.'[390]

The next step was for Israel and Jordan to settle their differences and a peace treaty was signed on October 26th, 1994. I was leading a pilgrimage at the time to Israel and Jordan. Our bus happened to be one of the first to cross the newly opened frontier at the Allenby/King Hussein Bridge. We were greeted with cheerful smiles and waves.

In September 1995, a further agreement, known as Oslo II, was signed by Rabin and Arafat - once again in Washington. This provided a clear timetable and pattern for the extension of Palestinian self-rule to the West Bank. Rabin, however, warned Arafat to 'prevent terrorism from triumphing over peace.' If that were not done by the Palestinians, Rabin added in prophetic words, 'we will fight it by ourselves.'[391]

There was strong opposition to the agreement in Israel. Sharon accused Rabin of collaborating with a terrorist organisation. The leader of a right-wing party said the government had committed 'national suicide.'[392] The vote in the Knesset could not have been closer: 61 to 59 in favour. At a rally in Jerusalem, Netanyahu denounced Rabin as a traitor.

To regain the initiative a mass peace rally was held in Tel Aviv on November 4th. Rabin insisted that despite the risks, 'the path of peace is preferable to the path of war.' The Rally ended with the singing of 'The Song of Peace':

Let the sun rise, and give the morning light
The purest prayer will not bring back
He whose candle was snuffed out
and was buried in the dust
A bitter cry won't wake him, won't bring him back
Nobody will return us from the dead dark pit
Here, neither the victory cheers
nor songs or prayer will help
So sing only a song for peace
Do not whisper a prayer
Better sing a song for peace
With a great shout.

As Rabin made his way to his car, he was shot dead by an assassin – Yigal Amir, a religious student at Bar-Ilan University. A friend, who is a rabbi in Jerusalem, had left the rally slightly early. It had been, he said, 'the best moment of his life.' When he reached his home, he turned on the news. 'It was the worst moment of my life.'

Three shots and it's over.
Now one talks about him in the past tense.
Suddenly, the present becomes the past,
And the past is only a memory.
We are standing, crying,
Wanting to believe it never happened.
That it is all a bad dream,
That we'll wake up tomorrow and it will be ok.
Instead we wake up to a sad reality,
Where pain is laced with hatred.
We cannot digest the enormity of the loss,
Or comprehend its harshness
In every sense of the word, we were beheaded
And now it crumbles.
It's as if he were the head, and we the body.
And when the head isn't functioning,
the body dies.[393]

A poem to Leah Rabin written by fourteen year old Bat-Chen Shahak

1996 to 2009

Shimon Peres now became Prime Minister, but a series of deadly attacks by suicide bombers shook popular confidence in the peace process. In the election in May 1996, Labour won two more seats than Likud, but Benjamin Netanyahu, the leader of Likud, won the vote for Prime Minister by just under 1 percent.

Netanyahu, whose slogan had been 'Peace with Security,' had promised to fulfil Israel's international commitments under the Oslo agreements, but more slowly. His period in office was one of increasing conflict between Israelis and Arabs.

When Ehud Barak became Prime Minister in 1999, hopes for peace revived. I remember the mood of optimism when I was in Jerusalem in the year 2000, shortly after Pope John Paul II's historic visit. Some Jewish women had started learning Arabic and one or two Jewish friends came with us to Bethlehem. Barak, keen to force the pace of the peace process, was willing to give up most of the West Bank, Gaza and East Jerusalem, but Arafat was unwilling to move so quickly and insisted on 'the right of return'. The Camp David negotiations, despite Clinton's best efforts, ended in failure.

The failure of the peace talks was followed by a renewed outbreak of violence known as the Second Intifada. This was in part provoked by a visit to Temple Mount by Ariel Sharon. Whereas the first Intifada was often a matter of stone throwing – which itself can be deadly – now the use of suicide bombers, so-called 'martyrs for Islam,' became more common. The Israelis reacted with much increased security, which involved long and frequent waits at check-points and the 'targeted killing' of known perpetrators of violence. In the aftermath of the attack on the Twin Towers in New York on 9/11, those Palestinians who sought self-rule by violence were now seen as terrorists – indeed often it seemed that the West regarded all Palestinians as terrorists - especially President Bush who saw Israel as a strong ally in the 'war against terror.'

Ariel Sharon, who had succeeded Netanyahu as leader of the Likud party, was elected Prime Minister in 2001. In an attempt to stop terrorism, Sharon sent Israeli troops to reoccupy towns in the West Bank and Gaza. Meanwhile Arafat - shut up in his compound by Israeli troops
- and his Fatah party were losing support to Hamas, which was an avowedly Islamic party. Arafat died in November 2004 and was succeeded by Mahmoud Abbas.

In the following summer, Sharon withdrew Israeli troops and all Jewish settlers from the Gaza strip. Palestinian authorities took charge and were responsible for law and order. Sharon also decided to implement a policy of 'disengagement,' which would involve a permanent separation of Israel from Palestine. This, however, was along boundaries, which were determined unilaterally and often unfairly by Israel and were marked by the notorious wall or fence. Bethlehem, for example, is now almost completely surrounded by 'the Wall' which is often at least twelve feet high. Some settlements were to be evacuated, but many were to be protected by special roads and defences within the West Bank.

Before Sharon, who had formed a new political party, could implement his plan, in January 2006 he suffered a massive stroke.

In the same month Hamas, won a surprise victory in the Palestinian election. Hamas was founded in 1987, soon after the First Intifada, as an offshoot of the Egyptian Muslim Brotherhood. Tensions between Hamas and Fatah, which had previously been the dominant party, had increased after the death of Yasser Arafat. In 1965 the Organisation of African Unity called for the formation of a unity government and a cessation of hostility between Hamas and Fatah. Eventually in 2017 they reached agreement and the Hamas government was replaced by a short lived national unity government. In June 2007, Hamas fighters took control of the Gaza Strip and removed all Fatah officials. President Abbas declared a state of emergency and appointed a new government.

The USA and UK and many other countries regarded Hamas, which seeks the destruction of Israel, as a terrorist organisation and refuse to negotiate with it. Since 2007, therefore, Hamas has been the *de facto* governing authority of the Gaza Strip and has fought several battles with Israel. On the other hand, the Israeli government and the Palestinian authority, not without tensions, have reached a *modus vivendi* but despite much talk, a 'Two States solution' has not been achieved and, as I write, seems further away than ever.

Following Sharon's stroke, his deputy Ehud Olmert, a former Mayor of Jerusalem, became prime minister and won the election. Ehud Olmert continued the policy of disengagement and of building walls and roads to separate the Arabs and the Israelis.

In 2008, just before Olmert left because of corruption and in the last days of Bush's presidency, Israel launched a massive attack on Gaza. Ever since Israeli troops had withdrawn, there had been repeated clashes on the Gaza-Israeli border. Despite some cease-fires, rockets have been regularly aimed at Israeli settlements. It is not clear whether at first the Palestinian authorities were unwilling or unable to stop them, but with the election of Hamas, attacks increased. These resulted in revenge attacks by the Israeli air force, targeted assassinations and restrictionson the movement of people and supplie. Finally, Israel's patience ran out, but the bombardment and the fighting in a crowded urban area caused many civilian deaths - shown on television around the world. Just before President Obama's Inauguration in Washington, Israeli troops withdrew.

2009-2023

In 2009 Benjamin Netanyahu once again became Prime Minister.

A second invasion of Gaza took place in 2014. Because of an Israeli blockade, tunnels into Israel and Egypt were the only way to move in people and supplies, including missiles, which Hamas used for launching attacks against Israel. The Israeli aim was to destroy these tunnels. Egypt's military government was also hostile toward Hamas, because the year before, General Abdel Fattah al-Sisi's junta had seized power from the Egyptian Muslim Brotherhood - a group with close ties to Hamas which had held power in Egypt for a short time. The fighting was intense and resulted in nearly two thousand Palestinian casualties – many of whom were children. There were 67 Israeli deaths. Both sides were accused of committing war crimes. The fighting caused massive disruption and destruction and still little has been done to repair the damage.

Whether these operations have been a deadly blow to Hamas or has strengthened its resolve to try to destroy Israel is not yet clear. The massive destruction and loss of life in Gaza further alienated public sympathy for Israel in many parts of the world. The greatest suffering, of course, is borne by the people of Gaza who, much of the time, are without power, clean water, adequate food and medical supplies.

There is little sign that either side is willing to enter into negotiations. Indeed rockets continue to be fired into Israel from Gaza - provoking a military response from Israel.

Even in the West Bank there has no progress toward a two state solution, partly because Israel continues to build 'settlements' President Trump's recognition of Jerusalem as the capital of Israel and his decision to move the American Embassy there have made clear that the USA is not even-handed and has reduced the hope for a lasting agreement.

Following the April 2019 election, after prime minister Benjamin Netanyahu was unable to form a government, the Knesset dissolved itself, thereby setting up a snap election that took place on 17 September 2019. Following the second election, again, no one was able to form a government, so a third election took place on 2 March 2020.

An agreement was finally reached on 20 April 2020, between Netanyahu and MK Benny Gantz on the formation of a national unity government: but the Knesset was again dissolved on 23 December 2020, resulting in the 2021 election. On 13 June 2021, in a 60–59 vote with 1 abstention, the Knesset voted to approve the thirty-sixth government of Israel. This was led by Naftali Bennett, leader of right-wing *Yamina* party, who was Prime minister for a year, and Yair Lap, leader of the centrist *Yesh Atid* party. Lapid inforrmed the President that the government would 'work for the service of all Israeli citizens, whether or not they voted for it and do all in its power to unite and connect all parts of Israeli society.'

By the end of 2022, the government failed and, early in 2023, Benjamin Netanyahu, with support from the extreme right-wing party, again became Prime Minister. The new government's attempt to take more control over the judiciary has provoked strong opposition.

As I write (July 2023) The major raid on the West Bank Jenin Refugee Camp, in which more than a dozen Palestinians were killed and many homes were badly damaged, has also been met with vociferous protest.

With the change of President in the USA and the confusion caused by the Coronavirus pandemic, there has been no progress towards a lasting solution. The question is being asked if a two-state solution is possible, but there are no obvious alternatives.

Yet, even if the situation is depressing, as Rabi Ron Kronish has written, 'There are still people in Israel and Palestine who care about peace.'

12. ISRAEL – THE PEOPLE

If the history of Israel/Palestine is complicated, it is also difficult at first to know to which community people belong and even whether to greet them with 'Shalom' or 'Salaam.' A CNN International producer asked an Israeli friend, 'Our viewers are confused. We have footage of Jews who look like Arabs, Arabs who look like Jews. We have black Jews; bearded sixteenth-century Jews; and sexy girls in tight jeans. Who are these people, anyway?'394

An observant Jew described the variety by picking up items used during the feast of Sukkot: the etrog, an aromatic lemon-like fruit and a lulav, which is a cluster of date, palm, myrtle, and willow branches. 'Each kind of branch represents a different type of Jew,' he said, 'those who study Torah, those who perform kind acts, those who do both, those who do neither. When we hold them together, we're a community, there is more uniting us than dividing us.' 395

Although for nearly fourteen hundred years Muslims were in the majority in Palestine, Jewish and Christian communities survived. The first census carried out by the British in 1922 showed a total population in Palestine of 757,000 people. There were nearly 600,000 Muslims, 84,000 Jews, and 73,000 Christians, 7,000 Druze and a few Baha'is, Samaritans and other minorities.

The Jews

The Yearning To Return

Through the centuries a small community of Jews lived in the Land, mostly in Jerusalem or Safed (Zefat), which was a centre for the study of Kabbalah or the mystical interpretation of scripture. Old people came from Europe as they wrote in their passports 'to die in Jerusalem,' and to be buried there. Some believed that those who were buried on the Mount of Olives would be the first to greet the long-awaited Messiah. Jews buried outside the Land, it was thought, would face a painful subterranean journey from their place of burial to Jerusalem when the End of Days arrived. Even while alive, the journey to Jerusalem could be hazardous. Of 1,500 Jews who travelled to Palestine in 1700 from Poland, Hungary and Moravia, nearly 500 died on the way.[396]

The Jewish Liturgy also makes clear the continuing attachment to Jerusalem of Jews, who through long centuries of exile, could never hope to go there. The Passover Seder ends with the words, 'Next Year in Jerusalem.' 'The thrice daily prayer, the Amidah contains a blessing entirely devoted to Jerusalem...while six of the nine stanzas of the hymn sung at the Friday evening service to welcome the Sabbath voices the longing for Jerusalem. And this is a physical Jerusalem as much as a celestial journey. As Rabbi Yohanan, a Palestinian scribe of the third century put it, "I shall enter Heavenly Jerusalem only after I have entered the Jerusalem on earth.' [397]

The Hasidic master, Nachman of Bratslav (1772-1811) invited friends to his daughter's wedding with these words, 'The wedding of my daughter will take place on such and such a date in the holy city of Jerusalem.' There was a mark beside Jerusalem indicating a note at the bottom of the invitation which, read, 'If in the meantime, the Messiah has not come, the wedding will take place in Bratslav.' [398]

For many Jews in Eastern Europe, the Land of Israel constituted a much more immediate reality through prayer and study than did the lands in which they lived. They knew its geography and history better – their knowledge of Hebrew was infinitely better than their knowledge of Russian and Polish.' [399] Many of the Ancient Jewish Novels in the anthology edited by Lawrence M Wills are set Jerusalem 'Throughout the centuries, the Jews kept alive the hope of Return to their old homeland,' wrote Benjamin Netanyahu, before he became Prime Minister. 'It is impossible to exaggerate the importance of the idea of the Return in Jewish history and its centrality to the rise of Israel. Yet the fashionable a-historicism prevalent today assumes that the Holocaust was the main force that propelled Jewish statehood.' [400]

At the beginning of the nineteenth century there were about 2,000 Jews in Jerusalem – one-fifth of the total population. The Jewish population in Palestine – mostly in Jerusalem - increased quite rapidly in the nineteenth century from 12,000 in 1839 to 35,000 in 1880 and 70,000 in 1900. Many of the Jews there were very poor and living conditions in the Old City were bad. The English Jewish philanthropist Sir Moses Montefiore, who visited the land seven times in the middle of the nineteenth century, built some houses to reduce the overcrowding and a windmill that he hoped would be the basis for a flour industry. A few hundred Jews lived in the holy city of Safed, some in the mountain village of Peki'in, which had a tradition of continuous Jewish settlement since Roman times and in Tiberias, on Lake Galilee, where Rabbi Akiva is buried. There were a few Jews in the port towns of Acre and in Jaffa.

The first Russian Jews arrived in the second half of the nineteenth century, and more followed after the renewed pogroms following the assassination of Tsar Alexander II. [401]

The First Aliyah

By the end of the nineteenth century, the Zionists' demand for a Jewish national home was growing. Most of the settlers, who made Aliyah (an ancient term for 'going up to Jerusalem') in the first half of the twentieth century, were Ashkenazi (or Jews of European descent

Many of the Jewish refugees made their way to Britain or the USA, but a few came to Palestine. Some 25,000 Jews from Russia reached Palestine `between 1882 and 1903 in, as already mentioned, what is known as the First Aliyah.[402] These settlers mostly worked on the land and received some support from the Rothschilds. Rishon Le-Zion, an agricultural settlement – minutes away from what is now Tel Aviv – was founded by Russian Jews in 1882. It was there that Benjamin Netanyahu's maternal great-grandfather arrived in 1896 when 'it was still a cluster of red-tiled whitewashed houses springing up in the middle of a sandy wilderness.'[403]

The first all-Jewish village, Petah Tikvah, also near Tel Aviv, dates back to 1909. The first settlers spoke Yiddish, Russian, Polish, Romanian or German, but the children began to speak Hebrew. In the nineteen thirties many Jews fleeing the Nazis tried to settle, but the numbers were strictly controlled by the British authorities.

Many of the settlers were inspired by socialist ideas – some of them creating Kibbutzim - pioneering agricultural communities where everything was held in common. If the kibbutz movement has now lost some of its early idealism, the divide between secular and religious Jews has intensified.

The Strictly Orthodox

The Strictly Orthodox or *Haredim* – which means in Hebrew 'those who tremble before God' - were only a small minority when the state was founded, but now number almost half a million. They are recognisable by their black hats and long black coats – although there are slight differences in how members of the various groups dress. The Ultra-Orthodox keep themselves to themselves and strictly observe the written and oral Torah. Marriages are still often arranged and most couples have large families. At the wedding celebrations, men and women do not eat or dance together, but are separated by a partition or *mechitzah*. There are unlikely to be televisions in the home lest children are corrupted by what they watch. For many ultra-Orthodox men, study is their livelihood and learning the Talmud their profession. As one student put it, 'The spiritual wealth of learning Talmud is worth more than any pay cheque.'[404]

There are divisions among the Ultra-Orthodox. Some follow Hasidic traditions, others the sober teaching of the Vilna Gaon.[405] Both are attracting new members, especially the Lubavitchers/Habad who are reaching out to non-observant Jews. This growth is adding to the tensions between the Haredi and secular Jews, who resent yeshiva students' exemption from military service, which is compulsory for other young Israeli men and women. One ultra-Orthodox explained, 'By praying to protect the nation, we are doing them more of a favour than serving in the army. More of their sons would die if we didn't pray.'[406] On Memorial Day, when most Israelis stand to observe a time of silence in honour of soldiers who have died, most Haredim ignore the ceremony.

The Chief Rabbis

Israel has two Chief Rabbis: one heads the Ashkenazi (Western) Jews, the other is leader of Sephardi/Mizrahi (Eastern) Jews. The concept of a chief rabbinate and rabbinical courts are not part of Jewish law and tradition and they are not recognised by the ultra-Orthodox groups. The system was started by the Ottoman Empire and continued by the British. For centuries, most Jews in Palestine were Sephardim, but in the early twentieth century the Ashkenazi became the larger group. Now with a higher birth rate there are again more Sephardim.

The Sephardim

The Sephardi community - Jews from Arabic countries, such as Morroco, Egypt, Algeria, Tunisia and Iran and Iraq - does not have the divisions which are to be found among the Ashkenazi, and their practice and interpretation of Torah is more relaxed. Their worship includes more singing of tunes akin to Arabic music. At first, when European influence was dominant, they found it hard to adjust to a new way of life.

The Ashkenazi Jews

Today, the Ashkenazi Orthodox Jews, many of whom had come from Europe – both religious and secular - increasingly define themselves over against non-Orthodox trends, insisting on the divine authority of the unchanging Torah. Many of them have settled in the West Bank, which, they claim is part of the land promised by G'd.[407]

Non-Observant/Secular Jews

A large number of Israeli Jews are non-observant, according to one survey. Some belong to non-Orthodox synagogues, which have no official status. Non-Orthodox conversions are not recognised and all marriages have to be conducted by Orthodox rabbis, so some Israelis fly to Cyprus or elsewhere to get married.

Of the 'secular' Jews, some are occasionally observant, most probably on Rosh Hashana and Yom Kippur as well as national holidays such as Purim, Pesach and Hannuakh. They will circumcise their sons. They will vary in how strictly they observe kosher. Most public catering is kosher. Some Jews, of course, are avowedly atheist and some are attracted by Eastern religions and new spiritual movements.

There is some concern that there is too little interaction between different communities.

Times of Israel

An orthodox and a secular Jew at the Western wall

Israel, 'is at once a secular state and a holy land. The state symbols are Jewish. The official emblem is the menorah ... The shekel was used as currency before the time of Abraham...The blue and white national flag, with a Star of David in the centre, is based on the prayer shawl or tallit... Israel runs on Jewish time. On the Sabbath public transport comes to a halt in Jerusalem and El Al, the national airline is grounded.' There is concern, however that there is too little interaction between secular and religious Jews.'[408]

The Western Wall and the Dome of the Rock

Place Of Origin

Israeli Jews are not only differentiated by their religious observance or non- observance, but also by their origins - whether or not they are *sabra* (born in Israel); or by which country they have come from. Recent arrivals are Jews from Russia, who were free to leave the country after the collapse of Communism and Jews from Ethiopia, who call themselves *Beta Israel* or 'House of Israel.'

Other Communities

Jews are not the only people who live in Israel/Palestine, but as this book is about 'Meeting Jews', I hope readers will consult other books that give greater attention to the non-Jews.

The population of Israel is now more than nine million people, of whom one in five is an Arab Israeli. Because the birth rate among Arabs is higher, the ratio is likely to be one to three within twenty years. Some 200,000 of the Palestinians live in East Jerusalem. Christian Arabs number about 123,000 or fourteen percent of all Israeli-Arabs. There are also the Druse, a few Messianic Jews, some Samaritans, Arameans, and Circassians and some Baha'is. The West Bank and the Gaza Strip have a population of one and a half million Palestinians – most of whom are Muslims. There are about 50,000 Christian Palestinians in the West Bank and Gaza.

Muslims

In some parts of the Land, the call to prayer, from the loudspeakers of the minarets or from the bells of the churches, is a familiar sound. All Muslims in the state of Israel are Sunnis. The Arabs of '48 who stayed in what had become Israel were disorientated, poor and mostly illiterate. Most upper and middle class Arabs had left and Islamic institutions had been destroyed or damaged. Those who remained had often been up-rooted from their native villages. Some have made a success of life in Israel. They are bilingual and if they are professional people they have a reasonable standard of living. Their practice of the faith is relaxed. Most take part in the political life of the country. Rabin's government depended upon the support of Arab Kenesset members.

Suhad, a Muslim from Acre, where about one third of the population is Palestinian, said that, 'From childhood I was aware that being an Arab in a Jewish state gives you the mentality of the "Other." All national holidays are Jewish. Everything is Jewish – including the flag and the 'Hatikvah', the national anthem. 'Everything Zionist makes me feel it is the cause of my disaster. The flag is the symbol of a state that destroyed over four hundred of our villages inside Israel.'410

Later Suhad was one of the few Arab students at Tel Aviv University. She found it almost impossible to discover a landlady who would have her. 'I'll have to ask my neighbours,' was a common reply – and Suhad heard no more. 'To more and more Jews the word "Palestinian" sounds more like "potential terrorist" than fellow citizen.'414

Christians

Worldwide, there are nearly half a million Palestinians who are Christian – that is approximately six and a half percent of all Palestinians. Palestinian Christians are often viewed with suspicion by Muslims as well as by Jews. A population census carried out by the Palestinian Central Bureau of Statistics in 2017 concluded that there are 47,000 Palestinian Christians living in Palestine – in East Jerusalem, the Gaza Strip. and the largest number (some 95 percent) of Palestinian Christians live in the West Bank – concentrated mostly in the cities of Ramallah, Bethlehem and Jerusalem. A tiny Christian community of merely 1,100 people, lives in the besieged Gaza Strip.413

The Christian population in the Holy Land has dropped

dramatically. Many bright young Palestinians emigrate – if possible to North and South America. This is because of the troubled and dangerous situation, but also because of hostility as much from Arabs as from Jews. Bethlehem used to be a predominantly Christian town. When Arafat assumed control, he changed the town's boundaries to include three refugee camps. Thousands of Muslims moved in. Christians became a minority.

Ancient Churches

Palestinian Christians mostly belong to three groups of churches, all of which claim to be direct descendants of the ancient Church of Jerusalem.

First, Oriental Orthodox Christians, who are usually Armenians, Copts, Ethiopians or Syrians. Some still use Aramaic, the 'language of Jesus' in their liturgy. On one visit to Jerusalem a Sister at the Syrian Church of St Mark's, which is perhaps located where Jesus shared his last supper with his disciples, recited the Lord's Prayer in Aramaic.

Secondly, are the Eastern Orthodox Christians, who are mainly Greek or Russian Orthodox.

The third group belong to Catholic churches, which accept the authority of the Pope. These ancient churches have quarrelled - and sometimes still do - about who should look after the holy sites.

Protestant Churches

Protestant churches were established in the Holy Land in the nineteenth century. Now most Protestant denominations are represented there. In 1841, the Anglican Church, with the support of the King of Prussia, founded a bishopric in Jerusalem. Soon afterwards, Christ Church was built, near to Jaffa Gate. St George's Cathedral is just outside the Old City.

Towards the end of the century the German Emperor William II built a fine Lutheran Church and also the Church of the Dormition on Mount Zion. During the nineteenth century Christian pilgrims visited the country in increasing numbers. In 1869 Thomas Cook, a Baptist lay preacher, led a party to Jerusalem.

Messianic Jews

It is difficult to estimate how many Messianic Jews there are but they are a very small number in Israe. Sarah Posner in her article Kosher Jews: Messianice Jews in the Holy Land estimates that 'there are 175,00 - 250,000 Messianic Jews in the USA 350,000 worldwide. They are a tiny minority Israel -- just 10,000-20,000 people by some estimates -- but growing, according to both its proponents and critics.

Because of the hostility which they often face, Messianic Jews may keep their allegiance private. Their status is, of course, as already mentioned, disputed. Is being Jewish just a matter of birth or also of belief? Does conversion to another religion mean that a person ceases to be a Jew? Rabbinical authorities would hold that it does. Messianic Jews claim that it does not. They point out that the disciples and the first believers in Jesus were Jewish. Many Messianic Jews observe the Sabbath and keep kosher and worship in Hebrew.

It should be added there are other people who are Jewish by birth, who belong to other churches.

To add to the complications, some recent Russian immigrants have turned out to be Christian – the Russian authorities marked people in their passports as Jewish on the grounds of birth not of faith.

Other Faith Communities

The Druze

The Druze are a distinct religious group with roots in Islam. They accept that Muhammad was a prophet but believe there have been subsequent messengers. Most Israeli Druze live in villages in the Golan Heights. They have been most welcoming when members of our pilgrimage groups have visited them. Some Druze live in Lebanon and Syria.

The Samaritans

The Samaritan community is even smaller, with some seven hundred people. Their faith is based on the first five books of the Bible and they reject subsequent developments. They are mentioned in the New Testament, especially in the Parable of the Good Samaritan and the story of the Samaritan woman who offered Jesus a drink of water.

According to the Samaritans, they derive from the biblical tribes of Menashe and Ephraim, the sons of Joseph who lived over 3000 years ago. They follow the traditions of Ancient Israel, without the later additions made by Jewish sages. 'In general, we are the same people,' says Benjamin Tsedeka, an affable Samaritan historian who is the leading voice on Samaritan history and an elder of his people. 'We are from the north (of the ancient Kingdom of Israel) and the Jews are from the south.' While their early history is mysterious, a popular belief among scholars is that they diverged from Judaism around the time of the Second Temple.

As the First Intifada broke out in 1987, (a five-year period of Palestinian uprisings), Samaritan families decided to flee the Palestinian city of Nablus to avoid being caught up in the violence, relocating to the nearby Mount Gerizim, the holiest site in the Samaritan religion, where I met with some of them and was shown their ancient scrolls.

Samaritans with Ancient Scrolls

The Baha'is

The world headquarters of the Baha'i religion, which dates back to the nineteenth century, is at Haifa, where there is a shrine and the Universal House of Justice, which has impressive formal gardens. The religion emphasises respect for all prophets. Baha'ullah (1817-1892), the founder of the Baha'i faith was imprisoned for a time at Akko (Acre) but ended his days at Baji, which is now a holy place with gardens of outstanding beauty.

The Baha'i Centre in Haifa

The Bedouins

The Bedouins, although they are Muslim, are not a religious group but traditionally a nomadic people, with a distinct culture. There are nearly two hundred thousand of them, mostly in the Negev. Loss of land and the attempts by the government to make them settle means that now only quite a small number of Bedouins are nomads. Many have become marginalized despite efforts to provide them with adequate facilities and education.

It is sometimes suggested that you can determine to which community a person belongs by what they wear on their head. Many Jews were a kippa or skull cap. But could you distinguish the large white crocheted kippa of a right wing Braslav Hassid Jew from the white crocheted skullcaps worn by Hajis, who are Muslims who have been on pilgrimage to Mecca?

'It does not matter what is on your head.
What counts is what is in it.'

A Druze saying

The Search For Peace

There have been many well-meaning attempts to find a lasting solution, so that the various communities in Israel/Palestine can live together.

A root cause of the difficulties is fear. My first visit to Israel was in the 1950s and I remember as we entered the church of the Dormition, in the then divided city of Jerusalem, an uneasy feeling as I saw that Jordanian rifles were trained on us. When we travelled in Galilee or to the Dead Sea our guide was armed.

Geography makes clear why a return to pre-1967 boundaries does not offer Israel security. For example, the Golan Heights, which Israel captured from Syria, overlook Galilee.

Israel was born in insecurity and fear. Once at the end of a study tour arranged by the Council of Christians and Jews in 1990, my wife Mary and I were waiting for a taxi at Safed in fact, it came so late that we were not allowed to board the plane - and as we chatted to the receptionist, who had come from Eastern Europe, she kept saying, 'I know one day they will come and drive us out.' The 'they', of course, were the Arabs, who would re-enact her childhood terror of the Nazis.

And then there was the Arab who had taken a photograph of our group at the Dome of the Rock. I asked him to bring the photos to our hotel, but when I told him where we were staying, at a hotel in West Jerusalem, his face dropped. I did not at first understand why he couldn't come to the hotel and then I realised he was terrified that, although his purpose was totally innocent, he was afraid that he would be picked up by the police, who would not believe his reason for being in West Jerusalem and that he might be put into prison and suffer what goes on in the prisons. The security situation is such that although you know you are innocent, the soldiers who search you may not think so. A husband driving his wife to hospital to have a baby may be shot at – but some 'patients' in ambulances are lying on suicide belts. An innocent bystander may be killed or injured when a 'terrorist' is attacked – one more example of collateral damage! Mothers who cannot stop teenage sons from joining in protests are anxious lest their children end up in prison.

Whole communities are fearful of each other. Israelis are afraid of their neighbouring countries, especially as the situation in Syria, Iran and Iraq is so unstable and there is the danger that these countries may soon have the potential to make nuclear weapons. There is sharp division amongst Israelis whether security is guaranteed by military strength or by forging a just and lasting peace agreement. If toward the end of the last century the emphasis was on a peace agreement, since 9/11 and the American and British attack on Iraq, the whole area has been in turmoil, so security has been the priority.

Interfaith and Peace Activists

Yet while the politicians struggle to find an answer, there are many initiatives to build trust between different communities as a contribution to the lasting solution that many in all communities long for. Rabbi Ronald Kronish, who was Founding Director of the Interreligious Coordinating Committee, describes thisvery well in his book, *The Other Peace Process*.[415] He highlights the work of the Alliance for Middle East Peace, which represents more than 160 organizations and 'tens of thousands of Israelis and Palestinians, Arabs and Jews, committed to people-to-people work and a more peaceful and just reality for all people in the region.'

Christians need to go on supporting the patient work of many interfaith and peace groups who seek to dispel fear, by helping people to see the other not as an 'enemy', but as a fellow human being. In part this is the work of education and of dispelling ignorance and prejudice. For example, there was at one time a project to produce common history and religious syllabuses, so that Israeli and Palestinian children could learn to see both sides of their complex history and gain a fairer picture of the other's religion. Even more important are the efforts of Neve Shalom, the Interfaith Encounter Association, Rabbis for Human Rights, Bereaved Parents and other groups which encourage Israelis and Palestinians, especially the younger generation, to meet.[416]

I hope and pray that they continue despite the difficulties. Small everyday behaviour can sow the seeds of peace. Of course, there is much interaction we never hear about. On one occasion I visited the Orthodox Jewish Shaare Zedek hospital, where more than 70% of those treated are Arabs. Those who give blood donate it for Israeli and Arabs alike. On one visit, I was particularly impressed by the rabbis whom I met, who campaigned for justice for Palestinian families. Some had helped to rebuild Arab homes that had been destroyed by members of the Israeli army; others had taken part in public protests. There are Israeli lawyers who defend accused Palestinians.

It is important that when we protest against the abuse of human rights, whether by some members of the Israeli army or by some Arabs, we do so together as Jews, Muslims and Christians. This is why the Alexandria Declaration of 2002, which called for peace in the area, was particularly welcome because it came from leaders of three faiths, during the height of the Second Intifada. They said, 'According to our faith traditions killing innocents in the name of God is a desecration of his Holy Name, and defames religion in the world. The violence in the Holy Land is an evil, which must be opposed by all people of good faith. We seek to live together as neighbours, respecting the integrity of each other's historical and religious inheritance. We call upon all to oppose incitement, hatred, and the misrepresentation of the other.'[417]

God of our fathers,
You chose Abraham and his descendants
To bring your Name to the Nations:
We are deeply saddened by the behaviour of those,
who in the course of history,
have caused these children of yours to suffer:
And asking your forgiveness
we wish to commit ourselves to
Genuine brotherhood with people of the Covenant ,
Jerusalem, 26 March 2000: Signed: John Paul II

Christian Attitudes

Christian attitudes to Israel are very varied. The Israeli-Palestinian conflict perhaps causes more misunderstanding between Christians and Jews than anything else – even more than the idea of "mission", i.e.

the notion that Christians still want to convert Jews to Christianity. Christians in the West often find it difficult to appreciate the importance of 'the Land' for Jews. Even so, many church statements recognise 'that disregard for Israel's safety and welfare is incompatible with the Church's necessary concern for the Jewish people... But Christians also have to balance this with acute concern for justice for the Palestinian people.'[418] Some Christians themselves, besides those Christians who live in Palestine - both Arab Christians and ex-patriot clergy and scholars - have a deep attachment to the Holy Land. Normally, many pilgrims visit it each year. The Christian sense of the Land's holiness is different to the Jewish one.[419] For Christians, its significance lies in the fact that this was the setting for the physical life and ministry of the Lord Jesus.

Whilst Arab Christians recognise that Christians from Western Europe and the USA feel guilty about the Holocaust, they may be resentful that, especially in the USA, this seems to be expressed in uncritical support for the state of Israel. They feel too that their concerns have all too often been ignored by Western Christians. Many Christian pilgrims who come to the Holy Land have no real meeting with Christians who live there.

Some Christians are very pro-Palestinian, for example, the Middle East Council of Churches. Aid workers, who see the suffering and abuse of human rights, see part of their role as 'advocacy' - championing the cause of the oppressed.[420]

Sometimes fundamentalist and Christian Zionists who identify closely with Israel, also expect the conversion of the Jews before the Messiah returns. Some Christians who recognise that God's covenant with Israel has never been broken, also hold that the Promised Land is part of God's promise and covenant.

Other Christians see the State of Israel as a political reality to be understood in terms of international law, with no particular theological meaning. A statement of the General Assembly of the Presbyterian Church (USA), for example, said, 'The State of Israel is a geopolitical entity and is not to be validated theologically'. This seems also to be the position of the Vatican, which eventually in December 1993 established full diplomatic relations with the modern State of Israel.[421]

I think it is important to make a clear distinction between criticism of the policies of particular Israeli governments and being anti-Israel – although some anti-Semites do exploit anti-Zionism. This is why protests about the abuse of human rights are best done through interfaith agencies. Christians should avoid giving the impression of telling Jews and Muslims how they should behave – 'Christian' nations have too much of which to be ashamed and in many countries minority communities, especially Jews, have suffered severe discrimination. Christians need to be aware of the suffering on both sides, to support all who work for peace and justice and particularly, as suggested above, to support interfaith groups, which continue their activities despite many difficulties and setbacks.

Conclusion

Even in the darkest moments, the faith in God, which Jews, Christians and Muslims share, can offer hope. Together they can affirm that there is another way. It is costly and risky - but so is violence. To quote former Archbishop Desmond Tutu, 'There is no future without forgiveness.'[422] Although there is so little that can be done from a distance, everyone can pray for all those who are involved in the conflict and especially for those who work for healing and reconciliation.

Pray not for Arab or Jew
For Palestinian or Israeli
But pray rather for yourselves,
That you may not divide them in your prayers
But keep them both together in your hearts
Pray for the Peace of Jerusalem

Psalm 122, verse 6

The last word should be given to Bat-Chen, who was murdered on her fifteenth birthday by a suicide bombing in Tel Aviv on March 4th, 1996. In her diaries, which were discovered after her death, there were two central themes. One was to be a poet. The other was to live in peace with her Arab neighbours. 'I have a dream for peace,' she wrote.[424] 'I call out, "Come on peace ... come on already.' Two years before she had written in a school magazine.

There is not much left to say;
We're in a halfway spot.
There isn't real peace in the Middle East,
Nor is there real war:
And for us,
we're marching forward towards peace.

May that dream come true.

Politico

13. JEWISH-CHRISTIAN RELATIONS

What do Jews think of Jesus? 'They don't' was Franz Rosezweig's blunt reply. Many Jews are aware of long ages of anti-Jewish preaching by Christians and have suffered from prejudice and persecution. They want to have nothing to do with Christians, who for centuries have tried to convert them when they have not been extorting money from them or shutting them up in ghettoes. They may put some of the blame for the Holocaust on Christians and are quite likely to ask 'Why didn't the Pope excommunicate Hitler?'

Rabbinic and Mediaeval Jewish references to Jesus are mostly hostile, although Maimonides conceded that, although Jesus was a false messiah, 'all the actions of Jesus. Only serve to pave the way for the coming of the (true) Messiah.' As a result of Christian preaching, more people outside the Jewish community were aware that a messiah would come.

Increasingly the recognition that Jesus was a Jew is bringing members of the two faiths together There has been in the last fifty years a transformation in Christian-Jewish relations. The great wartime Jewish leader Leo Baeck said, shortly before his death, 'I am convinced that the next great phase of the world's history will witness the emergence of a new sense of partnership between the Jewish and Christian worlds, within the kingdom and purpose of God.'[425] Many Ultra-Orthodox Jews and Jews who settled in Israel from Arab lands are unaware of this new relationship.

In Israel, the initiative in dialogue has been taken not by religious leaders but by Jewish scholars, who generously responded to those Christian theologians who recognised that centuries of anti-Jewish teaching had prepared the seedbed, in which Nazism could grow. Henry Siegman, former Vice-President of the Synagogue Council of America, wrote: 'What impels the Jew to dialogue with Christianity are not theological but historical considerations. For the Jew, the problematic of Christian-Jewish relations is determined by a history of Christian attitudes and actions towards the Jew which diminished his humanity and inflicted on him suffering and martyrdom ... His concern is for his present and future survival'.[426]

Yet although the horrors of the Holocaust gave an immediate urgency to Christian-Jewish dialogue, it had already started before the Second World War. This is important, because the changes in Christian teaching are not because of guilt feelings and a concern 'to be nice to the Jews,' but because the old teaching was false. Even now the motivation for dialogue of some Christians is a desire to learn more about the Jewish roots of their faith or a wish to make-up for the Holocaust. This is why the section on Jewish-Christian relations comes towards the end of this book, lest interest in Judaism, as in the past, is part of a Christian agenda and not because of a genuine desire for friendship with Jewish neighbours.

Christian Motivation

It is helpful to recognise the different motivations for dialogue among both Christians and Jews. Because Christianity grew out of Judaism, Christians have in every century defined themselves in relation to the Hebrew Bible and the Jewish people. That distinction is itself significant. Much of the discussion has been in terms of the Church's relationship to what Christians have called the Old Testament.

Christians have often concentrated on the Prophets and the Psalm, rather than on the first five books of the Bible. Christian have also often ignored both Rabbinic Judaism and the contemporary Jewish reality - so much so that even forty years ago Christian scholars could speak of the inter-testamental period as 'late Judaism', thereby ignoring the fact that Jewish life has continued to develop during the last two thousand years.

Rabbinic Judaism, which took shape during the early centuries of the Christian era, is, as we have seen, in significant ways, very different from the religion of the Hebrew people, as portrayed in the Hebrew Bible. Indeed, as already mentioned, some people see Rabbinic Judaism and the Early Church as two new religious branches growing from common roots.

Too often the Christian motivation for dialogue has been a desire to learn more about the Jewish origins of their faith. For Christians, the 'Old Testament' provides the frame of reference for the Christian story of salvation.

There are Christians throughout the world, as Dr Hans Ucko of the World Council of Churches has said, 'who know the road from Bethlehem to Jerusalem better than how to get from one suburb to another in their own city. In churches, chapels and cathedrals, Christian congregations may hear a reading about Jewish history or recite Jewish poetry or meditate on Jewish characters.[1427]

In the New Testament alone, Israel is mentioned at least fifty times and Jews one hundred and eighty times. Christian men and women have Hebrew names. Christian theology takes many of its starting-points from the Old Testament and has sometimes used Judaism and the Jews as an ugly background for its own story.

Other Christians have felt guilty about the suffering of the Jewish people, especially during the Holocaust, and have wanted to purge Christian teaching of its anti-Judaism.

The American Catholic Harry James Cargas, Harry James put this in strong words:

> To call myself a Roman Catholic is to describe my spiritual development incompletely. It is more honest for me to say that at this time in my life I am a post-Auschwitz Christian, in the wider context of Western Christianity. The Holocaust event requires my response precisely as a Christian. The Holocaust is, in my judgment, the greatest tragedy for Christians since the crucifixion. In the first instance, Jesus died; in the latter, Christianity may be said to have died. In the case of Christ, the Christian believes in a resurrection. Will there be, can there be, a resurrection for Christianity? That is the question that haunts me. Am I a part of a religious body that is in fact a fossil rather than a living

entity?

Can one be a Christian today, given the death camps, that, in major part were conceived, built, and operated by a people who called themselves Christians and some of whom - records prove, their own words prove, eyewitness accounts prove - took pride in this work? The failure of Christianity in the mid- twentieth century is monumental. Is it fatal? I need to know?[428]

Jewish Motivation

For many Jews, their history has been largely conditioned by Christian hostility and persecution. For nearly two thousand years most Jews have lived as a minority in Christian Europe. At different times, they have been tolerated, persecuted or exterminated.

In mediaeval France and Germany, carvings of the 'Judensau' were common, even sometimes on church buildings. It was supposed that Jewish children suckled from a sow, known as the 'Judensau' or Jewish sow. The 'Blood Libel' originated in England in 1144 with the case of William of Norwich. According to the libel, Jews showed their hatred of Christianity by re-enacting the Crucifixion and murdering a Christian child at Easter time. A later development suggested that the child's blood was used to make unleavened bread for Passover. Another version of the libel is to be found in The Prioress' Tale in Chaucer, Geoffrey's Canterbury Tales. Such virulent anti-Semitism persisted into this century and even in some quarters till the present day - for example, the notorious *Protocols of the Elders of Zion*, which has been clearly shown to have been an anti- Semitic forgery.

In Christian art through the centuries, Jews are depicted as the evil opponents of Jesus Christ, especially in pictures or stained glass windows of the Passion.[429] Indeed Christian teaching for centuries blamed the Jews for the death of Jesus, a teaching often called 'deicide.' The link between this false teaching and Jewish suffering through the centuries is obvious. This is one reason – as already mentioned - why some Jews have been willing to enter into dialogue. They hope to make Christians aware of the deep-rooted anti-Judaism of traditional church teaching. Other Jews hope to gain Christian sympathy for Israel.

Even so, as Rabbi Dr Michael Hilton, has shown in his book *The Christian Effect on Jewish Life*, Judaism has been deeply influenced by Christianity.[430] Through the centuries, because of Christian hostility, Jews have been defensive and were often forced to live in introverted ghettos. References to Christianity were usually hostile, although, as in Mediaeval Spain, there were periods of cultural exchange.

Orthodox Jews, on the whole, reject 'theological' dialogue, which grapples with questions of ultimate truth. The leading American rabbi, Joseph Dov Soloveichik, argued that faith communities can only communicate on 'secular grounds' or 'human categories'. The life of faith is so intimate that it cannot be communicated to those outside the community. He opposed 'any attempt to debate our private individual faith commitment.' He did, however, endorse dialogue on humanitarian and cultural concerns and admitted that these discussions 'will, of course, be within the framework of our religious outlooks and terminology.' [431] Individual Orthodox rabbis have been ready for a wider dialogue, as have many Liberal and Reform Jews in Britain and Reform and Conservative Jews in USA.

Nineteenth And Early Twentieth Century Developments

In the nineteenth century in Central and Western Europe, Jews were allowed out of the ghetto. Exchange on equal terms became possible. But emancipation brought its own temptations to assimilate. At the same time some Christians, often in missionary circles, began to take a more sympathetic interest in Jews and Judaism. It has been said of the late nineteenth and early twentieth centuries that Jews and Christians engaged not in dialogue but in double monologue. Christians wanted to prove the superiority of their faith; Jews were primarily concerned with bettering their lot in society. Christians wanted converts: Jews, civil rights. Jews were forced to talk religion where they meant social betterment.

Some Jews, however, were beginning to take an interest in Jesus and Christianity. Samuel Hirsch, who was one of the first Reform rabbis to do so, was followed by Abraham Geiger and the distinguished historian Heinrich Graetz spoke positively of Jesus, seeing him as a Jewish teacher. The trend continued in the twentieth century. Herman Cohen, (1842- 918) - author of *The Religion of Reason from the Sources of Judaism* - wrote extensive critiques of Christianity. He had a sense of the deep relationship between Judaism and Christianity, especially in its Protestant manifestations. Franz Rosenzweig proposed the doctrine of 'the Two Covenants.' Martin Buber accepted the reality of Christianity as a path to God and asked Christians to say the same of Judaism. Other scholars, such as Claude Montefiore, a Liberal Jew, wrote a commentary on the Synoptic Gospels. Joseph Klausner, a Jewish nationalist studied Jesus and Paul.

At the same time some Christian scholars were beginning a reassessment of Judaism, although their colleagues were slow to accept their findings. The pioneers included

Robert Travers (1860-1950), a Unitarian minister and scholar, whose many works on the Talmud and Midrash helped Christians - willing to question inherited prejudice - to appreciate the spiritual importance of Rabbinic Judaism. George Foot Moore, (1851-1931), of Harvard University, whose greatest work was his three volume *Judaism in the First Centuries of the Christian Era*, published between 1927 and 1930, gave a sympathetic picture of the Pharisees.

James Parkes

James Parkes (1896-1981), who because of his great influence deserves fuller attention, also challenged traditional stereotypes of Judaism. Parkes was ordained as an Anglican clergyman, although he never served as a parish priest. He worked at first with the Student Christian Movement and in 1928 was sent to Geneva to take charge of its International Student Service office. He soon became aware of the rising tide of anti-Semitism in Continental Europe. Very quickly Parkes made clear his rejection of missionary activity directed at Jews. 'To give the Jew a square deal to be a Jew' became James Parkes' life work. 'The absolute basis of my work is that the Jews with whom I am in contact know that I have no secret desire to convert them.'[432]

He insisted on the theological equality of the revelations at Sinai and in the Incarnation. He believed it was essential to a new relationship to recognise the equal validity of the two religions. He characterised Judaism as God's revelation to man as a social being and Christianity as God's revelation of Himself in terms of a human being to the individual person. Parkes also argued that Christian theology had been too Christocentric and that by stressing 'salvation in Christ', the Church had consigned the majority of humanity to hell. In 1930, the first of Parkes' many contributions to the cause of Jewish-Christian understanding was published. *The Jew and his Neighbour* was a study of the causes of anti-Semitism and, convincingly, showed the Christian roots of this insidious evil. Parkes was one of the first Christians to recognise clearly that the origins of much anti-Semitism lay in the teaching of the churches. He set out the details of his argument in his doctoral thesis, *The Conflict of Church and Synagogue: A Study in the Origins of AntiSemitism*, which was first published in 1934.

Parkes was clear that Christianity and Christian theologians were to blame for the unique evil of anti-Semitism. In his view, in the Greco-Roman world Jews were seen in both a positive and negative light. Jews were granted special privileges and many Gentiles were attracted by Jewish monotheism and by its high ethical teaching. He showed that one can find an anti-Jewish polemic in the Gospels themselves and that this became more vitriolic in an increasingly Gentile church. Parkes wrote of his doctoral research, 'The central and overpowering, indeed horrifying conclusion, which that research brought me, was the total responsibility of the Christian Church for turning a normal xenophobia (fear of foreigners) into the unique disease of AntiSemitism.'[433]

As he learned about Judaism, he saw the Church had misrepresented Torah and caricatured the Pharisees. It was, he said, totally wrong to accuse the Jews of deicide – responsibility for killing God's son. Parkes was, in due course, to be placed on Hitler's 'black list' of those marked out for immediate elimination in the event of a Nazi victory. Already in 1935, he had been a victim of a Nazi attack on his apartment in Geneva. Later that year, he came back to Britain and soon settled at Barley, in Hertfordshire, where he devoted himself to scholarly research and writing. His output was prodigious and his *History of the Jewish People* was translated into several languages. On his retirement in 1966, he gave his magnificent library of some 7,000 books and treatises on anti-Semitism and Christian-Jewish relations to the Parkes Library at Southampton University.

After the Second World War, Parkes gave considerable attention to the Palestine/Israel question. He stressed the continuing Jewish link with the Land, both in daily prayer and in the existence of a small community of Jews in Palestine through the centuries.

Lev Gillet

Another prophetic figure was Father Lev Gillet, an Orthodox monk who wrote under the pse, he has been neglected because his *Communion in the Messiah* was first published in 1942, at the height of the war. Father Gillet was Secretary of the World Congress of Faiths when I joined the Congress in the nineteen sixties. I regret not having talked more to him about his work.

In his *Communion in the Messiah*, he not only called for support for persecuted Jews, but also showed the inter-relationship of the two religions - in theology, spirituality and religious practice. He makes clear the difference between Jewish and Greek ways of thinking. 'What is needed,' he said, 'is a "translation of meanings": a rethinking of Christology in Jewish terms - not only in Hebrew words, but in Hebrew categories of thought. He notes that Philo in his *On Abraham* gave a 'trinitarian' interpretation of the visit of the three strangers to Abraham. Philo wrote 'The One in the Midst,' attended by his two powers, presents to the mind's vision the appearance of the One and sometimes the appearance of Three.'

Gillet recognises the 'God-given mission of the Christian Church to Israel', but adds that 'we should no less strongly

JEWISH FRIENDS AND NEIGHBOURS

believe in the God-given mission of Israel to the Christian Church'. He quotes from a sermon by Cardinal Faulhabrer on the lasting damage caused by the fact that 'After the death of Christ, Israel was dismissed from the service of Revelation.' Gillet ends his book with the hope that Christians will come to see that "Israel the Beloved" has never ceased to be the First Born Child.

Beginnings Of A Change

Besides the work of scholars, a few intellectuals were beginning to meet to talk about their religions. In Britain, one of the first initiatives to encourage friendly conversation is associated with The London Society for the Study of Religions, which was founded in 1904, largely under the inspiration of Baron von Hugel. From the beginning, the society included some Jewish members, of whom the most notable was Claude Montefiore. He was one of the first members to present a paper, which was on 'A Jewish view of the New Testament'. Between the world wars, the Society often met in his home.

In 1924, the Presbyterian Church of England began to discuss its relationship with Jews. Professor Elmslie from Cambridge asked what useful purpose the mission served. The following year at a meeting of the Jewish Mission Committee, Professor Elmslie spoke sympathetically and appreciatively of Judaism. Then, at the General Assembly of the Presbyterian Church of England, for the first time, a Jew, Herbert Loewe, was invited to speak. He was conscious of the special nature of the occasion. 'I do not know whether such a meeting has been held before. To my mind, it is the Lord's doing, and marvellous in our eyes'. Whilst recognising differences, Herbert Loewe stressed what the two faiths shared, 'The love of God and love of man are the foundations of our Faith and

224

of yours.' Recognising the differences between Jews and Christians, Herbert Loewe went on to say, 'I am convinced that our partnership in the fight against oppression and injustice and race-hatred can never be successful, and our efforts can never be blessed until we learn to respect the standpoint of each other.'[434]

1924 was also the year in which the Social Service Committee of the Liberal Jewish Synagogue felt that 'in spite of serious differences of belief, Jews and Christians were at one in their desire to bring nearer the Kingdom of God on earth'. The Committee, with some other organisations, convened a gathering for Jews and Christians to confer together on the basis of their common ideals and with mutual respect for differences of belief.[435] This aroused so much interest that the *ad hoc* committee was given a more permanent status and eventually in 1927, a (London) Society of Jews and Christians was established. It is still active today. Several Jews also supported the World Congress of Faiths - founded in 1936 - which promotes fellowship between people of all faiths.[436]

By the time the Second World War broke out, certain changes in Christian attitudes to Jews and Judaism were beginning to take place. A few scholar had shown the usual view of Judaism and of the Pharisees, was grossly distorted. Some Christians were questioning whether the Church should seek to convert Jews. Some spoke out against fascism and anti-Semitism and a few were recognising the link between anti-Semitism and traditional Christian teaching and that implied a critical approach to scripture and a willingness to rethink traditional Christian theology. A few Christians were meeting Jews for friendly discussion of religious matters. But in every case, it was only a few Christians.

The Rise Of Nazism

By the mid-thirties, the rise of the Nazis to power in Germany also made practical action necessary, both to combat anti-Semitism and to help refugees. Anti-Semitism was exploited by the British Union of Fascists (BUF),which was led by Sir Oswald Mosley. A provocative march through the East End of London, on the 4th of October 1936, was resisted by local inhabitants, in the so-called 'Battle of Cable Street. In the London County Council elections in 1937, the BUF polled 19 per cent of the vote in Shoreditch and 23 per cent in Bethnal Green.

At the same time, refugees from Germany began to make their way to Britain. Various groups tried to offer help. There were several Jewish organisations, which found it increasingly difficult to cope with the flood of refugees. In 1936, an Inter-Aid Committee was formed, which included representatives of both Jewish and Christian caring agencies. In 1938, following Kristallnacht "The Night of the Broken Glass", when synagogues and Jewish property across Germany were attacked, the situation deteriorated.

LOOTING MOBS DEFY GOEBBELS
Jewish homes fired, women beaten
Berlin, Thursday Night. Pogrom goes on till night

All over Germany tonight the Jews are cowering in terror. Their shops are wrecked and looted, their synagogues are burning, their homes are at the mercy of gangs drunk with destruction. Not even the proclamation of Dr. Goebbels, the propaganda minister-

broadcast this afternoon and again tonight-ordering the stoppage of pogroms could curb the madness of the mobs.

The wave of violence sweeping through the cities has moderated now only for lack of further damage to be done. So dangerous did the situation become in Berlin that at eight o'clock the entire police force were called out. They were reinforced by hundreds of Black Guards. But the wrecking and pillaging went on until even the Nazi gangs were exhausted by their orgy.

BEATEN UP

Jews who had managed to elude their persecutors earlier in the day were hunted out and beaten up. Crouching fearfully in corners, they anxiously await the next stroke of the Terror ---the anti-Jewish decrees already threatened following the assassination of von Rath, the Embassy official in Paris. One of them, they believe, will empower the State to confiscate all their property. "Compensation," fixed by the Nazis themselves, would take the form of shares in one of the nationalised industries, such as the Hermann Goering Ironworks. The revival of ghettos is another thing they expect. Such a decree would force them out of their present homes. Their only alternative to being herded together in special areas would be flight from Germany.

All this afternoon they crowded foreign consulates, pleading for visas. In peril of being beaten up as they hurried along the streets they begged, prayed, the officials to grant them permits, particularly to Britain, her Dominions, or the U.S.A. They filled the passages, stood round in huddled groups outside, waited with pitiful patience for their turn. "How much capital have you?" was the invariable question. "None," was often the answer, with a despairing shrug. Others, with money, had to be turned away on other grounds. Only about five per cent were successful in their pleas. Even these must now get Nazi permits to leave Germany. If they are lucky they may be allowed to take away with them twelve per cent of their own money; the rest must remain here.

From The Daily Express, 11/11/1938 © 1938 The Daily Express

Kindertransport.

The atrocity made clear the seriousness of Nazi anti-Semitism. Concerned citizens appealed to the Prime Minister, Sir Neville Chamberlain. The immigration process was speeded up. Priority was given to rescuing children.

The rescue mission, known as Kindertransport would ultimately bring some 10,000 children from Germany, Austria, Czechoslovakia, Poland and Danzig to Britain. The first train left Berlin in December 1938 and the last train left Germany on 1 September 1939, which was the same day as that on which the Nazis entered Poland and Britain and the Allies declared war.

Each child carried a single suitcase, a little money and a name tag. On arrival they were soon taken to a foster home. It was a traumatic experience for young children to be suddenly taken from their homes and challenging for them (and their hosts) to relate, when language, religion and customs were different.

Whenever a Jewish child was placed in a Christian home, it was laid down as a principle of the movement, and clearly understood by the host, that there was to be no proselytization. Further, the child was put in touch with the nearest resident Rabbi, or religious instruction was arranged by correspondence.

https://www.rainbowpilgrims.com/event/crossing-borders

Brave Diplomats

During the war, some diplomats, such as Sir Nicholas Winton in Czechoslovakia, Raol Wallenberg in Hungary, Chiune Sugihara, the Japanese ambassador in Lithuania and Aleksander Ładoś, the Polish government-in-exile's *de facto* ambassador to Switzerland, helped many Jews to escape. Their stories and that of other rescuers is very inspiring.

The Council Of Christians And Jews

A few courageous voices were quick to speak out against the Nazis and anti-Semitism. The outbreak of war convinced Christian leaders in Britain that besides help to refugees, efforts should be made to promote better relations between Jews and Christians.

In response to several approaches, Archbishop William

Temple agreed to call together a meeting of leading Christians and Jews. As a result, in March 1942, with the backing of the Cardinal, the Chief Rabbi and Free Church leaders, a Council of Christians and Jews (CCJ) was established. It is at first sight surprising that there is no mention of anti-Semitism. This was deliberate, because Archbishop Temple persuaded those responsible for setting up the Council that anti-Semitism was only one of many expressions of racial and irreligious intolerance, which in turn are symptomatic of deeper disorders. It may also be that a focus on anti-Semitism would not have enlisted as much support, because at that stage the full implications of Hitler's policies were not recognised.

The Council devoted itself to educational work: helping members appreciate the teachings, beliefs and practices of the other religion. No attempt was made to mask the distinctiveness of either faith community. Together Jews and Christians agreed to combat all forms of discrimination and to promote the ethical values, which they held in common.

When the Council was established, W.W. ('Bill') Simpson, a Methodist minister who, as we have seen, had been active both in helping refugees and in the initial work to set up the Council, was the obvious choice to be secretary. This was a post which he held, with great distinction, until 1974.

It is interesting that in a pamphlet called 'The Christian and the Jewish Problem', published by the Epworth Press in 1939, W. W. Simpson was already looking beyond the immediate tragedy of the refugees and the horrors of Nazi persecution, to recognise the Christian share of responsibility for Jewish sufferings. Simpson mentioned the charge of deicide, the attacks of the Crusaders, the institution of the Ghetto and the Inquisition. 'It is important to realize that one of the chief factors in forcing the Jews into a negative kind of separatism has been the attitude generally adopted by the Christian community'[434]

A New Relationship

Nostra Aetate

The decree *Nostra Aetate*, 'In Our Age', promulgated in October 1965 by the Second Vatican Council, was a decisive turning point not only in Catholic-Jewish relations, but also more broadly for Christian-Jewish relations.

Nostra Aetate began by recalling the spiritual bond that links the people of the New Covenant to Abraham's stock and by affirming God's continuing covenant with the Jewish people. The document commended dialogue.

Most important the charge of deicide was repudiated. The decree also condemned all persecution and particularly displays of anti-Semitism.

Nostra Aetate not only closed the era of friction and enmity, it also left behind the 18th century concept of religious tolerance. In proclaiming mutual respect as the guiding principle in inter-religious relations for the future, the Decree constitutes a milestone in Christian-Jewish relations and opened a new vision for the future.

Gerhard Riegner, Gerhard who for many years was Secretary General of the World Jewish Congress said of the

Declaration that:

'It stresses the spiritual bond between the Church and the Jewish people. It acknowledges that it received the 'Old Testament through the people with whom God concluded the Ancient Covenant'.

It acknowledges the Judaic roots of Christianity, starting with the Jewish origin of Jesus himself, of the Virgin Mary and of all the Apostles.

It declares that God does not repent of the gifts He makes and the calls He issues and that Jews remain 'most dear to God'.

It states that what happened in the Passion of Christ cannot be charged against all Jews without distinction then living, or against the Jews of today.

It declares that the Jews are not rejected or accursed by God.

It proclaims the Church's repudiation of hatred, persecution, and displays of anti- Semitism at any time and by anyone.

It fosters and recommends mutual understanding and respect through biblical and theological studies and fraternal dialogues.'

The last principle, in Riegner's view, was the most important with its stress on mutual understanding and respect.[439]

It is interesting that when in 1986, Pope John Paul II visited the Great Roman Synagogue, he also concentrated on the general acceptance of a legitimate plurality on the social, civil and religious levels.[440] At the Synagogue, the Pope also repeated the words of Vatican II that the Church 'deplores the hatred, persecutions and displays of anti-Semitism directed against the Jews at any time and by anyone' – adding 'I would like once more to express a word of abhorrence for the genocide decreed against the Jewish people during the last War, which led to the holocaust of millions of innocent victims.'[441]

A considerable number of subsequent Vatican documents as well as statements by national and provincial synods have sought to extend and apply the teaching of Nostra Aetate.[442] Even so, many Christians seem unaware of the need to reject and revise traditional teaching.

A New Approach

When I first studied theology, however, nearly fifty years ago, the books we were told to read spoke of 'mortal enmity' between the Pharisees who insisted upon 'the letter of the law' and Jesus 'who spoke with the authority of the living God.'[443] Jesus when he overthrew the tables of the money changers, I was taught, was 'determined to replace the tables of legalism tended by the merchants of hypocrisy. These tables, like the Temple, will be replaced by him.'[444]

Martin Noth, in his *History of Israel* - a standard reference book - declared that, 'Jesus himself ... no longer formed part of the history of Israel. *In him the history of Israel had come to its real end*. (my italics).' [445] By implication, for two thousand years, Jews had become a non-people.

A Religion Of Covenant

Judaism and especially the Pharisaic movement have been seriously misrepresented. Judaism is a religion of Covenant. This is made clear, as we have seen when a Jewish boy is circumcised. It is also evident in the Passover Seder.

God promised to Abraham that he would bless his descendants. God rescued the people of Israel from slavery in Egypt and chose them to be God's own people. The Torah was given by God to those whom God by grace had chosen. The Torah was the way of life for a community and God gave Israel the Land of Promise where it could be a holy people. Circumcision was the sign of membership of the holy people.

To obey the Torah was to affirm the covenant and to accept God's promise. It was the loving response to God's gracious act of rescue and choice of Israel. In Psalm 119 the Psalmist says, 'I love your commandments more than gold, more than the finest gold' (v.127) or 'Lord how I love your law, it is my meditation all the day long' (v.97). In fact joyful obedience, springing from thankfulness for God's mercy, is characteristic of Jewish devotion. Often Christians have, mistakenly, pictured the Law as a burden rather than as a delight. The influence of Luther and the way Paul has often been interpreted has been strong. This attitude is reflected in hymns, like 'Rock of Ages', which has the lines, 'Not the labours of my hands Can fulfil thy law's demands'.

The Pharisees

The Pharisees have been much maligned. My 1991 Concise Oxford Dictionary's second definition of the word 'Pharisee' is 'a self-righteous person, a hypocrite.' There is debate about the origins and teaching of the Pharisaic movement. It is clear, however, that they had a new perception of the relationship of God to human beings. God was not just the God of the patriarchs or just the parent of Israel, but the God of every individual. God watched over and cared for each person. New names were given to God, such as Makom 'the all present' or Ha-Kadosh Baruch Hu 'The Holy One Blessed Be He' or Abinu She-Bashamayim 'Our Father in heaven'. [446]

As a direct result of the new understanding of the God-human relationship, the Pharisees taught belief in the resurrection - a teaching, which brought them into conflict with the Sadducees, who were the high priestly party. It was amongst the Pharisees, that the position of rabbi, or teacher, emerged. They also developed the synagogue as a place for communal assembly. After the destruction of the Temple, as we have seen, the rabbis gave a symbolic interpretation to the sacrifices and insisted that they had no efficacy apart from genuine repentance and reparation. The Pharisees' teaching about the Covenant and Torah was true to the Biblical teaching as already outlined. Jesus' arguments with the Pharisees, as reported in the Gospels, were no greater than the arguments amongst the Pharisees themselves. There were, as we have seen, sharp differences amongst the Rabbis, for example, between Hillel and Shammai, and their respective followers. It needs also to be remembered that the Gospels were written down at least thirty years after the death of Jesus and in part reflect the growing tension between the synagogue and early church, which is clearly illustrated in the Acts of the Apostles.

It is worth again emphasizing that the split between church and synagogue took place over a long period and only in part for theological reasons. There was no sudden break. Rather, Christianity and Rabbinic Judaism are two developments, drawing on similar sources in first century Judaism, which gradually moved further and further apart, rather like a couple becoming estranged, who discover that in more and more ways their lives have drifted apart. By the end of the second Jewish revolt in 134 CE, despite some remaining links, 'Christian and Jew were clearly distinct and separate.'[447] Over the centuries bitterness and hostility between the two communities increased and only began to be reversed in the twentieth century, but is still too evident in many sermons.

Deicide

The most dangerous aspect of Christian emphasis on Jewish opposition to Jesus was the teaching of 'deicide,' which has now been repudiated by the churches. Through the Christian centuries, the death of Jesus has been blamed on the Jews. Often Jews would lock themselves in their homes on Good Friday for fear of the Christians. Several Jews have told me of times when they were attacked and called 'Christ- killers.'

Sadly, mention must be made of popular calumnies, such as the 'Blood Libel', which was invented in England. This is the pernicious accusation common in the Middle Ages that Jews – sometimes called 'children of the Devil' – murdered Christian children in order to use their blood for ritual purposes at the time of Passover.

It is now widely agreed that it is historically, morally and theologically wrong to hold the Jews guilty of the death of Jesus.

Historically, Jesus suffered crucifixion, which was a Roman penalty. It is known that Pilate was a cruel ruler and anyone who was said to claim to be a king was likely to be in trouble. By the time the Gospels were written, Christians wanted to gain legitimacy in Roman eyes and seem to have shifted the blame for Jesus' death on to the Jews. Some Jews opposed him, especially the high priests, who felt their vested interests, and indeed the limited freedom allowed to the Jews by the Romans, would be threatened by trouble with the Romans, and may have been involved in a plot to be rid of him. The Pharisees were not involved.

There is also considerable doubt about the nature and legality of 'the trial' of Jesus before the chief priests and the Council. Jesus had his supporters. There is no evidence, despite some hymns, that the Palm Sunday crowd, which cried 'Hosanna,' was the same as the mob which shouted 'Crucify'. Jesus seems to have been popular with the people. He was arrested at night to avoid a public outcry. Presumably, the secret that Judas betrayed was where Jesus could be secretly captured.[448] When he was crucified, other Jews mourned and lamented over him.[449] Those who became his first disciples were, of course, all Jewish.

Morally it is wrong to hold a whole people guilty of the supposed wickedness of some of their ancestors. Young Germans today, for example, cannot be blamed for the evil deeds of the Nazis.

Theologically, as the Vatican Council and other church synods have affirmed, God's covenant with his people has never been broken. Traditionally, also the churches have taught that Christ died for all people. All humanity, not one special group bears collective guilt for the death of Christ. It has also been Christian teaching that the death of Jesus was willed by God.

Messiah

Greater awareness of the Judaism of the first century has led some scholars to rethink the response to Jesus of his contemporaries. Jews looked for the coming of the Messiah. Speculation about the coming of the Messiah was as varied and as imprecise as is Christian thinking today about the Second Coming.

Most Jews hoped for an earthly deliverer who would free them from Roman occupation. Some saw the Messiah as the key figure in the New Age. The Gospels suggest that, if Jesus saw himself as Messiah, he radically reinterpreted the role as an embodiment of the Suffering Servant foretold in Isaiah. The fact that the Messiah would suffer and be rejected is frequently repeated in the Gospels. As a result it is clear that Jesus did not fit traditional Messianic expectations. It is wrong, therefore, to accuse Jews of failing to recognise their Messiah. Jews continue to wait for the coming of the Messiah or Messianic Kingdom in which poverty and violence and abuse of human rights will finally be a thing of the past.

There is a story that a Jewish-Christian dialogue meeting in Jerusalem was interrupted when someone broke in saying, 'the Messiah has come.' The group hurried out to meet him. The first question he was asked was, 'Is this your first or your second visit?' The answer was 'No comment, your calling is to bring in the kingdom of God.'

Son Of God

It is also recognised that the Jewish use of the term 'Son of God' is radically different from its use by Gentile Christians. In the Hebrew Bible both Israel and the king are called 'Son of God' - a term suggesting special favour and responsibility. To the first believers, who were Jewish, Jesus' sonship would probably have been understood in moral not ontological terms. It would have implied his total obedience to the Father's will.

The Hellenistic world thought in terms of divine paternity. Gentile Christians, therefore, came to understand the title Son of God more literally than the first Jewish believers. The American Catholic theologian Monika Hellwig has written, 'This is really where the serious and apparently intractable difficulties in Christology begin - in a simplification in gentile context and language of the elusive and allusive Hebrew way of speaking about the mystery of God and of God's dealings with creation and history.'[450] Some Christians argue the need to reverse the process, changing, as the American Catholic scholar John Pawlikowski suggests, 'our attitude toward the statement 'Jesus is Son of God' and 'Jesus is divine' from simple equation to interpretation.'[451]

This, however, is to stray into a Christian theological debate which is dealt with in many other books and which I tried to address in my *Time to Meet* and *Christian-Jewish Dialogue: the Next Steps.*[452] The new appreciation of Judaism does, however, raise theological questions, which have far-reaching implications for the Churches. Are Christians of the future bound by Creeds from the past? What do Christians mean when they speak of themselves as 'the people of God?' Are they God's only people?

Areas of Tension

Many in both communities are unaware of the dramatic changes in Christian-Jewish relations.There are also areas of continuing tension, especially in relation to Israel, missionaries, and inter-marriage.[453]

Pope Benedict XVI also caused controversy by some his actions. In 2007, Pope Benedict XVI relaxed restrictions on use of the old Latin Mass. In doing so, the Pope restored to prominence a Good Friday prayer for the conversion of the Jews. Attempts to diffuse the situation by issuing a new prayer were unsuccessful because this prayer also implied that Jews need to be converted to Christianity to find salvation.

The Pope also pressed ahead with moves to recognise Pope Pius XII as a saint, although his role during the war, as we have seen, is still a matter of hot debate. Another cause of tension was a decree to welcome back into the Catholic Church four bishops, who are members of the Society of Saint Pius X, which was founded by Archbishop Lefebrve to oppose the modernizing reforms of the Second Vatican Council, particularly because one of the four bishops, Bishop William Richardson was on record as a Holocaust denier.

There are also continuing difficulties relating to Israel/Palestine. Some at the Vatican feel that Israel has not honoured the undertakings given in 1993 when the Vatican established diplomatic relations with the state of Israel. The status of expropriated church property is unresolved; there are travel restrictions on Arab Catholic priests; and the state's failure to remove taxes on Church-owned property in the Holy Land.

Hope for the Future

Relations have improved under Pope Francis, who was quick to go to the Rome Synagogue. In 2014, Pope Francis visited Israel, where he urged Israeli and Palestinian leaders to show courage to seek peace in the Middle East. Subsequently he hosted joint prayers at the Vatican with Israeli President Shimon Peres and his Palestinian counterpart, Mahmoud Abbas. He also has allowed scholars access to the records of Pope Pius XXII.

Nostra Aetate not only closed the era of friction and enmity, it also left behind the 18th century concept of religious tolerance. In proclaiming mutual respect as the guiding principle in inter-religious relations for the future, the Decree constitutes a real milestone in Christian-Jewish relations and opens a new vision for the future.

Missionary Activity

The new appreciation of Judaism calls in question traditional missionary efforts to convert Jews to Christianity. Jews now see their calling to be, by example, 'a light to the Gentiles.' Although in the inter-testamental period, Jews may have engaged in missionary activity or proselytism, this became impossible once Christianity became the official religion of the Roman Empire.

The fact that the great universal monotheisms have not yet formally endorsed a plural world is the still unexorcised darkness at the heart of our religious situation.

Jonathan Sacks, former Chief Rabbi

Rabbis have often spoken of three covenants: God's covenant at creation with Adam and all people;[457] God's covenant with Noah, which required Gentiles to observe seven commandments which included the setting up of law courts and the prohibition of idolatry; and, thirdly, God's covenant with Israel. In contemporary Jewish writing there is frequent reference to God's covenant with all people through the covenant with Noah.[458] Most Jews accept a pluralist position and affirm that the righteous of all nations will have a share in the world to come.[459]

Jews have a deep fear of Christian missionary activity. In the middle Ages, some disputations between Jews and Christians were held. Some of these allowed for genuine inter-religious debate, others were arranged to ensure a Christian 'victory'. There was also occasional friendly interchange between scholars and considerable mutual influence of the two religions on each other. Yet the word 'mission' evokes memories of forced conversions and persecution. The nineteenth century saw both pogroms and renewed conversionary efforts.

Few people question the right of individuals freely to change from one religion to another, but there is strong Jewish dislike of organised Christian missionary activity or 'targeting,' as it is sometimes called. Jews resent the active and well financed missionary groups, often based in the USA, which harass some of the Jewish community. The Jewish community has an understandable insecurity, not just because of the past, but because in most European countries, Jews are a small minority.

A particular difficulty is caused by some Messianic Jews' desire to convert Jews. The activities of 'Jews for Jesus' have been much resented by the Jewish community.

Questioning Missionary Work.

A growing number of Christians are no longer happy with a missionary approach. The division of opinion among Christians was reflected in the Church of England Report, *Sharing One Hope* (2001).

It says: 'Some people feel it is not appropriate for Christians to believe that they have any kind of 'mission to the Jews.' This may be because of a particular theological understanding of God's covenant. It may be because they feel Christians have forfeited any moral right to seek the conversion of Jews because of the 'teaching of contempt' for centuries. It may be because of the importance of not disturbing dialogue. Some Christians speak of a shared mission with Jews to the world that God's name may be honoured.

Others think it is entirely appropriate that Christians who establish relationships of genuine friendship and trust with Jews should continue to see these relationships in the context of Christian mission. There is no place for 'targeting' Jews or any manipulation, but while seeking genuine understanding it is right to share one's deepest convictions.

Other Christians say they have a responsibility to try to convince Jews about Jesus as Messiah. Some quote Paul's words about 'to the Jew first, and also to the

Greek,' (Romans 1, 16) as a reason to give priority to missions to Jews. The Jewish community, who dislike all missionary efforts, are especially uncomfortable with 'Jews for Jesus'. [461]

A later Church of England report, *God's Unfailing Word* makes clear that these differences remain. It says, 'differences of perspective on the place of evangelism are to be expected among Christians. Others reinterpret the missionary command as shared mission. An Orthodox Jewish document of 2015 does the same. It says: 'We Jews acknowledge the ongoing constructive validity of Christianity as our partner in world redemption... Neither of us can achieve G-d's mission in the world alone.'[462]

The key question is whether or not Christianity has replaced Judaism. Those Christians who reject the traditional missionary approach usually affirm that 'God's covenant with the Jews has never been revoked.' Their views are based on their interpretation of Paul's teaching, especially in the complex chapters 9-11 of the Epistle to the Romans. They recognise also the continuing 'spiritual fecundity' of the Jewish people – in other words that Judaism is a living religion, with many spiritual gifts to share.

Again, we are straying into Christian territory. Most Jews are not particularly interested in the theological twists and turns by which some Christians distance themselves from the scriptural command to preach the Gospel to all people, but are thankful to get the Christians off their backs – even if they are still targeted by American-based fundamentalists.

Jewish Responses

Until recently most statements on Christian-Jewish relations have been issued by Churches. Many individual rabbis and Jewish scholars have engaged in dialogue and there have been a number of statements from joint meetings of Jews and Christians. *Dabru Emet: a Jewish Statement on Christians and Christianity*, issued in September 2000, was one of the first responses from a purely Jewish group - in this case a number of well-known rabbis and scholars.

Dabru Emet affirms that:

Jews and Christians worship the same God. 'While Christian worship is not a viable choice for Jews, as Jewish theologians we rejoice that, through Christianity, hundreds of millions of people have entered into relationship with the God of Israel.'

Jews and Christians seek authority from the same book. Christians can respect the claim of the Jewish people upon the land of Israel. Jews and Christians accept the moral principles of Torah.

Nazism was not a Christian phenomenon, but adds 'Without the long history of Christian anti-Judaism and Christian violence against Jews, Nazi ideology could not have taken hold nor could it have been carried out. Too many Christians participated in, or were sympathetic to, Nazi atrocities against Jews. Other Christians did not protest sufficiently against these atrocities. But Nazism itself was not an inevitable outcome of Christianity.'

The humanly irreconcilable differences between Jews and Christians will not be settled until God redeems the entire world as promised in Scripture.

A new relationship between Jews and Christians will not weaken Jewish practice. Jews and Christians must work together for justice and peace.[464]

Some Jewish Views of Jesus

This approach has allowed some Jews to separate Jesus from the anti-Judaism of the Church and to view him sympathetically. There have been a considerable number of recent studies of Jesus by Jewish scholars.

Franz Rosenzweig was asked, 'What do Jews think about Jesus?' His answer, as we have seen, was 'They don't'. Whilst Christianity cannot be understood without reference to Judaism, the reverse is not the case. In the last century, Heinrich Graetz, (1817-91) and Abraham Geiger, (1810-74) included fairly neutral studies of Jesus in their histories of the Jewish people. Both recognised his Jewishness, which at the time was not emphasised in Christian writings.

The emphasis on Jesus' Jewishness has recurred in subsequent studies, for example by Claude Montefiore, Joseph Klausner, Geza Vermes, Ben-Chorim Schlom or Pinchas Lapide. The presumption of several Jewish writers is that it is possible to have a historical picture of Jesus. The Israeli scholar David Flusser says of his book *Jesus* that 'the main purpose of this book is to show that it is possible to write the story of Jesus' life'.

Jewish scholars have helped Christians acquire a more accurate picture of the Pharisees. They have also challenged the Gospel accounts of the trial of Jesus.

Pinchas Lapide gave five reasons, which, he said, 'bring Jesus closer to me than to many a Christian theologian in Europe today'. He and Jesus share the setting in life - which includes the geography and topography of Israel, with its fauna and flora – they also share the languages of Hebrew and Aramaic, the Hebrew Bible as sacred literature, Oriental imagination, and a concern for Israel.[465]

When Jewish scholars attempt to assess the significance of Jesus they do so within Jewish categories, but with sympathetic identification with him. Instead of the traditional Jewish view that he was a false Messiah some have suggested that he was a failed Messiah. Others such as Geza Vermes, especially known for his work on the Dead Sea Scrolls, who emphasises the miracles, see Jesus as a Galilean Hasid or holy man. In Vermes' view, Jesus did not belong to the Pharisees or Zealots. Rabbi Harvey Falk, however, holds that Jesus was a Pharisee of the School of Hillel. The *Jewish Annotated New Testament* is entirely written by Jewish scholars.[466]

The influential American Rabbi Irving Greenberg wrote, 'Out of defensiveness, the Rabbis confused a "failed" Messiah (which is what Jesus was) and a false Messiah. A false Messiah is one who has the wrong values ... a failed Messiah is one who has the right values, upholds the covenant, only did not attain the final goal (Bar Kokhba is given as an example) ... (Moses and Jeremiah are then discussed as "failures").All these "failures" are at the heart of divine and Jewish achievements. This concept of a "failed" but true Messiah is found in a rabbinic tradition of the Messiah ben Joseph. The Messiah ben David (son of David) is the one who brings the final restoration. In the Messiah ben Joseph's idea, you have a Messiah who comes and fails, indeed is put to death, but this Messiah paves the way for the final redemption. Christians also sensed that Jesus did not exhaust the achievements of the final Messiah. Despite Christian claims that Jesus was a total success ... even Christians spoke of a second coming. The concept of a second coming, in a way, is a tacit admission - if at first you don't succeed, try, try and try again.'[467].

A few Jews are willing to recognise that whilst God has spoken to them at Sinai, God is also present in Jesus. Rabbi Tony Bayfield, a former Head of Britain's Movement for Reform Judaism, has written: 'Christ comes to the dialogue room and I experience him perhaps in something of the same way in which Christians experience the God of Abraham, Isaac and Jacob. Fascinating, perplexing, enlightening, puzzling, distinctive - not my God. And yet, as it were, - and paradoxically - an outpouring and an outreaching of the Ein Sof, the "Without End", who I believe, both Jews and Christians address.'[468]

Dialogue for a Better World

From the early days of Christian-Jewish dialogue there has been a desire to speak together on moral matters and to act together to combat prejudice and discrimination. 'The ultimate aim of dialogue,' according to a statement by the International Council of Christians and Jews, 'is to contribute towards a better world - a world in which the will of God is done; a world of justice and peace.'[469] Christians and Jews have talked together, for example, about the values of family life. They campaigned together for religious freedom in the former Soviet Union.

Even so, recognising the measure of friendship that has grown up between individual Jews and Christians and their co-operation on many social and moral issues, the period since the Second World War has been dominated by the need to remove inherited misunderstanding and suspicion between Jews and Christians.

Several people are suggesting that now is the time to move forward to affirm the moral values, which are shared by the two faith communities and to reject extremism and religiously sanctioned violence. Professor Ewert Cousins has written that in concert with other religions, Christianity and Judaism should put their energies into solving the common human problems that threaten our future on the earth ... Just to meet, even creatively, on the spiritual level is not enough. They must channel their spiritual resources towards the solution of global problems.[470]

At a service to mark the fiftieth anniversary of the Council of Christians and Jews in 1996, Lord Coggan, a former Archbishop of Canterbury, said:
'There is a very real danger that we may rest content with dialogue and fail to push on from it to the next stage of our journey together. If we get stuck in dialogue, we may rest content with mere words, with theoretical niceties, with the luxury of intellectual debate. We must advance from dialogue to a sense of joint-trusteeship.

At the heart of the Jewish faith and of the Christian faith is the conviction that Jews and Christians alike have been recipients of divine truths, which are of immense importance. Lord Coggan went on to enumerate some of these: Belief in a God who cares for each individual and for the creation; a recognition that the body is a temple for God's abiding presence; the necessity of a break from the routine of work (the Sabbath).[471]

Can Jews and Christians Pray Together?

Increasingly, Jews and Christians are coming together to pray and/or to pray with people of other faiths, especially at times of national emergency, for example, after an act of terrorism or during a pandemic.

Sometimes where Christians and Jews have been together for a weekend conference, members of one faith have been present at a service of the other faith. At one such conference, the Jewish participants met in one room for their morning prayers, while the Christians met in another. Afterwards, one rabbi asked, 'Which room would Jesus have gone to?' Perhaps hospitals, prisons, and airports with their 'multi-faith chapels' or quiet rooms point to an answer to such questions.

Christian-Jewish dialogue has occasioned some remarkable joint events. In 1986, the world premiere of Ronald Senator's *Kiddush for Terezim* was performed at Canterbury Cathedral. This was a musical work commemorating the victims of the Shoah. The text, which was prepared by Albert Friedlander, included some of the poems and diaries written by children of the Terezin concentration camp.

In 1990 to mark the 800th anniversary of the Massacre at Clifford's Tower in York, a special commemorative weekend was held in the city. This included a seminar, concert, and service at York Minister and at the Synagogue. Then at Clifford's Tower itself, a cantor sang on this tragic site the Jewish prayer of mourning and Christians joined in the Amen.[472] Following, the London bombings, several synagogues hosted acts of remembrance in which Muslims and Christians were invited to participate.

Alan Brill in *Interfaith Worship and Prayer* makes a helpful distinction between 'universal prayer' and 'specific liturgies.' 'A joint service is not intended by either side to fulfil the obligation for statutory prayer. For example, a Catholic's participation in a joint service does not fulfil her obligation to attend Mass. It would be inappropriate for a synagogue to have a joint service instead of its regular Shabbat service.' Yet, a Rabbi may be invited to preach at a Christian service or a priest at a service in a synagogue.

Aaron Rosen, in the same book, discusses the use of shared space and gives as an example the plans to build on the new Museum Island in the centre of Berlin a house which is both a fully functional church, synagogue and mosque. He adds, 'A space need not be exclusively Jewish to be genuinely Jewish' and quotes the poet Yehudah Leib Gordon's saying, 'Be a man of the streets and a Jew at home.'[473]

Public Life

Another question is how to acknowledge the growing number of faith communities in Britain, where one denomination of one religion, the established Church of England, has historically had a privileged and dominant position. Should the Monarch be 'Defender of Faith' rather than 'Defender of the Faith?' Should the Coronation be a multi-faith ceremony? Should bishops be the only designated religious voice in the House of Lords?

The questions themselves are a reminder that dialogue is not now confined to Jews and Christians but increasingly also involves Muslims and people of other faiths.

It was to encourage understanding between Jews, Christians and Muslims that the Three Faiths Forum was founded by Sir Sigmund Sternberg, a Papal Knight and winner of the Templeton Prize for Progress in Religion,

Sheikh Dr Zaki Badawi, who founded the Muslim College, and myself. The Woolf Institute of Abrahamic Faiths, based in Cambridge, is doing similar work at a more academic level. Perhaps it is worth pointing out that both organizations avoid the term 'the Three Monotheistic Religions,' because this particularly offends Zoroastrians and Sikhs and members of some other religions.[474]

Jewish Muslim Dialogue

There is now increasing Jewish-Muslim discussion. Although this is not really the concern of Christians, perhaps they can listen-in and perhaps it will help them in their understanding of Judaism. Jewish interaction with Muslims is, of course, nothing new. The Prophet Muhammad had at least one Jewish wife. Initially, Muhammad's relations with the Jews were good, although they later deteriorated.

A recent statement by Muslims, acknowledging current tensions, looks back to more congenial relations in the past.

'Many Jews and Muslims today stand apart from each other due to feelings of anger, which in some parts of the world, translate into violence... For many centuries our communities co-existed and worked together fruitfully and peacefully such as in the Iberian Peninsula. As Muslims and Jews we share core doctrinal beliefs - most importantly, strict monotheism. We both share a common patriarch, Ibrahim/Abraham, other Biblical prophets, laws and jurisprudence, many significant values and even dietary restrictions. There is more in common between our religions and peoples than is known to each of us.'[475]

Talmudic literature pre-dates the rise of Islam, but even thereafter, there is little reference to Muhammad in pre-modern literature. This may be because Jews were reluctant to offend Muslim rulers. It is also suggested - on dubious evidence - that Jews were forbidden from studying the Qur'an and were not allowed to teach the Torah to Muslims.[476] Some Jews seem to have questioned the authenticity of Muhammad's prophecy, although the Yemenite Jewish scholar Netanel ibn Fayyumi acknowledged it.

Abraham Geiger, who we have already met as one of the first Jews seriously to write about Jesus, also, as a young man, wrote *'Was hat Mohammed aus dem Judenthume aufgenommen?* (What did Mohammed take from Judaism?). Other Jewish scholars have learned about Islam in the context of the study of religions.

There is no Jewish view of Muhammad, Rabbi Norman Solomon insists, because he does not figure as a person in Jewish theology. 'At the same time, Islam itself is increasingly seen not as a rival or usurper with a competing claim to exclusive truth, but as another manifestation of the infinite self-revelation of God.' [477]

Much of the contemporary Jewish-Muslim dialogue, which is always under threat from developments in the Middle East, is on practical matters, especially how faith communities should adjust to the modern world and life in a plural society. 'In a nutshell, the dialogue is about jointly promoting the moral and ethical codes that underpin our two traditions... about engaging in the national struggle against racism ... and ensuring our cultural distinctiveness as equal and active members of the community. And it is about ensuring that the wider society in which we live accepts our "otherness" and celebrates our diversity.'478 There is, besides, now some shared study of the Scriptures among young people and also between scholars.

A Community of Communities

Maintaining a faith community's identity, while its members play a full part in the life of the wider society is a challenge to all religions in our modern pluralistic world.

The late Jonathan Sacks – a former Chief Rabbi - claimed that Jews have shown how it is possible to be both Jewish and British and have provided a template for other newer arrivals.

A community 'needs two kinds of religious strength; one to preserve our own distinct traditions, the other to bring them to an enlarged sense of the common good.'478 He compares this to speaking two languages. 'There is a delicate interplay between our second languages of identity and our first language of common citizenship. If we recognise only the first language, we are in effect calling for the disappearance of minorities. If we insist on second languages to the exclusion of a common culture, we risk moving to a society of conflicting ghettoes.'

Social cohesion' and 'multi-culturalism' are not in opposition. By being true to one's own faith, one learns to respect the faith of others and discovers that beyond our rich diversity, we share the moral values which flow from a belief in One God, 'whose glory the heavens are telling.'

(Jews) constantly strive to recognise that all people are created in the divine image... We believe that God is the hidden ideal to which we always aspire through our daily routines, our religious practices, our learning and our prayers. The higher world is the world to which we aspire, but it is also one that we can realise only within ourselves, in our relationships, and in our community. Touching the transcendent reality greater than ourself is the spiritual goal of Judaism. The realisation of our aspiration can only be achieved within the world.[479]

14. EPILOGUE

I hope, dear reader, that you will be as much enriched as I, as a Christian have been, by meeting Jews and learning about Judaism. Our shared vocation is 'to struggle to bring God down to earth.' We are called, together with all people of faith, to oppose racism, anti-Semitism and all forms of discrimination and by our prayers, words and actions to prepare for God's rule of mercy, justice and peace.

Let the time come, O God, when there shall be peace
on earth, friendship among all races,
freedom from fear, freedom from want,
freedom to think and speak at the dictates of conscience,
when our systems of justice will be protective and healing
and when all people shall live closer to the principles of Your Kingdom

A prayer (adapted), written by George Appleton,
former Anglican Archbishop in Jerusalem

BIBLIOGRAPHY

Abraham's Children, ed. Norman Solomon, Richard Harries and Tim Winter, London, 2006

Aguilar, G, History of the Jews of England, Edinburgh, Chambers Miscellany, vol.18, no 153,

Alderman, Geoffrey, Modern British Jewry, Oxford, Clarendon Press, 1992

Amos Oz, A Tale of Love and Darkness, E.T. Nicholas de Lange, London, Vintage, 2005 and many other books by the same author.

Approaches to Auschwitz, Eds. Rubenstein, R and Roth, J K London, SCM Press, 1997.

Ariel, David, What Do Jews Believe, London, Rider 1966.

Ateek, Naim, A Palestinian Cry for Reconciliation, Orbis, 2008,

Ateek, Naim, Justice and Only Justice, Orbis Press, Maryknoll, NY, 1989

Authorised Daily Prayer Book of the Hebrew Congregations of the British Commonwealth.

Barrett, C.K ,The Gospel According to St John, London, SPCK, 1958.

Bat-Chen, The Bat-Chen Diaries, Minneapolis, Kar-Ben Publishing (Lerner Publishing), 2008

Bayfield, Tony and Braybrooke, Marcus, eds, Dialogue with a Difference, London, SCM Press,

Bayfield, Tony, Deep Calls to Deep, London, SCM Press, 2017

Bayfield, Tony, Being Jewish Today, London, Bloomsbury Continuum, 2019.

Bayfield, Tony, Brichto, S, and Fisher, E, He Kissed Him and They Wept, London, SCM Press, 200

Bemporad Jack and Shevack M, Our Age, The Historic New Era of Christian-Jewish relations, New York, New York City press, 1996

Benjamin, Disraeli, Coningsby or the New Generation, May 1849,

Blackwell Reader in Judaism, Ed Jacob Neusner and Alan J Avery-Peck, Oxford, 2001

Blumenthal, David, Facing the Abusing God: a Theology of Protest, Louisville, Westminste Press, 1993

Bousset, W, Jesus, 1911, (Forgotten Books, 2018)

Boys, Mary C, Redeeming Our Story, New York, Paulist Press, 2013

Braybrooke, Marcus Children of One God, London, Vallentine Mitchell, 1991.

Braybrooke, Marcus ed. Bridge of Stars, London, Duncan Baird, 2001.

Braybrooke, Marcus Time to Meet, London, SCM Press,1990

Braybrooke, Marcus, Faiths Together: the World Congress of Faiths and the Global Interfaith Movement, Teignmouth, Braybrooke Press, 2019

Braybrooke, Marcus, Christian-Jewish Dialogue: the Next Steps, London, SCM Press, 2000.

Braybrooke, Marcus, Christians and Jews Building Bridges, Braybrooke Press, Teignmouth, 2012

Braybrooke, Marcus, How to Understand Judaism, London, SCM Press, 1995.

Buber, M, Ich und Du was published in 1923. The first English translation wa s published in 1937.

Buber, Martin Between Man and Man, Routledge, 1947.

Burridge R A and Sacks J, Confronting Religious Violence, London, SCM Press, 2018

Bursting the Bonds, eds Leonard Swidler, John Eron and
Lester Dean, New York, Orbis, 1990

Cahill, Thomas, The Gifts of the Jews, Oxford, Lion Publishing, 2000

Cantor, Norman, The Sacred Chain, London, HarperCollins, 1995

Catholics, Jews and the State of Israel Ed. Anthony Kenny, Paulist Press 1993

Celebration: The Book of Jewish Festivals, Ed Naomi Black, London, Collins 1987.

Cesarani, David, The Jewish Chronicle and Anglo-Jewry 1841-1991, Cambridge Cambridge University Press, 1994

Challenges in Jewish-Christian Relations, eds Aitken, J A, and Kessler, E, Mahwah, New Jersey, 2006

Challenging Christian Zionism, Ed Naim Ateek, Cedar Duaybis and Maurine Tobin, London, Mellisende, 2005

Christians and Jews: A New Way of Thinking, Council of Churches for Britain and Ireland,

Clements, Keith, Bonhoeffer and Britain, London, Churches Together in Britain, 2006

Cohn-Sherbok, Dan and Dawoud el-Alami, The Palestine-Israeli Conflict, Oxford, Oneworld, 2001

Cohn-Sherbok, Dan Chryssides, G and Usama Hasan, People of the Book, London, Jessica Kingsley, 2019

Cohn-Sherbok, Dan, Holocaust Theology, Exeter, University of Exeter Press, 2002.

Cohn-Sherbok, Dan, Israel: the History of an Idea, London, SPCK, 1992.

Cohn-Sherbok, Dan, Judaism and Other Faiths, Basingstoke, Macmillan Press, 1994.

Cohn-Sherbok, Dan Exodus, London, Bellew Publishing, 1992

Cohn-Sherbok, Modern Judaism, Basingstoke, Macmillan, 1996

Contemporary Jewish Religious Thought, ed. Arthur A Cohen and Paul Mendes-Floret,

Courage to Care: Rescuers of Jews During the Holocaust, Eds Carol Rittner and Sondra Myers, New York, New York University Press, 1996

Cowan, P.R, Mixed Blessings: Overcoming the Stumbling Blocks in an Interfaith Marriage, Penguin, New York, 1987

Cragg, Kenneth, Palestine::the Prize and Price of Zion, London, Cassell, 1997

Disraeli's Jewishness, ed. Todd M Endelman and Kushner Tony, London, Vallentine Mitchell, 2002

Doni, Hayim Halevy, To Be a Jew, New York, 1972.

Dow, M, The Star of the Return: Judaism After the Holocaust, West Point, CT, Greenwood Press, 1991

Dunn, D.G. The Parting of the Ways, London, SCM Press, 1991,

Eban, Abba, Personal Witness: Israel through my eyes, Jonathan Cape, London, 1993.

Ellis, Marc H, Unholy Alliance, London, SCM Press, 1997

Everett, Robert A, Christianity Without Antisemitism: James Parkes and the Jewish Christian Encounter, Pergamon Press, 1993.

Fackenheim, E L, To Mend the World: Foundations of Future Jewish Thought, New York, 1994.

Feminist Interpretation, Schottroff, Luise; Schroer Silvia; Wacker, Marie-Theres,

Minneapolis, Fortress Press, 1998.
Fifteen Years of Catholic-Jewish Dialogue, Rome, Libreria Editrice Vatican, 1985
Figes, Eva, Journey to Nowhere, Granta Books, London 2008.
Forms of Prayer, The Movement for Reform Judaism, London, 2008.
Franz Rosenzweig, The New Thinking, New edition, Peter Lang, 2020
Fried, Stephen, The New Rabbi: A Congregation Searches for Its Leader, New York, Bantam, 2002
Fry, H, (ed.), Christian-Jewish Dialogue, Exeter, Exeter University Press, 1996..
Fry, Helen, Montagu, Rachel and Scholefield, Lynne,(eds) Women's Voices:
Gager, J G, The Origins of Anti-Semitism, Oxford, Oxford University Press, 1983
Gartner, Lloyd P, History of the Jews in Modern Times, Oxford University Press, 2001.
Gilbert, Martin, Israel, London, Doubleday, 1998.
Gilbert, Martin, The Jews of Hope: the Plight of Soviet Jewry, London, Macmillan, 1984
Gold, M, Jews Without Money, New York, Caroll and Graf, 1930.
Goldberg, David and Rayner, John,The Jewish People: Their History and Their Religion, London, Penguin, 1989
Goldhagen,Daniel, Hitler's Willing Executioners, Abacus, 1992
Gospels and Rabbinic Judaism, ed. M Hilton and G Marshall, London, SCM Press, 1988
Gryn, Hugo, Chasing Shadows, London, Viking, 2000.
Harris, K, Attlee, Weidenfeld and Nicolson, 1982.
Hartman, D, Jews and Christians Between Past and Future
Hear Our Voice: Women Rabbis Tell Their Stories, Ed. Sybil Sheridan, London
Hilton, M, The Christian Effect on Jewish Life, London, SCM Press, 1994
Holocaust and Genocide Studies, Pergamon Press. 1988
Holocaust Poetry, Complied by Hilda Schiff, London, HarperCollins (Fount), 1995.
Interfaith Worship and Prayer, eds, Lewis, C and Cohn-Sherbok, London, Jessica Kingsley, 2019
Iturbe, A (English translation, Thwaites, L Z), The Librarian of Auschwitz (the story of Dita) London, EburyPress, 2017
Jacobs, Louis, Helping with Inquiries: An Autobiography, London, Vallentine, Mitchell, 1989,
Jacobs, Louis, The Jewish Religion, Oxford, Oxford University Press, 1995
Jerusalem Perspectives, Ed Peter Schneider and GeoffreyWigoder, London
Jewish Annotated New Testament, eds Amy-Jill Levine and Marc Zvi Brettler, Oxford,Oxford University Press, 2010
Jewish Ladies' Visiting Association 10th Annual report, 1893-4
Jewish Year Book 2008.
Jews and Christians Speak of Jesus, Ed. Arthur Zannoni, Mineapolis, Fortress Press, 1944
Johnson, Paul A History of the Jews, London, Weidenfeld and Nicolson, 1987,
Jones, Pamela Fletcher, The Jews of Britain, Moreton in the Marsh, The Windrush Press, 1990,
Jews and Christians in Conversation, eds Kessler,E; Pawlikowski, J; Banki, J, Cambridge, Orchard Academic, 2000
Judaism and Ecology, ed Rose A; London, Cassell Publishing, 1992.
Karlen, Neal Shanda: The Making and Breaking of a Self-Loathing Jew, New York,
King, Andrea, If I'm Jewish and You're Christian, What Are the Kids? New York, UAHC Press, 1993

Klassen, William, The Contribution of Jewsih Scholars to the Quest for the Historical Jesus, Cambridge, CJCR Press, 200

Klenicki, Leon ed., The Passover Celebration, Ed. Chicago, Liturgy Training Publications,

Kraemer, Lottie A Lifelong House, Sutton, Surrey, Hippopotamus Press, 1983.

Kronish, R, The Other Peace Process, Plymouth, Hamilton Books, 2017

Küng, H, Judaism, (e.t., John Bowden) London, SCM Press, 1992

Lapide, Pinchas and Küng Hans, Brother or Lord, Fount Books, 1977,

Lewis, C and Cohn-Sherbok, D, Interfaith Worship and Prayer, London, Jessica Kingsley, 2019

Lindsay, Paul, The Synagogues of London, London, Vallentine Mitchell, 1993

Lipman, V D, A Century of Social Service, 1859-1959, London 1959.

Littell, Marcia, Liturgies on the Holocaust, Lewiston, The Edwin Mellen Press, 1986.

Maccoby, Hyam, Judaism in the First Century, London, Sheldon Press, 1989

Magonet, Jonathan, The Explorer's Guide to Judaism, London, Hodder and Stoughton, 2003.

Magonet, Jonathan, Talking to the Other, London, Tauris, 2003.

Magonet, Jonathan, The Subversive Bible, London, SCM Press, 1997

Magonet, Jonathan, Bible Lives, London, SCM Press, 1992

Magonet, Jonathan, A Rabbi Reads the Torah, London, SCM, 2013

Magonet, Jonathan, A Rabbi's Bible, London, SCM Press, 1991

Making of Modern Anglo-Jewry, Ed David Cesarani, Oxford , Blackwell, 1990

Martin, Gilbert, Israel, London, Transworld Publishers, Doubleday, 1998.

Mendes-Flohr, Paul and Reinharz, Jehuda, The Jew in the Modern World, Documentary.

Miller, Ronald, Dialogue and Disagreement Franz Rosenzweig's Relevance, Lanham, MD, University Press of America, 1998

Montefiore, Hugh, On Being a Jewish Christian, London, Hodder and Stoughton, 1998

Modern Jewish Philosophy, Ed Michael L Morgan and Peter Eli Gordon, Cambridge

Modern Judaism, Ed Nicholas de Lange and Miri Freud-Kandel, Oxford, Oxford University, 2005

Montefiore, S S, Jerusalem: the Biography, London, Weidenfeld and Nicholson, 2011

Moyaert Marianne and Geldhof Joris, Ritual Participation and Interreligious Dialogue, Basingstoke, MacMillan, 2019:

Muir, Edwin Collected Poems by, Ed by Willa Muir. Oxford, Oxford University Press,1960

Neuberger, Julia, On Being Jewish, London, William Heinemann (Mandarin Pbk), 1996.

Neusner, Jacob, Invitation to the Talmud, San Francisco, Harper and Row, 1989

Nicholl, Donald, The Testing of Hearts, London, Marshall Morgan and Scott, 1989

Nickelsburg, George W E Jewish Literature Between the Bible and the Mishnah, London, SCM Press, 1981

No Going Back, Edited by Carol Rittner and Stephen D Smith, London, Quill Press.

Noth, Martin A History of Israel, London, SCM Press, Second edtn, 1958

On Being a Jewish Feminist: A Reader, ed Susannah Heschel, New York, Schocken Books. 1995

Our Lonely Journey, Remembering the Kindertransports, Ed Stephen D Smith, Newark, Paintbrush Publications, 199 1996.

Oxford Dictionary of World Religions, Ed John Bowker, Oxford, Oxford University

Press, 1997

Parkes, J, The Conflict of Church and Synagogue, London, Socino Press, 1934.

Pawlikowski, John, Christ in the Light of the Christian-Jewish Dialogue, Ramsey, N. J. Paulist Press, 1982

Pawlikowski, John, What are they saying about Jewish-Christian Relations, New York, Paulist Press, 1980

Peck, A J, Philadelphia, Fortress Press, 1982

Plaskow,Judith, Standing Again at Sinai: Judaism from a Feminist Perspective, New York, 1991

Polack, Albert and Lawrence, Joan, Cup of Life, London, SPCK, 1976

Remembering for the Future, Eds John K Roth and Elisabeth Maxwell, Basingstoke, Palgrave, 2001

Riah Abu El-Assal, Caught in Between: The Extraordinary Story of an Arab Christian Israeli Palestinian, London, SPCK, 1992.

Riff, M, The Face of Survival: Jewish Life in Eastern Europe Past and Present, London, Valentine Mitchell, 1992

Rittner, C, Smith, Stephen D, Steinfeldt, , Irena, The Holocaust and the Christian World, London,

Romain Jonathan, Till Faith Us Do Part, London, Fount/HarperCollins, 1996

Romain, Jonathan, Faith and Practice, London, RSGB, 1996

Romain, Jonathan, The Jews of England, London, Jewish Chronicle Publications, 1985

Ross, Tamar, Expanding the Place of Torah: Orthodoxy and Feminism, Waltham, Brandeis University Press, 2004

Rubenstein, William and Hilary, Philosemitism, Basingstoke, Macmillan, 1999.

Sacks, Jonathan, Community of Faith, London, Peter Halban, 1995

Sacks, Jonathan, Future Tense, London, Hodder and Stoughton, 2009

Sacks, Jonathan, Manchester University Press, 1992

Sacks, Jonathan, The Great Partnership, London, Hodder and Stoughton, 2011

Sacks, Jonathan, The Dignity of Difference, London,Continuum 2002.

Sacks, Jonathan, Faith in the Future, London, Darton, Longman and Todd, 1995,

Sacks, Jonathan, The Persistence of Faith, London, Weidenfeld and Nicolson, 1991

Sacks, Jonathan, To Heal a Fractured World, The Ethics of Responsibility, London, Continuum, 2005

Sanders, E P, Judaism: Practice and Belief, 63 BCE-66CE, London, SCM Press, 1992

Sandmel, Samuel, Juidaism and Christian Beginnings, New York, Oxford University Press, 1978

Sands, P, East West Street, London, Weidenfeld and Nicholson, 2016

Schimmel, S, Wounds Not Healed by Time, The Power of Repentance and Forgiveness, Oxford, Oxford University Press, 2002

Schwartz, Mimi, Good Neighbours, Bad Times Lincoln,, University of Nebraksa Press, USA,

Select Poems of Jacob Glatstein, New York, October House. Date

Shapira, A, The Seventh Day: Soldiers talk About the Six-Day War, London, Deutsch, 1971.

Shapira, A, What Israel Means to Me, Hoboken, New Jersey, Wiley and Sons, 2006.

Sharing One Hope, London, Church House Publishing, 2001.

Simon, Maurice, Israel Baalshem, His Life and Times, London, Jewish Religious Educational Publications, 1953

Simpson, W W, Jewish Prayer and Worship, London, SCM Press, 1965

Simpson, W W and Weyl, Ruth, The Story of the International Council of Christians and Jews, ICCJ, 2010

Solomon, Norman Judaism and World Religion, London, Macmillan, 1991.

Stemberger, G, Jewish Contemporaries of Jesus, London, Fortress Press, 1995h,

Stifan Justice, and only Justice, Maryknoll, NY, Orbis Books 1989;

Soul Searching – Studies in Judaism and Psychotherapy, Ed Cooper, Howard, 1988

Then and Now – Recollections of Jewish Life in Oxford, ed Jackson, Freda, Oxford, Oxford Jewish Centre, 1992

Tolan, Sandy, The Lemon Tree, London, Transworld Publishers, 2006

Wiesel, E and Friedlander (eds.), The Six Days of Destruction, London, Pergamon, date

Wilchinski, Myer, A History of a Sweater. Video on u-tube

Wollaston, Isabel, Auschwitz and the Politics of Comemoration:

Wouk, Herman, This is My God, (1960), London, Fontana Books, 1979, York, Penguin, 1987

Zuidema,Willem, God's Partner: An Encounter with Judaism, London, SCM Press, 1987.

NOTES

1 See Marcus Braybrooke, Children of One God,
2 Jonathan Magonet, The Explorers Guide to Judaism, Hodder and Stoughton, 1998, p.9
3 Quoted by Willem Zuidema, God's Partner: An Encounter with Judaism, London, SCM Press, 1987, p. 1
4 Martin Gilbert, Israel, London, Transworld Publishers, Doubleday, 1998, p. 270.
5 http://www.israelnationalnews.com/News/News.aspx/221859
6 bod.org.uk/jewishfaith.info
7 Quoted by David Goldberg and John Rayner in The Jewish People: Their History and Their Religion, London, Penguin 1989 edtn,
8 See, for example, Neal Karlen, Shanda: the Making and Breaking of a Self-Loathing Jew, New York, Touchstone, 2004, passim
9 Dow Marmur, The Star of the Return: Judaism After the Holocaust, West Point, CT, Greenwood Press, 1991, quoted by Tony Bayfield, Being Jewish Today, London, Bloomsbury Continuum, 2019, p.27
10 Elliott Abrams, Faith or Fear, New York, The Free Press, 1997, p.193
11 See further Norman Cantor's gloomy view in The Sacred Chain, London, HarperCollins, 1995
12 Jonathan Sacks, The Persistence of Faith, London, Weidenfeld and Nicolson, 1991
13 See further Jonathan Romain, The Jews of England, London, Jewish Chronicle Publications, 1985
14 See Pamela Fletcher Jones in The Jews of Britain, Moreton in the

Marsh, The Windrush Press, 1990, p.75.
Like Barabas in the play, Lopez was put to death in 1594, falsely accused of plotting against the Queen's life. Marlowe, who wrote his play in 1590, can hardly have foreseen this.
15 Romain, op.cit, p. 77
16 Geoffrey Alderman, Modern British Jewry, Oxford, Clarendon Press, 1992, p. 6
17 Romain, op.cit pp 117-121.
18 Quoted by Alderman, p. 51

19 Roman Catholics were granted political rights in 1829.

20 Alderman, p. 64

21 Disraeli's Jewishness, Ed. Todd M Endelman and Tony Kushner, London, Vallentine Mitchell 2002, p. 3.

22 Quoted in The Jew in the Modern World, A Documentary History, ed. Paul Mendes-Floh and Jehuda Reinharz, Oxford, Oxford University Press, 1995, pp. 258-9

23 Disraeli's Jewishness, op.cit, p.3

24 The Making of Modern Anglo-Jewry, Ed David Cesarani, Basil Blackwell, Oxford 1990. p.2.

25 Quoted by Alderman, p. 71

26 From the Preface to the Fifth Edition of Benjamin Disraeli' Coningsby or the Generation, May 1849

27 David Cesarani, The Jewish Chronicle and Anglo-Jewry 1841-1991 Cambridge University Press, 1994, p.45.

28 Alderman, pp. 69-70

29 From the Preface to the Fifth Edition of Benjamin Disraeli's Conningsby, May1849, pp. 19-25

30 G Aguilar, History of the Jews of England, Edinburgh, Chambers Miscellany, vol.18, no 153, 1847, p. 16

31 Alderman, p. 73.

32 V.D Lipman, A Century of Social Service, 1859-1959, London, 1959, p.10.

33 The Jewish Chronicle and Anglo-Jewry p. 248

34 The Jewish Chronicle, 4.5.1883.

35 Quoted by Alderman, p. 120.

36 Adler, p. 114

37 Beatrice Potter in Life and Labour of the People of London, quoted by Romain, p.124

38 Myer Wilchinski, A History of a Sweater, quoted by Romain, p. 125

39 Rev G S Reaney in The Destitute Alien in Great Britain, quoted by Romain, p.131.

40 J L Silver in The Royal Commission on Alien Immigration, quoted by Romain, p. 131

41 Arthur Balfour in 1905, quoted by Romain

42 Yiddish iderived from German dialects with added vocabulary drawn from Hebrew and Slavonic languages. It is written in Heb rew characters and was spoken in Eastern European countries.

43 Alderman, p. 128

44 Alderman, p. 138

45 Rosalyn Livshin in The Making of Modern Anglo-Jewry, p. 81

46 Jewish Ladies' Visiting Association 10th Annual report, 1893-4I, quoted by Livshin, p. 82

47 Quoted by Livshin, p.86.

48 Quoted by Livshin, p.86.
49 Quoted in Lipman, Social History, p. 147
50 Quoted by Livshin, p. 93.
51 Alderman, p. 233
52 Jewish Chronicle, 23.4.1909.
53 Quoted by Alderman, p.222
54 Quoted by Alderman, p.229
55 Quoted by Livshin, 94
56 Quoted by Alderman, p. 251.
57 The letter is reproduced in The Jew in the Modern World: p. 580
58 From a Home Office note by Sir Samuel amuel Hoare, quoted by
    Alderman, p. 279
59 Report of the speech of Chief Rabbi Hertz in the Jewish Chronicle,
    17.3.1944.
60 Figures are taken from the Jewish Year Book 2008.
61 The title of a Runnymede Trust Report, 1997.
62 Tony Bayfield, Being Jewish Today, London, Bloomsbury, 2019,
    p. 66.
63 https://www.thejc.com/education/education-news/orthodox-jews- no-
future-warns-rabbi-aaron-
64   https://www.jpost.com/diaspora/jewxit-could-300000-jews-flee-the-
uk-592214
65   https://www.timesofisrael.com/uk-chief-rabbi-election-is-over-but-
concerns-over-anti- semitism-racism
66 Board of Deputies Report www.boardofdeputies.org.uk/page.php/
Publications/242/1/1
67 Alderman, p.389.
68 See also below in the chapter 'At the Synagogue.'
69 See below
70   https://www.theguardian.com/uk-news/2015/oct/16/majority-of-
british-jews-will-be- ultra-orthodox-by-end-of-century'
71 Alderman, p.145
72 Alderman, p.150
73 Alderman, p.396
74 Nurit Stadler in Modern Judaism, Ed Nicholas de Lange and Miri
    Freud-Kandel, Oxford, Oxford University Press, 2005, p. 222. See
    also Louis Jacobs, Oxford Concise Companio to the Jewish Religion.
75 The Jewish Year Book 2008, p. 11.
76 Alderman, p. 203
77 Quoted by Alderman, p. 204.
78 L H Montagu, 'Spiritual Possibilities of Judaism Today,' Jewish
    Quarterly Review, January 1899, p. 216 and p. 218.
79 www.liberaljudaism.org
80 L. Jacobs Helping with Inquiries: An Autobiography, London,
    Vallentine, Mitchell, pp.179- 80

81 p. 137
82 p. 138
83 p. 155
84 p. 156
85 p. 198.
86 The full list of Jewish Presidents in 2019
   The Most Revd and Rt. Hon Rowan Williams, The Archbishop of Canterbur, Sir Jonathan Sacks, The Chief Rabbi of Great Britain and the Commonwealth
   H.E. Rt. Rev. Cormac Murphy O' Connor, The Cardinal Archbishop of Westminster Rabbi Abraham Levy, Spanish and Portuguese Sephardic Congregations
   H. E. Rt. Rev Gregorios, the Archbishop of Thyateira and Great Britain
   Rabbi Dr. Tony Bayfield, Head: Movement for Reform Judaism Commissioner
   Elizabeth Matear, Moderator of the Free Church Group
   Rabbi Danny Rich: Chief Executive Liberal Judaism.
   Rt. Revd David Lunan, The Moderator of the General Assembly
   of the Church of Scotland
   Rabbi Jonathan Wittenberg. Assembly of Masorti Synagogues
87 https://chiefrabbi.org/history-chief-rabbinate/
88 https://www.bod.org.uk/who-we-are/
89 Alderman, pp. 409-410
90 Faith or Fear, pp. 189
91 faith or Fear p. 193. Author's italics.
92 https://www.woolf.cam.ac.uk/
93https://religionmediacentre.org.uk/factsheets/faith-schools-in-the-uk/
94 Hayim Halevy Donin, To Be a Jew, New York, 1972, p.35 Quoted by
   David S Ariel,in What Do Jews Believe, London, Rider, 1995, p. 135
95 David Ariel, What Do Jews Believe: the Jewish Faith Examined,
   New York, Schocken and London, Rider, 1996, p. 135
96 Norman Solomon, Judaism and World Religion, London,
   Macmillan, 1991, p.7
97 Men. 29b
98 The Torah: A Modern Commentary, Ed W G Plaut, New York,
   Union of American Hebrew Congregations, 1981, p. xviii
99 The Torah: A Modern Commentary, p. xviii
100 Tony Bayfield, p. xix
101 Romain, p. 9
102 Louis Jacobs, p. 211
103 Romain, p. 134
104https://www.churchtimes.co.uk/articles/2016/15-july/news/uk/
more-jews-are-intermarrying
105 Angela Topolski in Ritual Participation
106https://www.thejc.com/news/uk-news/shuls-prepare-for-same-sex-

marriages-1.52595

107 www.chiefrabbi.org.

108 www.cardiffreformsyn.org.uk, quoting Rabbi Tony Bayfield.

109 Quoted on www.liberaljudaism.org/news_liturgypresscoverage.htm

110 Quoted on www.liberaljudaism.org/news_liturgypresscoverage.htm

111 Quoted on www.liberaljudaism.org/news_liturgypresscoverage.htm

112 David S Ariel, p.

113 The Authorised Daily Prayer Book of the Hebrew Congregations of the British Commonwealth of Nations, (English translation by S. Singer), London, Eyre and Spottiswoode, 1962, pp. 93-95.

114 Exodus 33, 20.

115 Genesis 26

116 Quoted by Ariel, p. 55.

117 Micah4, 1ff

118 Jonathan Sacks, To Heal a Fractured World, The Ethics of Responsibility, London, Continuum, 2005, p. 275

119 Deuteronomy 6, 9.

120 Forms of Prayer, London, The Movement for Reform Judaism, 2008, p. 437.

121 Genesis 2, 2.

122 Exodus 23, 12.

123 Deuteronomy, 5,12.

124 I Maccabees, 2, 41.

125 Quoted from 'The Shabbat Laws,' which discusses the rules in some detail

126www.chabad.org/library/article_cdo/aid/95907/jewish/The- Shabbat-Laws.htm

127 Quoted by W Zuidema, God's Partner, p. 73.

128 The reference is to Chief Rabbi R Dreyfus.

129 Psalm, 119, 5.

130 Forms of Prayer, p.447 Proverbs, chapter 31.

131www.chabad.org/library/howto/wizard_cdo/aid/113425/jewish/ What-is-Kosher.htm
    Exodus 23, 19

134 This is based on material from www.koshercertification.org.uk/ whatdoe.html   where more details are to be found.

135 Exodus 12, 15

136 Julia Neuberger, On Being Jewish, William Heinemann Mandarin, 1996, p.91

137 Quoted by Neuberger, p 96-7

138 Exodus 21, 10

139 Ber 9.5

140 The translation and comments are from the website of the Orthodox Union in USA

141 Deuteronomy 6, 8

142 Deuteronomy 22, 12 and Numbers 15, 38

143 Barabara Borts, Women and Tallit, quoted by J Romain, p. 94

145 Board of Deputies

146 Megillah 29a

147 Psalm 74, 8

148 Luke 4, 16

149 For example, See Acts 14, 1

150 Tamid, 5,1; Yoma,7,1

151 Quoted by Paul Lindsay, The Synagogues of London, London,
    Vallentine Mitchell, 1993, p. 38.

152 A casting is a metal, often silver, container

153 Deuteronomy 5, 8.

154 David Ariel, What Do Jews Believe, p. 188

155 Louis Jacobs, Jewish Religion, p. 181.

156 W. Zuidema, p. 12.

158 Exodus 37, 17-24

159 Forms of Prayer, p. 154

160 Genesis 17, 1-14

161 The Daily Prayer Book, pp 401-2

162 Jonathan Romain, Faith and Practice,pp.45-6

163 Forms of Prayer, p. 350

164 Singer, p. 396 - p. 397

170 D. Hartman, Jews and Christians between Past and Future.

171 Herman Wouk, This is My God, (1960), London, Fontana Books,
    1979, p.167

172 George W E Nickelsburg, Jewish Literature Between the Bible and the
Mishnah   London, SCM Press 1981. See also www.chabad.org/library/
article_cdo/aid/901656/jewish/ Introduction-to-Mishneh-Torah.htm

173 Quoted in The Blackwell Reader in Judaism, Ed Jacob Neusner
    and Alan J Avery-Peck, Oxford, Blackwell, 2001, pp. 60-61.

174 Sanhedrin, 88b

175 Passages are quoted by Lee I A Levine in Christianity and
    Rabbinic Judaism, p. 135.

176 Quoted by Levine, p.136.

177 Acts of the Apostles, 5, 38-9 (Jerusalem Bible).

178 Quoted by Levine, p. 138.

179 Quoted by J Magonet, the Explorer's Guide to Judaism, p. 112.

180 J Magonet, p. 105.

181 Mishnah Gittin, 9, 10, quoted in The Gospels and Rabbinic
    Judaism, ed M Hilton and G Marshall, London, SCM Press, 1988,
    p. 126

182 Gittan, 90, quoted in The Gospels and Rabbinic Judaism, p. 127.

183 John, 20, 16

184 Numbers 27, 22

185 Stephen Fried, The new Rabbi, A Congregation Searches for Its Leader, New York

186 *op.cit.*

187 Rosh-Ha-Shanah, 16a

188 Quoted in Celebration: The Book of Jewish Festivals, Ed Naomi Black, London, Collins 1987, p. 15

189 From the Rosh Hashana mussaf service

190 Nehemiah, 8, 1-10.

191 Days of Awe in Forms of Prayer, 8th edtn, 1985, p. 273

192 Leviticus, chapter 16ff. Critical scholars assume the passages are a description of how Yom Kippur was observed in the Temple.

194 Isaiah, 58, 6-7.

193 Forms of Prayer, p.240.

194 Jeremiah, 29, 7.

195 Exodus 32.

196 Leviticus 23, 24

197 Genesis 22, 13..

198 Leviticus 23, 42-3

199 Qouted in Celebration, *op cit.*

200 From the Rosh Hashana mussaf service.

201 Hugo Gryn, Chasing Shadows, London,Viking 2000, pp 250-251

202 Quoted from Days of Awe. The words are by Jan Fuchs (b. 1912)

203 op cit p. 792

204 *ibid*

205 Ahasuerus is also known as Ahashverosh and Ahashuerus

206 Megillah, 7b

207 Quoted in Days of Awe, p.589 The words are by Jan Fuchs (b.1912), a Jewish community worker. See also p.792

208 The term 'Hebrew' is a social designation for the Israelites. The word is used in the early books of the Bible, especially by non-Jews (Genesis 4,13; Genesis 39, 14;I Samuel 4, 6). The word may be derived from 'avar, which means to pass beyond or over. Israel was the name given to Jacob (Genesis 32,22-32). His descendants became known as Israelites, a term often used in the Bible. The word 'Jew' is derived through Latin from the Hebrew word Yehudi, meaning from the tribe of Judah. When after Solomon's death, the kingdom was divided, the north became known as Israel. The south was located in Judea, the territory of the tribe of Judah. In the book of Esther (2,5) Mordecai is described as a Jew, althoug he was from the tribe of Benjamin. The word 'Hebrew' is, of course, also still used of the language.

209 Exodus 2, 1

210 Quoted by Louis Jacobs, Jewish Religion, University Press, Oxford, 1999, p. 240.

211 The Ethics of the Fathers 6, 6, quoted by Louis Jacobs, p. 240
212 The Ethics of the Fathers, 6,4, quoted by Louis Jacobs, p. 241
213 Quoted by Louis Jacobs, p. 241 from Joshua, 1, 8.
214 See Psalm, 119, 105
215 Avot, 3,2.
216 David S Ariel, What Do Jews Believe, London, Rider, 1995, p. 22
217 Forms of Prayer, p. 226. The quotation is from Isaiah, 6, 3.

   Similar words are used in the Sanctus at Christian services of
      Mass or Holy Communion.
218 W.G. Plaut, The Torah, p. 503
219 Psalm 78, 23-28
220 See further in the chapter 'At the Synagogue
222 Psalm 119, verse 97 and 101.
223 For information about the British Holocaust Memorial Day and
               for resources go to www.holocaustmemorialday.gov.uk.
resources are also available from The Council of Christians and Jews
www.ccj.org.uk
 and The Holocaust Centre at Beth Shalom www.bethshalom.com
224 See further Wollaston, Isabel, Auschwitz and the Politics of Com
      memoration: the Christianization of The Holocaust, Holocaust
      Educational Trust, 2000.
225 A Fiedlander, p.161 also Six Days of Destruction
226 Marcia Littell, Liturgies on the Holocaust, The Edwin Mellen
      Press, Lewiston, 1986 pp. 11-17 344 Albert Friedlander, The Six
      Days of Destruction, Ed. E Wiesel and Albert Friedlander,
      London, Pergamon Press, 1988, p. 60
230 Maimonides
231 Louis Jacobs, Jewish Religion, p. 236
232 Jonathan Sacks
233 A Bayfield p.149
234 Steven Nadler in Modern Jewish Philosophy, Eds Michael L
      Morgan,Peter Eli Gordon, Cambridge University Press, 2007, p.16
235 Sometimes spelt 'Chasidic.' See further Maurice Simon, Israel
      Baalshem, His Life and Times, London, Jewish Religious
      Educational Publications. 1953.
236 Deuteronomy 10, 20 says 'Thou shalt cleave to Him.'
237 Quoted in The Oxford Dictionary of World Religions, Ed Joh n
      Bowker, Oxford, Oxford University Press, 1997, p. 309.
       No reference is given
238 Paul Johnson, A History of the Jews, London, Weidenfeld and
      Nicolson, 1987, p. 299.
239 This teaching is known as 'deicide' and since the Holocaust has
      been repudiated by almost all churches.

240 Jerusalem, p.97

241 Zechariah, 8, 22.

242 Quoted in The Jew in the Modern World, p. 258.

243 Paul Johnson, p. 300.

244 David S Ariel, What do Jews Believe?   'Identity theory' is defined in the Enyclopaedia Britannica (15th edition, 1977) as the philosophical view of Materialism that mind and matter, however capable of being logically distinguished, are in actuality expressions of a single reality that is material. It may also be used to imply that certain characteristics pertain to certain races.

245 www. quora.com

246 These words from a letter are quoted by Peter Eli Gordon in Modern Jewish Philosophy, p. 125.

247 Franz Rosenzweig, 'The New Thinking' quoted by Peter Eli Gordon, p. 123

248 Peter Eli Gordon, p. 126

249 Encyclopaedia Britannica, 1977, 3, p. 358

250 Although written in the first decade of the twentieth century, these books were not translated into English until after the Second World War.

251 *Ich und Du* was published in 1923. The first English translation was published in 1937. Walter Kaufman, a critic of Buber, who produced a second translation of the work, preferred 'You' – arguing that 'Thou' was archaic and impersonal.

252 Martin Buber, Between Man and Man, Routledge , 1947, 2002, pp. 250-51.

253 David Novak in Modern Judaism, p. 285

254 Abraham Joshua Heschel, God in Search of Man, New York, Farrar, Strauss and Cudahy, 1955, p. 185

255 Quoted by Novak, p. 286

256 Heschel, God in Search of Man, p. 240-3.

257 Quoted from 'No Religion is an Island,' by Katie Chowdhury in Interreligious Insight, April 2009, p. 31.

258 Quoted by Tamar Rudavsky in Modern Jewish Philosophy from Tamar Ross, Expanding the Place of Torah: Orthodoxy and Feminism, Waltham, Brandeis University Press, 2004. p.xiii., quoting from Yeshayahu Leibowitz

259 Expanding the Place of Torah: Orthodoxy and Feminism, p.xvii

260 Susan Grossman in The Blackwell Reader in Judaism, Ed by Jacob Neusner and Alan J Avery-Peck, Oxford, Blackwell, 2001, p. 323

261 Jonathan Magonet, Talking to the Other, London, Tauris, 2003, p. 87

262 Rabbi Alexandra Wright in Hear Our Voice, Women Rabbis tell their Stories p. 156.

263 Rachel Montagu in Hear Our Voices:

264 Quoted in The Torah, edited by W G Plaut, p. 159.

265 Ellen M Umansky in The Blackwell Reader in Judaism, p. 322.

266 Judith R Baskin in The Blackwell Reader in Judaism, p. 331.

269 Rachel Montagu is Women's Voices: New Perspectives for the
     Christian-Jewish Dialogue, Ed Helen Fry, Rachel Montagu and Lynne
Scholefield, London, SCM Press, 2005, p. 28. The quotation from Judith
Plaskow (1982), is from 'The Right Question is Theological' in On Being
a Jewish Feminist: A Reader, ed Susannah Heschel, New York, Schocken
Books, p. 222-33

270 Judith Plaskow, Standing Again at Sinai: Judaism from a
     Feminist Perspective, New York, 1991

271 See further my Christian-Jewish Dialogue: the Next Steps,
     London, SCM Press, 2000, p. 7

272 From 'We All Stood Together' by Rachel Adler, quoted in
     The Blackwell Reader in Judaism, p. 321

273 C.K Barrett, The Gospel According to St John, London, SPCK,
     1958, p, 469

274 Numbers 27, 22-3.

276 Louis Jacobs, Jewish Religion, see entry under 'Rabbi'.

279 www.religionmediacentre.org.uk/factsheets/faith-schools-in-
     the-uk/

280 The Yad Vashem Memorial has stated that the Nazis did not produce
soap with fat which was extracted from Jewish corpses on an industrial
scale, saying that the Nazis may have frightened camp inmates by
deliberately circulating rumors in which they claimed that they were able
to extract fat from human corpses, turn it into soap,
mass-produce and distribute it.

280 E L Fackenheim, To Mend the World: Foundations of Future
     Jewish Thought, New York, Schocken Books, 1982, p. 12

281 Arthur Waskow, Quoted from Out of the Whirlwind, ed Steven
     Jacobs, East Rockway, Cummings and Hathaway, 1996,
     pp. 370-371

282 Eva Figes, Journey to Nowhere, Granta Books, London 2008,
     pp. 139-140.

283 Journey to Nowhere, p. 7

284 Mimi Schwartz, Good Neighbours, Bad Times, University of
     Nebraksa Press, Lincoln, USA, 2008, p. 63

286 From, Lottie Kraemer, A Lifelong House, Sutton, Surrey,
     Hippopotamus Press, 1983, p.45

287 Websters New International Dictionary, 1924 Edition.

288 From, Lottie Kraemer, A Lifelong House, Sutton, Surrey,
     Hippopotamus Press, 1983, p.45

289 Remembering for the Future, Eds Joh n K Roth and Elisabeth
     Maxwell, Basingstoke, Palgrave, 2001, vol 1, p. 21.

290 Paul Johnson, A History of the Jews, Weidenfeld and Nicolson,

1987, pp. 510-11. The quotation is from Samuel Rajzman, which Johnson quotes from Martin Gilbert, The Holocaust : the Jewish Tragedy, London, Collins 1986, p. 457 See also

http://www.hitlerschildren.com/article/638-holocaust-gas-chambers'

291 Churchill was referring, in a letter written on 11 July 1944 to Anthony Eden, Foreig Secretary, specifically to the slaughter of Hungarian Jewry, in his The Second War, VI, Triumph andTragedy, Boston 1953, p. 693.

292 The figures are quoted from Lloyd P Gartner, History of the Jews in Modern Times, Oxford University Press, 2001, p. 377.

293 Poem by Nelly Sachs, translated by Ruth and Matthew Mead from Holocaust Poetry, Complied by Hilda Schiff, London, HarperCollins (Fount), 1995, p. 67

294www.thejc.com/comment/analysis/what-is-the-ihra-definition-of-antisemitism-and- why-has-labour-outraged-jews-by-rejecting-it

295 The word is sometimes spelt without a hyphen

296 Quoted from The Face of Survival: Jewish Life in Eastern Europe Past and Present, ed. Michael Riff, London, Vallentine Mitchell, 1992, pp.129-130

297 Johnson, pp. 472-3.

298 Quoted by Fred Wright, Father Forgive Us, Monarch Books 2002. In his last testament, dictated to Goebbels and others, Hitler blamed the Jews for starting the war.

299 Librarian at Auschwitz

300 From the Lambeth Conference of Anglican Bishops 1988 statement on 'Jews,Christians and Muslims: the Way of Dialogue.'

301 The Holocaust and the Christian World, Ed Carol Rittner, Stephen D Smith, Irena Steinfeldt, London, Kuperard, 2000, p. 62-3

302 The Holocaust and the Christian World, p. 62

303 Pope John Paul

304 Quoted, without reference, in the Encyclopaedia Britannica.

305 For more information see Keith Clements, Bonhoeffer and Britain, London, Churches Together in Britain, 2006

306 See The Holocaust and the Christian World, pp. 64-67.

307 Vera in Our Lonely Journey, Remembering the Kindertransports, Ed Stephen D Smith Newark, Paintbrush Publications, 1999, p.10 308 op.cit. 18.

309   https://en.wikipedia.org/wiki/List_of_Righteous_Among_the_Nations_by_country

310 Quoted by David Blumenthal, F acing the Abusing God: a Theology of Protest, Louisville, Westminster/JohnKnox, p.223

311 Quoted in The Holocaust and the Christian World, p. 163. No source is given.

312 *Goldhanger*

313 Quoted by Blumenthal, op.cit, pp. 222-3, from E Kurek-Lesik, 'The Role of Polish Nuns in the Rescue of Jews, 1939-45. See also Eva
    Fleischner in The Holocaust and the Christian World,
        pp.156-7 and *Mimi Schwartz in No Going Back*. p.

314 Quoted in The Six Days of D: Meditations Towards Hope, Ed Elie
    Wiesel and Friedlander, Oxford, Pergamon Press, 1982

315 The Reader's Digest Universal Dictionary, London 1987, revised edtn. 1998, p. 1566.

316 Steven Katz 'Jewish Faith After the Holocaust: Four Approaches' in Post-Holocaust Dialogues:Critical Studies in Modern Jewish Thought, New York, New York University Press, pp. 141-173, - 2.

317 Quoted in Dan Cohn-Sherbok, Holocaust Theology, London,
    Lamp, 1989, p. 16

318 Jeremiah 31, 29.

319 See Norman Solomon, Judaism and World Religion, p. 181 and
    footnote p, 271.

320 Gershon Greenberg, 'Orthodox Theological Responses to the
    Holocaust' in Holocaust and Genocide Studies, III, 1988, p. 439,
        quoted by Solomon, pp.180-1.

321 Genesis 6, 5 and Jeremiah 3, 17.

322 See Isaiah 45. v. 7 and the first two chapters of Job

323 Deuteronomy 31, 18, Isaiah 45, 15, and Psalm 44, 23-24

324 Genesis 18, 24-25.

325 Exodus 32, 11-14

326 Dan Cohn-Sherbok, Holocaust Theology, p. 120, but see the
    whole of chapter 10.

327 Isaiah, chapter 53.

328 Approaches to Auschwitz, Eds Rubenstein, R and Roth,
    J K London, SCM Press, 1997, pp. 302- 336

329 See Emil Fackenheim, 'The Holocaust and the State of Israel:
    Their relation,' in Auschwitz:The Beginning of a New Era'
    Ed Eva Fleischner,1977, pp.205-15

330 Jacob Glatstein, ' Dead Men Don't Praise God' in Select Poems of
    Jacob Glatstein, New York, October House, pp.68-70

331 The Scribe – Journal of Babylonian Jewry, March 1986, No. 18.

332 Emil Fackenheim in Contemporary Jewish Religious Thought,
    Ed Arthur A Cohen and Paul Mendes-Flohret, Simon and Schuster
    Macmillan 1987, pp.309-408 quoted i The Holocaust Now, ed.
    Steven Jacobs, p. 381.

333 See Dan Cohn-Sherbok, pp. 81-82

334 Quoted by Marcus Braybrooke, Time to Meet, London, SCM Press,
    pp.123-6. See also Dialogue with a Difference, ed Tony Bayfield
    and Marcus Braybrooke, SCM Press

335 Phippe Sands, East West Street, London, Weidenfeld and

Nicholson, 1916

336 See, for example, the rather misleadingly named Forgiving
    Hitler – the Kathy Diosy Story as told by Kel Richards,
    Matthias Media, Sydney2002 and also Schimmel,
    Wounds Not Healed by Time, The Power of Repentance and
    Forgiveness, Oxford, Oxford University Press, pp. 67-70.
337 Schimmel, Wounds Not Healed by Time p. 69
338 Quoted by Marcus Braybrooke, Time to Meet, SCM Press, 1990, p. 113.
339 Julia Neuberger, On Being Jewish, p. 138.
340 Quoted in Time to Meet, p. 113.
349 For example, Kenneth Cragg, Palestine: the Prize and Price of Zion,
London, Cassell, 1997; Naim Stifan Ateek, Justice, and only Justice,
Maryknoll, NY, Orbis Books 1989; Naim Stifan Ateek, A Palestinian Cry
for Reconciliation, Orbis, 2008, Riah Abu El-Assal, Caught in Between: The
Extraordinary Story of an Arab Palestinian Christian Israeli, London, SPCK,
1999. See also, Dan Cohn-Sherbok and Dawoud el-Alami, The Palestine-
Israeli Conflict, Oxford, Oneworld, 2001, Justin Butcher, Walking to
Jerusalem, Hodder
    and Stoughton, 2018
350 Sandy Tolan, The Lemon Tree, London, Transworld Publishers, 2006
351 See The Seventh Day: Soldiers Talk about the Six-Day War, London,
1971, quoted by Kenneth Cragg, p.106 or see publications of 'Soldiers
Against Silence', see Gilbert, p106
352 Ari Shavat, My Promised Land, scribepublishing.co.uk, 2014 *passim*
353 Bat-Chen Shahak, The Bat-Chen Diaries, Minneapolis, Kar-Ben
    Publishing (Lerner Publishing), 2008, p.40
354 Daily Telegraph, 22.4.09, p. 11
355 p. 347
356 What Israel Means to Me
357 What Israel Means to Me p. 65
358 www.jewishvirtuallibrary.org/latest-population-statistics
359 What Israel Means to Me p. 291
360 What Israel Means to Me p. 284
361 What Israel Means to Me p. 347
362 What Israel Means to Me p. 119
363 What Israel Means to Me p. 54
364 What Israel Means to Me p. 255
365 Herod the Great was a Idumean
366 Quoted by Martin Gilbert in his authoritative book *Israel*,
    London, Doubleday pp. 34-5 and to whom, with his permission,
    I make frequent reference.
367 Herod the Great.
368, 1998, p.99
369 Quoted by Eva Figes in Journey to Nowhere, p. 127. No reference given.
370 http://www.yadvashem.org

371 Abba Eban, Personal Witness. Israel Through My Eyes, Jonathan Cape, London, 1993, quoted by Gilbert, p. 145

372 United Nations Special Committee on Palestine.

373 What Israel Means to Me, p.73

374 Gilbert 151

375 K Harris, Attlee, Weidenfeld and Nicolson, 1982, p. 390.

376 A vivid and deeply felt account from a Palestinian perspective is Kenneth Cragg's Palestine: The Prize and the Price of Zion, London, Cassell, 1997.

377 The capture of Lydda and Raala are vividly described in The Lemon Tree. The notes give details of the sources.

378 J Magonet, The Explorer's Guide to Judaism, Hodder and Stoughton, 1998, p. 265

379 Gilbert, p. 384.

380 The Seventh Day: Soldiers talk About the Six-Day War, London, 1971, quoted b K.Cragg, p. 95

381 Gilbert, p. 460

382 www.independent.co.uk/voices/robert-fisk-sabra.

383 Gilbert, p.534. 384 Gilbert , p.540. 385 Gilbert, p. 547

386 Gilbert, p. 543.

387 Gilbert, p. , p.555

388 Gilbert, p.567

389 Gilbert, p.570

390 Gilbert, pp. 569-70

391 Gilbert, p. 584-5

392 Sky News 31.3.09 - website 393 The Bat-Chen Diaries, p.6 394 The Israelis, p. 1

395 The Israelis, p. 250

396 In 1777 some 300 Hasidic Jews journeyed from Poland to Palestine and in 1812 about 400 followers of the learned Vilna Gaon made the journey from Lithuania

397 Tudor Parfit in Jerusalem Perspectives, Ed Peter Schneider and Geoffrey Wigoder, London Rainbow Group, 1976, p-. 6

398 Quoted by J.Magonet, p.251

399 Ibid

400 Benjamin Netanyahu, A Place Among the Nations: Israel and the World, London, Bantam, p. 29

401 Pogrom is a Russian word which means 'bloody mass attack'

402 Psalm 122 begins, 'I was glad when they said unto me, we will go up to the house of the Lord.'

403 Benjamin Netanyahu, p.35

404 Israelis, p. 187.

405 See below in the chapter 'At the Synagogue.'

406 p. 202

407 Many Jews avoid using the Hebrew name of God and dislike the

Jerusalem Bible's use of 'Yahweh.' Some Ultra-Orthodox extend this to the English word God and write it with an apostrophe instead of an 'o'- 'G'd.'

408 The Israelis, p. 250 For a detailed survey of religious observance by Israeli Jews, see jcpa.org/dje/ articlesZ/howrelism.htm
See also Amos Oz A Tale of Love and Darkness, London, Vintage, Random House 2005 and other books by the same author.

409 Named, quite appropriately, after the 'prickly pear,' a plant, which is widespread in the Negev.

410 Suhad in What Israel Means to Me, p. 269.

411 Naila in What Israel Means to Me, p. 321

412 What Israel Means to Me, p. 272

413. www.counterpunch.org/2019/10/31

414 Luke 10, 25-37

415 Ron Kronish, The Other Peace Proces, Plymouth, Hamilton Books, 2017

416 For more information contact The Israel Interfaith Co-ordinating Committee.
http://www.english.icci.org.il
also https://www.stories.allmep.org/

417 See http://www.anglicannifcon.org/Alexand-Declaration.htm

418 Christians and Jews: A New Way of Thinking, Council of Churches for Britain and Ireland, 1994, p. 14

419 See further The Spiritual Significance of Jerusalem for Jews, Christians and Muslims, Ed Hans Ucko, Geneva, World Council of Churches, 1994.

420 See further Stephen Sizer, Christian Zionism: Road Map to Armageddon, Leicester, Inter-Varsity Press, 2004 and Challenging Christian Zionism, Ed Naim Ateek, Cedar Duaybis and Maurine Tobin, London, Mellisende, 2005

421 Statement of the General Assembly of The Presbyterian Church (USA) 1987. For Roman Catholic statements see Catholics, Jews and the State of Israel Ed. Anthony Kenny, Paulist Press 1993 and Jack Bemporad Our Age, The Historic New Era of Christian-Jewish Understanding, New City Press 1996. pp. 74-81.

422 The title of a book by Desmond Tutu, No Future Without Forgiveness, London, Rider, 1999

423 Quoted by Ayelet Shahak in No Going Back, Edited by Carol Rittner and Stephen D Smith, London, Quill Press, 2009, p. 131

424 The Bat-Chen Diaries, p. 107

425 Leo Baeck, quoted in Marcus Braybrooke, Children of One God, London, Vallentine Mitchell, 1991, p. 144

426 Quoted in Fifteen Years of Catholic-Jewish Dialogue, 10-1985, Rome, Libreria Editrice Vaticana, p.31

427 Sadly, the practice in many Church of England churches today is

only to read from the New Testament and not to sing the Psalms.

428 Harry James Cargas Shadows of Auschwitz, New York, Crossroad, 1990, p.1

429 See further Heinz Schreckenberg, The Jews in Christian Art, London, SCM Press, 1996.

430 Michael Hilton The Christian Effect on Jewish Life, London, SCM Press 1994

431 Quoted by Geoffrey Wigoder, 'Jewish-Christian relations since the Second World War,' Manchester University Press, 1990, p. 62 from the journal Judaism, Winter 1971, p. 95

432 From a letter of Parkes to Hoffmann, 9.12.1930.

433 Quoted by Robert A Everett, Christianity Without Antisemitism: James Parkes and the Jewish Christian Encounter, Pergamon Press, 1993, p. 25

434 In the journal The Promise, No 26, July 1925, pp.2-3.

435 See further Marcus Braybrooke Children of One God, London, Vallentine Mitchell, 1991, chapter one.

436 See further Marcus Braybrooke, Widening Vision: the World Congress of Faith and the Growing Interfaith Movement, www.lulu.com, 2016

432 Children of One God, p. 7

433 Theguardian.com/world/2018/nov/10/the-kindertransport-children-80- years-on

439 Gerhard Riegner in Fifteen Years of Catholic-Jewish Dialogue, pp. 277-8.

440 Fifteen Years of Catholic-Jewish Dialogue, p. 322.

441 Ibid.

442 A large selection of relevant documents is to be found on three web sites: www.jcrelations.net/en/?area=Statements www.bc.edu/research/cjl/resources/documents; - the website of Boston College and www.scarboromissions.ca

443 W Bousset, Jesus, 1911, pp. 67-9

444 G.I.A. Quarterly 11.2 Winter 2000, p. 22 Quoted by John Pawlikowski. op.cit.

445 Martin Noth, A History of Israel, London, SCM Press, Second edtn 1958. (My emphasis)

446 John Pawlikowski, Christ in the Light of the Christian-Jewish Dialogue, Ramsey, N. J. Paulist Press, 1982 pp. 76-89

447 James D G Dunn, The Parting of the Ways, London, SCM Press, 1991, p.243

448 Luke 22, 4 and Mark 12, 12.

449 Luke 23, 27 and 48.

450 In Jews and Christians Speak of Jesus, Ed. Arthur Zannoni, Mineapolis, Fortress Press 1994, p.139.

451 Pawlikowski, p. 10

452 See, for example, Marcus Braybrooke, Time to Meet, London, SCM Press, 1990

453 See further No Going Back, ed Carol Rittner and Stepehen Smith, London, Quill Press, 2009

454 Letter dated 16.2.2010 on the Catholic News Service website

455 CNN report to be found at Haaretz.com

456 Jonathan Sacks, The Persistence of Faith, London, Weidenfeld and Nicolson, 1991, p. 81.

457 Ecclesiasticus 17.

458 Genesis 12, 9ff.

459 See further chapter 9 of Dan Cohn-Sherbok, Judaism and Other Faiths, Basingstoke, Macmillan Press, 1994,

460 www.jweekly.com 8.8.2003

461 Sharing One Hope, Church House Publishing, 2001, pp. 26-7.

462 Quoted by Michael Ipgrave in Common Ground , Spring 2020

463 Certainly in origin a Christmas tree is pagan rather than Christian. See further P and R Cowan, Mixed Blessings: Overcoming the Stumbling Blocks in an Interfaith Marriage, New York, Penguin 1987;
     Jonathan A Romain, Till Faith Us Do Part, London, Fount/Harper Collins, 199; Andrea King, If I'm Jewish and You're Christian, What Are the Kids? New York,UAHC Press, 1993.

464 The statement is printed in Braaten Carl (ed.), Jews and Christians, People of God

465 Pinchas Lapide and Hans Küng, Brother or Lord, Fount Books, 1977, p. 13f

466 Quoted in Bursting the Bonds, eds Leonard Swidler, John Eron and Lester Dean, New York, Orbis Books 1990, p. 110

467 The Jewish Annotated New Testament, eds Amy-Jill Levine and Marc Zvi Brettler, Oxford University Press, 2011.

468 Dialogue with a Difference,op.cit, p. 27

469 Current Dialogue, Geneva, World Council of Churches, No.28, June 1995, pp. 11-15

470 Ewert Cousins, The Journal of Ecumenical Studies, Summer-Fall, 1993, Vol 30, 3-4, p. 425

471 Common Ground, London, Council of Christians and Jews, 1993, 1, pp. 4-5.

472 Children of One God, pp. 95-6 and p. 81

473 Interfaith Worship and Prayer, Ed Christopher Lewis and Dan Cohn-Sherbok, London, Jessica Kingsley publishers, 2019, pp 69-86

474 For example the 'Open Letter: A Call to Dialogue and Understanding Between Muslims and Jews,' www.woolfinstitue.cam.ac.uk/cmjr.

475 See further Normal Solomon in Abraham's Children, ed Norman Solomon, Richard Harries and Tim Winter, London, T and T Clark, 2005, pp. 132 ff. Norman Solomon refers to the work

of the distinguished scholar, Lazarus-Yafeh.

See also Jonathan Magonet, Talking to the Other, London
I B Tauris, 2003, pp. 147-160

476 Norman Solomon, op. cit, p.139

477 Jonathan Magonet, op.cit, p. 176

478 Jonathan Sacks, The Persistence of Faith, p.94

479 Jonathan Sacks, Faith in the Future, London, Darton, Longman
and Todd 1995, p. 119

Index

Netanyahu, 184, 185, 186, 189,190, 194
Nicholson, 18
Niebuhr, R 139
Niemoller, 134, 137 -8
Noth, 236
Novak, 110

Olmert, 188
Omar, Caliph, 164
Oneklos, 93
Orpah, 87

Pacelli , Cardinal and later Pope Pius XII, 138, 139
Parkes, James,
Patterson, D, 4
Pawlikowski, 241
Pepys, 36
Peres, 179, 181, 185, 243
Pfister, Oskar, 105
Pharaoh, 76-80
Philo, 225
Pinchas Lapide, 248
Pius XII, 134, 136, 139, 142
Plaskow, 100, 191, 201
Plaut, 37, 198, 200, 201
Polack, 63
Pompey, 89
Pontius Pilate, 164
Pope Francis, 243
Pope John Paul I, 133
Potter, xlix

Raab, 159
Rabin, 178, 181 - 185
Rachel, 76
Rambam, 93
Rameses II, 77
Rashbam, 93
Rashi, 92, 93
Rav Amnon, 66
Reinhart, lxx
Reigner, 214,
Robinson J, lxxiv, 108
Roderigo, xl

Apologies for the use of Roman and Arabic numbers and any inaccuracies caused by a technical fault

Books by Marcus Braybrooke

All in Good Faith - *A Resource Book for Multi-faith Prayer, edited by Jean Potter and Marcus Braybrooke*

Beacons of Light - 100 holy people who have shaped the history of humanity

Bridge of Stars - 365 Prayers, Blessings and Meditations from around the World; *'With a prayer to reflect on every day, I hope readers will develop in themselves the warm-hearted peace of mind that is the key to enduring happiness.'* The Dalai Lama

Children of One God - a history of the Council of Christians and Jews (CCJ)

Christianity; An Explorer's Guide - *'ideal for the enquirer of any and no belief and will also inform Christians under-standing of the faith of the Church'* Revd David Winter

Christians and Jews Building Bridges - *an updated history of CCJ*

Dialogue with a Difference - *reflections of pioneers of Christian-Jewish dialogue.* Edited by Rabbi Tony Bayfield and Revd Marcus Braybrooke

Explorer's Guide to Christianity - *an introduction for the*

questioning

Faith and Interfaith in a Global Age - *the story of the interfaith movement from 1893-1997*

Faiths Together for the Future - *the story of the World Congress of Faiths and the interfaith movement*

Hinduism - *the author's personal reflection of how he has been enriched by Hindu scriptures and Hindu friends*

Interfaith Pioneers 1893-1939 - *'an inspiring story of people of faith who dedicated their lives to creating a more peaceful and caring world community* - John Singleton

Islam: A Christian Approach - *what Christians and Muslims can learn from each other and do together to promote peace and relieve poverty*

Learn to Pray - *a practical guide for beginners to discover how prayer can enrich one's life*

Peace in Our Hearts: Peace in Our World - *a meditation for every day*

Pilgrimage of Hope - *a history of the interfaith movement from 1893-1993*

Promoting the Common *Good* - *Bringing Economics and Theology Together Again* - with Dr Kamran Mofid.

Sikhism - *A Christian Approach*

Testing the Global Ethic - edited by Peggy Morgan and Marcus Braybrooke

Time to Meet - *Towards a deeper relationship between Christians and Jews*

Together to the Truth *- A Comparative Study of Some developments in Hindu and Christian Thought since 1800*

Widening Vision - *The World Congress of Faiths and the Growing Interfaith Movement*

1,000 World Prayers - *an anthology of prayers from many faiths and spiritual tradtions*

Marcus Braybrooke

Revd Dr Marcus Braybrooke grew up in Cranleigh in Surrey, UK , where he went to school. After National Service in Libya and Cyprus and a short visit to Israel which was to have a lasting affect on him, he won a scolarship to Magdalene College, Cambridge, where he studied history and theology and, more important, met Mary Walker, a social worker, whom he married in 1964.

Marcus was then awarded a scholarship from the World Council of Churches to study Hinduism and other world religions at Madras Christian College. He also travelled widely in India and also helped at a clinic for those suffering from leprosy.

On his return, he studied for a year Wels Theological College and was ordained in 1964 at St Paul's Cathedral. He also, at this time, joined the World Congress of Faiths and studied for a Master's degree at King's College, London. His thesis was the basis for his first book *Together to the Truth.*

Marcus has served in a number of parishes and was for the time Director of the Council of Christians and Jews. His 'hobby' has been interfaith work, as well as writing books and gardening. During a sabbatical, he studied at Tantur Ecumenical Institute, which is half way between Jerusalem and Bethelehem

He was awared a Lambeth Doctorate for his interfaith work and has received other awards.

Marcus has worked closely with many international interfaith organizations and played a key role in the 1993 Year

of Interreligious Co-operation and Understanding.   He has
spoken at several Parliaments of World Religions

Mary, who was a social worker, shared in their interfaith is
work, often travelling with Marcus and also speaking at the
conferences. She did pioneering work on the attitude of people
of different faiths to kidney transplants.

They has two children and six granddaughters.

Printed in Great Britain
by Amazon